How I Wrote My First Book
The Story Behind the Story

Twenty authors tell amazing stories about the efforts that went into writing their first book.

Anne K. Edwards and
Lida E. Quillen, Editors

Twilight Times Books
Kingsport Tennessee

How I Wrote My First Book

Copyright © 2011. Lida E. Quillen

All rights reserved. No part of this book may be reproduced, stored in a retrieval system or transmitted in any form by any means electronic, mechanical, photo-copying, recording or otherwise, except brief extracts for the purpose of review, without the permission of the publisher and copyright owners.

Paladin Timeless Books, an imprint of
Twilight Times Books
P O Box 3340
Kingsport, TN 37664
http://twilighttimesbooks.com/

First Edition, February 2011

Articles copyright by the contributing authors. Used by permission.

    Library of Congress Cataloging-in-Publication Data

How I wrote my first book, the story behind the story : twenty authors tell amazing stories about the efforts that went into writing their first book / Anne K. Edwards and Lida E. Quillen, editors. -- 1st ed.
   p. cm.
   ISBN-13: 978-1-60619-149-1 (trade pbk. : alk. paper)
   ISBN-10: 1-60619-149-7 (trade pbk. : alk. paper)
   1. Authorship. 2. Authors, American--20th century--Biography. I. Edwards, Anne K., 1940- II. Quillen, Lida E.
   PN149.H68 2011
   810.9'005--dc22
                            2011004672

Cover art by Ardy M. Scott

Printed in the United States of America.

Table of Contents

Christine Amsden: "My Million Words of Crap" / 7

Darrell Bain: "The Story Behind *The Pet Plague*" / 20

Bob Boan: "How I Came to Write *Bobby becomes Bob*" / 27

Mayra Calvani: "Tips on Writing Your First Novel" / 43

D Jason Cooper: "Understanding Numerology" / 52

Lee Denning: "Two Beginnings" / 59

Susan Goldsmith: "How I Wrote *Abithica*" / 70

Ginger Hanson: "Ten Lessons I Learned from Writing *Quest for Vengeance*" / 82

Toby Fesler Heathcotte: "The Manuscript from a Mystifying Source" / 96

Darby Karchut: "Wings" / 109

Linda Langwith: "The Serendipity Factor" / 122

Aaron Lazar: "The Writing of *Double Forté*" / 132

Celia A. Leaman: "Writing *Mary's Child*" / 140

Beverly Stowe McClure: "How I Wrote *Shadows on the Desert*" / 148

Gerald Mills: "How I Wrote *No Place for Gods*" / 157

Erica Miner: "How I Wrote *Travels With My Lovers*" / 178

Stephanie Osborn: "How a Rocket Scientist Becomes a Writer" / 184

Bob Rich: "How I Came to Write Novels" / 190

Dorothy Skarles: "Tales of Intrigue, Adventure and Learning" / 200

Dan Starr: "A Solution and a Seed: Novel Writing as Growing a Crystal" / 208

My Million Words of Crap

by Christine Amsden

During a writers' boot camp I attended in 2003, Orson Scott Card said something that has stuck with me ever since. He said that before a writer can turn out worthy material, each one will generate at least one million words of pure crap. At the time, I wasn't sure whether or not I had finished writing mine.

Shortly after the boot camp, I wrote a truly awful short story that somehow started me on the path to writing *Touch of Fate*, though if you asked me now, I could not possibly trace the chain of thoughts that took me from an other-world fantasy tale featuring a crippled woman lying helpless in a ditch to a modern-day paranormal featuring a troubled clairvoyant. That story, like so many others, was part of my million words of crap, but I didn't know that as I wrote. I only realized this later, when I gave the story to my husband (then fiancé) to read, and he told me, quite brutally, that it was the worst story of mine he had ever read.

Those were words to lift the spirit! I believe that after blinking back a few tears and stammering a bit, I asked for specifics, but didn't listen to his answers. There are times when we are receptive to feedback and times when we aren't. This was one of the latter.

For the record, if you're going to show your work to your significant other and expect an honest response, you'd better make sure you have a good relationship. If you don't trust yourself to hear honesty from your spouse, then at least be honest about your expectations. Say you want ego stroking and in the meantime, find someone whose opinion you trust and whose friendship you could potentially live without.

Luckily for me, I have a pretty solid marriage, because my husband is almost incapable of saying anything but the truth as he sees it. He'll never live down a moment in college when he told a chubby friend of ours, "Oh, I assumed you'd want *diet* soda." I knew all of that when

I handed him the story, though of course I'd hoped the honest truth would be pleasant.

If there's one thing I've learned about writing, it's that true growth in writing doesn't come from pleasant feedback. That's the big difference between the million words of crap and the better-known adage, "Practice makes perfect." Practice alone does not make perfect, and writing a million words of crap won't get you anywhere until you realize that the words are crap. Without that spark of realization, the next million words will be just as bad.

So there I sat, not quite listening to what my husband was saying about my painfully awful story, while the last vestiges of illusion shattered. I was not done writing my million words of crap. About two thousand of them sat in my clammy hands, daring me to smell them.

Let me just put something into perspective for you. Your average mainstream mystery or suspense novel is about eighty to one-hundred-thousand words. First science fiction or fantasy novels tend to be about ninety to one-hundred-ten-thousand words. So one million words is, roughly speaking, about ten novels. I started writing regularly when I was eleven, so by 2003, I had been writing for fifteen years, more often than not, and had probably written a million words in bits and snatches, but I had never really finished a novel. Part of the reason was that I kept rewriting the same story over and over and over again. I had this idea, which now [finally] exists as a rough draft, but for the longest time it only served to hold me back.

Orson Scott Card didn't specifically say so, but looking back, I think that the million words have to be largely unique. It's not just the words, it's the story. At some point you have to write an entire story, from beginning to end, and then do it again. This is why some so-called writing experts (really, it's all just opinion backed up by success) suggest beginning with short stories, so you can get the feel for creating a whole story again and again.

I read an article with that very suggestion shortly after my ego-blow. Write short stories, it said, lots of them. So I did.

Now I have a confession to make. I'm not a short story writer. I'm a novelist. A handful of the short stories I wrote in the following months were published, but by and large I wasn't proud of my short story efforts. The trouble is that by the time I do real character development and real world building, I've got a bigger investment than 2,000-7,500 words. I don't read short stories for much the same reason - by the time I start getting into the story, it's over, and I want more. I've been a voracious reader for as long as I can remember, but after I set the early readers aside, it was always novels.

Writing short stories is an art form all it's own, so while I agree somewhat with the idea that beginning writers should practice finishing things by writing short stories, I think that some of us are meant to be novelists, and that sooner or later we need to practice finishing novels.

Of the short stories I did write, two stood out. One, alas, for reasons that go beyond the scope of this article. The other, *Signs* would eventually become the prequel to my first published novel, *Touch of Fate*.

The rest of 2003 ended in a blur of life changes. In October, I had my perfect fairy-tale wedding, complete with a vaguely Elizabethan-style gown.

Up until that point, I was doing some computer consulting work, but my husband encouraged me to follow my dream and devote my time to writing full time. He brought in enough money for the two of us and so, despite misgivings, I gave it a shot.

One of the questions I'm supposed to address is: What made you decide to write a novel? I realize that I'm skirting the issue, but you have to understand that for me, I never made a conscious decision to write a novel. Writing has always been as natural as breathing to me, and I could no more not write than I could not eat. My college career was choppy and indecisive, ending in two degrees simply because I had so much trouble making up my mind that by the time I graduated, I had the credits for both of them. Most of the time I tell people this happened because I was unfocused - unsure what I wanted to do - but I always knew I wanted to write, I just didn't know what I wanted to do to earn a living in the meantime.

While I had misgivings about not entering a more traditional career path, they were largely external misgivings. I had preconceived notions about what I should be doing, largely involving bringing home a regular paycheck. Inside, I knew that writing was the only thing I had consistently wanted to do since I was about eight years old. (The year I wrote my first masterpiece about Cabbage Patch Dolls going to Mars.)

By spring of 2004, almost a year after Card's boot camp, I was working on yet another draft of THE novel. This time it was going to be great. I had grown up a lot since I'd started writing it at the age of eleven. My characters were more complex, the world better developed, and the story itself had grown too large for a single volume. Now it was no longer THE novel, but THE trilogy.

Which is why it came as something of a shock when my father told me precisely what he thought of it. I'd moved past giving everything to my husband, partly because he didn't have time and partly because I wasn't sure I wanted him to be quite as honest as he'd been about the short story I mentioned. So I sent my father bits of the novel, a chapter at a time, until one dismal April afternoon. I can't be entirely sure if it was raining or not, but since it was April in the Midwest, it's a good bet. In my memory of the event, it was one of those nasty spring thunderstorms that turns the sky as black as night.

I was working on chapter eighteen when he called. I was pretty nervous, because he had been reading chapter sixteen, in which the main character killed someone. It was a daring scene, I'd told myself, but a necessary one. Even good people can make bad decisions, especially when pressured by outside influences. [Rationalization continues here.]

"Hi, Dad."

"Hi Christine." He sounded a bit nervous. "I read chapter sixteen today and I'm done reading."

"What?"

"I won't read anymore. If this were a published book, I would put it down. I can't forgive Clarica for killing that woman."

Devastating silence.

I can't really remember the rest of the conversation, but I'm afraid the biggest mistake I made wasn't in chapter sixteen. Something I said to my father that day made him useless as a wise reader from then on. He got the distinct impression that he'd hurt my feelings, which he had, but I still needed to hear it. Like I said, true growth doesn't come from pleasant feedback. Nowadays, though; he's a little too inclined to tell me what he likes about my novels.

That day, though, he told me the truth. There went sixty thousand more words of crap.

It wasn't that very day, but definitely within a few days that I stumbled upon an on-line site called Writer's Village University. The site offers a number of writing classes in fiction, non-fiction, literature, and poetry, and is very affordable. There are a number of such sites springing up on the Internet nowadays, including Savvy Authors, where I now teach an occasional workshop. Some of the writing courses out there are prohibitively expensive, and since I didn't have the money to spend, I can't say whether or not they're worth the money, but the cheap or free sites worked for me.

Writers Village University cost something like sixty or seventy dollars a year for all the courses I could take. And I took them. I loaded my schedule up with more classes than I really needed. In my state of temporary insecurity, I even signed up for some beginning classes that were entirely unnecessary for me, such as grammar and punctuation.

A few weeks later, I cleared away most of the rubbish and focused on a few classes that I hoped would spark my creativity. Among these was a class called "Writing the Mystery Novel," and that is where I conceived of the novel version of *Touch of Fate*.

From that point in May of 2004, it would only take me ten months to have a finished, marketable draft of my novel, but bear in mind that at this time I was working on my craft forty hours a week. I didn't have any children yet. I wouldn't expect most people to be able to finish a novel that quickly, especially a first novel, but after I made the decision to become a writer, instead of pursuing some more traditional career, I was determined to make it count. At times, I think, I pushed myself too far and too hard and I burned out. Having had this experience, I don't actually think it's a bad idea for a writer to have a day job. Ironically, I have become more productive since becoming a mother and cutting the number of hours I dedicate to writing each week by half. (Many of those hours are stolen during nap times and at night.)

The thing I've learned about creativity is that it can't always be forced. Some things just take time. So writing forty hours a week for a year is not quite the same thing as writing five hours a week for eight years, or writing twenty hours a week for two. Writing is simply not a linear process.

Besides, living life gives you something to write about when the writing itself is such solitary work. I spent hours a day alone in my office, either in silence or listening to a variety of soft and classic rock. I do like this kind of environment since I've always been a bit of a loner, but there's always the balance to consider. Writing is first about living, growing, experiencing, dreaming, and only then, if you're very lucky, is it about creating.

I didn't know any of that when I started *Touch of Fate*. At that time, I was determined to prove something, whether to myself or everyone else I have no idea. All I know is that in May of 2004, I had been "writing full time" for about half a year and all I had to show for it was another hundred thousand or so words of crap.

If only I'd known then how important writing those words had been, I might not have burned myself out later.

The mystery writing class was fun. I read about the traditional format of a mystery novel from the laying down of clues and red herrings to the revelation of whodunit. The only thing missing from the wonderful, albeit formulaic, approach was an idea. What in the world was I supposed to write about?

In answer, I found myself going back through my old short story files until I came across *Signs*, the story of a clairvoyant who predicted her own death. Since she survived, I decided she'd make a good amateur sleuth.

It's hard to say whether I was particularly enthusiastic about the idea at the time. I wasn't unenthusiastic, but it might be more accurate to say that I was determined. My most recent attempt at writing a novel had hit a seemingly insurmountable stumbling block (though I did eventually figure out how to solve the problem) and I still didn't have a single complete novel to show for my "career" as a "full time writer." For better or worse, I decided, I was going to finish this one.

I began with background. Who had died? Why? Who killed her? The last question took the longest to answer, since even when I began writing my first draft, I had no idea. I had over half a dozen possible suspects but none of them would confess.

The victim in a mystery novel is often not well liked. Why? Because it's more interesting if a lot of different people had a good reason to kill her (or him) and generally speaking, nice people won't have multiple suspects out for their blood.

I couldn't do it, though. I do sometimes enjoy solving a good puzzle, but writing one is a different matter. It's too cold and impersonal. If I was going to spend a year or more of my life writing the story of someone's death, I wanted to care that the person had died, grieve for her loss, and curse the scum of the earth who had done it to her.

So I had to come up with a likable victim who many people wanted to kill. The answer came easily, far more easily than most of the other questions I had to ask, and it had to do with my sleuth - the troubled clairvoyant. What if she wasn't alone? What if there was someone else with the same gift, someone who had learned to control it as she never had, but whose heroic actions had led to her death?

Suddenly I realized I had more than a formulaic mystery novel on my hands; I also had a real character story to tell. I'm glad I took the mystery writing course because nearly every novel I've written since then has made use of the things I learned there, but first and foremost, I write about people. The moment I realized this about myself, brute determination gave way to real enthusiasm and I could finally ease myself into writing the book.

They say that if you write 1,667 words each day, you can write a complete fifty-thousand-word novel in a month. That's the logic behind NaNoWriMo, National Novel Writing Month (November, for those of you who were unaware), which was a useful challenge when I was working on my first book. I have since abandoned the rigors of a daily word count goal in favor of an hourly devotion goal, largely due to lessons I learned while writing *Touch of Fate*. Technically, the word count goals worked. By mid-summer, I had penned about seventy thousand words of something resembling a book, but I prefer to think of that first draft as yet another seventy thousand words of crap.

I had a sleuth. I had a victim. I liked my victim and was very sad to have had to kill her. I even wrote journal entries from her point of view, after which I spent several days feeling so guilty over her demise that I considered trying to come up with another victim. (Maybe that's another reason that murder mystery victims tend to be unlikable.)

There was just one tiny issue that I was sure I could work out in the revisions: At the end of my rough draft, I still had no idea who killed her. I had suspects galore, along with clues and red herrings (I wasn't entirely sure which were which), but who actually pulled that trigger?

I don't get out much. When I was sixteen years old, I was diagnosed with a degenerative eye condition that leaves the world blurry and me incapable of driving. I am currently typing this article in twenty-six-point font, though I'll shrink it down to size before I send off the file. I did go on to college and ended up doing many of the things that any normal person might have done, but I won't pretend that my disability wasn't at least some part of the reason that I decided to stay home and write. In many ways it was easier.

I'd always lived a lot of my life in my own head, but the first year I spent largely locked away inside an apartment with nothing but my computer for company until my husband came home from work was pretty lonely. I found comfort and companionship in writing communities on the net. There was the Writer's Village University site I mentioned, but there was one I enjoyed even more - Hatrack. This is Orson Scott Card's web site, and it includes a large and friendly community for aspiring young writers. It's been a few years since I frequented the site, but it was practically home for me when I was writing *Touch of Fate*.

Daily, I would post there, answering questions and asking a few of my own. With the help of the moderator, Kathleen, I joined several e-mail critique groups, forming friendships that I still maintain to this day, despite the fact that I have outgrown the site.

Critique groups come and go. They have to. If you use the same group for too long, you will stop growing as a writer as your stories become more and more attuned to that group and its preferences. Fresh perspectives are important, especially since you will (hopefully) be selling your book to more than the five people in your critique group. That's why I eventually wandered away from Hatrack, but it still holds a special place in my heart and I continue to highly recommend it to new speculative fiction writers looking for a supportive community.

At one point, the site helped me come up with the title of my book. Titles have never been my strong suit, so I posted about ten different possibilities and polled the community. At the time, all I had was my painful rough draft, but it had the words "The End" on the last page and so I figured it also deserved a title.

That was when *Touch of Fate* was truly born, I think. I've always felt that things are more real when they have names, which was why I named both of my children long before they were born. When *Touch of Fate* was *Title Unknown*, it was easy to dismiss it as a sort of writing exercise with vague, nebulous possibilities but no real substance. With a title in mind, I could go on to have mock interviews in my head. (Admit it, I'm not the only one who's done these.)

Interviewer: So, tell me what made you decide to write *Touch of Fate*?

Me: Well, you see, it was a combination of a lot of things going on in my life at the time and everything leading up to it. I lived that story for the better part of a year. It affected my life and my life affected it, the two blurring together until, looking back, I'm not sure where one began and the other ended.

Interviewer: So would you say the story is about your life?

Me: In a way, yes. It was a hard year, living much of my life by myself in a new city with nothing but unseen Internet friends for company. Until that time, I had tried to pretend that my visual problems didn't matter much, that I was in control of my life despite it all, but that year taught me some hard lessons. In some ways, I may have been taking out my frustrations on Marianne when I gave her the power to predict but not change the future.

By now, I was in full burnout mode, despite the small success of unveiling my title. Burnout is not the same thing as writer's block, although I think the two are sometimes used interchangeably. Writer's block happens in the middle of a project when you quite simply do not know where to go next. It can often be cured by going back to the drawing board, reorganizing and rethinking the original plans.

Burnout happens when you've taken something you used to love and turned it into something you dread or even hate. Sometime in the fall of 2004, this happened to me. I had a rough draft of *Touch of Fate* and I even had a title, but I had forgotten how to have fun with the written word. I kept writing, but without the spark that brings it to life. Only one reason remained for my continued writing efforts at that time: to prove (To myself? To the world? To my mother?) that I hadn't wasted the last year of my life. To prove that I could write and publish a novel.

In short, the forces which drove me to write the second draft of *Touch of Fate* were so far removed from the forces that drove me to write *Cabbage Patch Dolls go to Mars* (when I was eight) that I'm pretty sure the latter outshone the former, at least in pure childish enthusiasm. There is a lot to be said for finding the child within. (I'm pretty sure thousands of self-help books would agree with me, but I'm not intentionally being corny.)

The only good thing about my second draft was that I did identify a killer. In fact, after writing several practice scenes from the killer's point of view, I decided to write it as a suspense-thriller rather than a straight mystery in order to give the reader some real insights into the killer's character and add to the dramatic tension.

So while it wasn't a total loss, it became increasingly clear that something was wrong. I didn't identify the problem with words until 2008, over three years later, when I read an enlightening book called *The Artist's Way: A Spiritual Path to Higher Creativity*. At that time, I realized that what I needed then, need now, and will always need, is to play.

Instinct has always served me well, however; and I did figure out that I'd taken all the fun out of writing with my rigorous eight to five schedule, with my daily word count goals, and with my devotion to quantity over quality.

I'd always done well in school. For years, I lived for seeing the letter 'A' circled in red at the top of my papers, maybe with a smiley face or a "Great job!" written off to the side. In psychology, we talk about external vs. internal motivations, and for me, it was all about the pat on the back.

Writing doesn't do that, at least not until you get a book published, and even then the praise is inconsistent and intermingled with harsh criticism. One day you're on top of the world because an honest-to-goodness publisher says they want to print your book and the next day some blow-hard who must have skimmed the book instead of reading it because he clearly missed the point is saying that your work is crap.

Before that first publication it's even worse, because the best praise you might get is from a wise reader (critiquer) who will probably also have many suggestions for improvement.

So in the increasingly chilly days of the fall of 2004, I asked myself over and over again: Why do I write? It can't be for praise or recognition; there has to be something else. Why did I write nearly every day in middle school and high school? Why did I turn to it from time to time during college and gravitate back to it with fresh vigor after college?

I didn't stop writing entirely, but I did put a hold on any project that I intended for sale. I still had my membership at Writer's Village University, so I signed up for a couple of classes to stretch my comfort zone a bit, including one on romance writing. I spent a month or two working on a science fiction romance novel that will never in a million years see the outside of my hard drive but which served a much greater purpose: It was fun.

That November, my husband and I decided to take a trip to London, kind of a last getaway before we started our family. At the time, I thought I would find exotic new stories in an exotic new location, but it didn't happen quite that way. The best bit of wisdom I've ever heard about traveling is that no matter where you are, you bring yourself with you. So while it might have been interesting to wander through the Tower of London, learning a bit of history and catching glimpses of the crown jewels from moving sidewalks while armed guards watched my every move, no story ideas popped into my head.

Nevertheless, it was a healing week. I wrote in a journal every day (something I highly recommend that all artists do), I wandered aimlessly through Hyde Park, breathing in the sooty air, and allowed myself to relax for the first time in over a year.

When I returned, I didn't have a new idea that I wanted to work on, but something had turned my thoughts back to the old idea. I wasn't feeling rushed and I wasn't feeling forced. I didn't have to write *Touch of Fate* for any particular reason, but I wanted to do it anyway. It called to me and being the dutiful artist, I answered its summons.

I won't go into a lot of details about my final draft except to say that it was a bittersweet experience. It was the end of a journey, and I knew even as I wrote it that it was nearly over. After that draft there would be no more excuses, no more sweeping revisions, and no more stalling. The novel would go off into the cold, cruel world and I would find something else to write, something that hadn't even occurred to me at the time.

There are times to let the creative process sweep you away and times to force your butt into a chair. For me, the editing process is nothing but BIC (butt in chair). Luckily, at the end of January 2005, I heard about a novel contest for first-time novelists (thanks to Kathleen at Hatrack). The deadline was March 1st, giving me a hair over four weeks to put the polish on and put together a query package (yet another aspect of writing that requires a great deal of forced BIC for me). I didn't win that contest or get a novel deal the first time I sent my baby out into the world (I've never heard of anyone who did), but it was great motivation and on February 28th, 2005, *Touch of Fate* was complete, spell checked, and most importantly, out in the world.

The timing couldn't have been better. That same week, I found out I was pregnant with my first child, which made it truly feel as if I had closed a chapter in my life and was about to move on to the next. There would be more books over the next few years, one of which ended up in the crap pile with my first million words. There would be more challenges, more lessons learned, and of course, the actual publication of *Touch of Fate*, but even if no one had wanted that first book, (and on February 28th, 2005, no one did), there was still an enormous sense of accomplishment. I had written my million words of crap and come through it with a sweetly scented work of art of which I could truly feel proud.

About the author

Christine Amsden was born and raised in the St. Louis area, which inspired the setting for her first novel, *Touch of Fate*. She started writing shortly after learning to pick up a pencil, and though she majored in Computer Science and Psychology in college, she never lost her love of the written word.
http://www.christineamsden.com

Upcoming release: *The Immortality Virus*, SF suspense

The Story Behind *The Pet Plague*

by Darrell Bain

I believe Robert A. Heinlein, the famed science fiction author, gave some of the soundest advice I know of for prospective authors: *Finish what you start!* I didn't read that until a long time after I began trying to write and even after reading the advice, it took me a long time to begin following it.

From the time I learned to read, before starting school, I loved it. I read everything I could get my hands on, whether it was meant for children or not. Admittedly, attending a country school, growing up on an isolated farm and subsequently in a very poor, dysfunctional family in the country greatly limited my reading material but never stopped me from wanting to read.

Aside from the very sparse school library, a couple of shelves of books in a former closet, there was little reading material available. From somewhere, I don't remember now, a book on the history of astronomy found its way to our house. It was old and tattered but I read it through several times. It certainly widened my horizons to learn how astronomers had discovered so much about the solar system and our galaxy since the invention of the telescope. Someone gave us a few of the Big Little Books (which were out of date even then), all science fiction. Mostly Flash Gordon as I remember. Perhaps that type of reading, plus the book on astronomy and a few Tom Swift books in the elementary school library are what pointed me in the direction of liking science, and in turn, good science fiction when I discovered it somewhere around puberty. Science fiction became my favorite genre but was by no means all I read. I read everything that came my way but I really liked science fiction. It tied in perfectly with my attraction to science, generated by that astronomy text and some classes in elementary school. I think it was the idea of delving into the unknown that sparked a lot of my interest in science and science fiction.

From reading, I progressed to the desire to write fiction. From the age of eleven or twelve I began wanting to write—and did so, mostly stories about spaceships and going to Mars or Venus and fighting weird aliens while settling and exploring the planets. Unable to type (and barely knowing what a typewriter even was), I very carefully printed all the stories I began in order to make my writing look as much like a book as possible. I'm sure hand printing the words didn't contribute much to the worthiness of what I wrote and I was considered an odd kid for even wanting to write fiction. Because I had few interests other than reading and a developing interest in girls, I had plenty of time to write. If memory serves, most of the stories I wrote in early adolescence were imitations of Heinlein's young adult novels.

I think I suffered from a limited attention span or possibly a touch of laziness because somehow none of those early books I started ever got finished. On the other hand, perhaps not completing any of them was because I had not the least idea of *how* to write fiction other than imitating (or trying to imitate) the style of my favorite author, Robert A. Heinlein. Whatever the reason, up until my middle years, my late forties I guess, I periodically began novels that never saw an end, even after I taught myself to type. By the time I was nearing fifty I had pretty well given up the hope of ever writing a complete book. Plotting was the most difficult area for me. I would get to a certain point in my story, then eventually abandon it and start another because I couldn't figure out how to get my characters out of the trouble I'd gotten them into. Becoming a real published author was the farthest thing from my mind, nothing more than a wild, wild dream. Then an amazing change came over the world: home computers with word processors became affordable.

When I bought my first computer, a Tandy 1000X with exactly 64 Kilobytes of RAM, the word processor seemed like magic to me. It made typing so easy, correcting mistakes so simple, that it was almost unbelievable. I took to it with all the enthusiasm of a starving man who'd stumbled into an unguarded kitchen.

One of the first things I wrote using my new computer was a ten page article of speculation about what kind of changes the science of genetics might inflict upon the world, particularly in the area of manipulation of the genetic makeup of our pets. I wrote about this subject because I had always had an interest in science and even after dropping out of high school in the ninth grade, I had eventually managed a degree in Medical Technology in my thirties. Genetics was not only a required subject for my degree but I also found the subject to be endlessly fascinating.

When I wrote that little piece I had no intentions of trying to have it published anywhere. It was simply something to write about with my new toy, but something funny happened by the time I got to the end of it. I thought, *you know, the ideas in this article might make a good science fiction novel.* I also thought it was the perfect format if I wanted to try again to complete a novel, since science fiction was, and always had been, my favorite genre of fiction.

Mind you, at that point I had never bothered studying or even reading anything about the actual methodology of producing a fiction novel, much less a good one. I was as innocent of such techniques as a baby is of Boson particles. I just knew the kind of book I liked to read and began to sort of put words together in a similar fashion, using my little article to set the theme.

One of the first decisions I had to make after beginning to write my book using that magic word processor was deciding on a title. At that point I had only a vague notion of how the book would develop and what the plot was going to be. Heck, I didn't even have a notion of *how* to plot a book! One thing I was sure of, though: if my future geneticists succeeded in inserting the genes for human intelligence into our pets and zoo animals, then inevitably some of those animals such as dogs, cats, ferrets, hamsters, rats, pigs, tigers and so forth would escape to become feral animals and multiply in the wilds. And, given greater intelligence than their naturally born cousins, they would take over their habitats and multiply virtually unhampered until it was too late to contain them. That reasoning went on to form a catchy phrase in my mind. A Plague of Pets! No, even better, the title of my prospective book would be *The Pet Plague.* I did know enough about writing, and from my voluminous reading, to realize that a good title will at least draw a prospective reader to give it a curious first look. I think it must have been right then that I first began thinking of possible publication.

So far I had accomplished two things. I had the beginning of a novel and a title for it. Now all I had to do was follow Heinlein's dictum and finish it before I got distracted by a good book or a vacation or any number of other factors that had foiled my previous attempts, including plain old laziness. If I didn't know much about writing I had at least discovered that it was hard work, even if it was enjoyable, way before I got that first computer.

At the time my wife and I owned a choose-and-cut Christmas tree farm. As you may guess, the month of December is the busiest time of the year for a Christmas tree farm, especially the choose-and-cut variety. As you may also guess, I began writing *The Pet Plague* just before Thanksgiving, our opening day for the selling season.

At the time, there was no way to take my computer to the shop since we didn't have a shop yet, and anyway, on weekends we were so busy that I had very little energy left for writing at the end of the day. Even after closing at dusk I still had to do our accounts, clean up and get ready for the next day, and that went on seven days a week until Christmas Eve. Still, I managed a few words each evening during the four days of the Thanksgiving weekend. I was becoming more and more interested in what I was doing and didn't want it to fall by the wayside like all my other efforts had over the years. Weekdays were my salvation since things didn't really get busy then until after school let out and parents picked up the kids.

Most of the day Monday through Friday, I would sit in my truck and write longhand when I didn't have other farm chores and wasn't otherwise occupied. I found myself resenting it when customers showed up wanting to buy a tree and interrupting my train of thought. Nevertheless, I usually got quite a few words written in my paper tablet and after closing the farm at the end of the day I would type what I'd written into the computer before going to bed. I found myself becoming more and more involved with the characters I had created, good guys and bad guys alike—but also found myself knowing less and less about what to *do* with them.

Nevertheless, I was going along pretty well until the week after Thanksgiving week even though I was beginning to have problems with plotting and giving my characters believable personalities. I was determined to finally finish a novel, though, so I kept dredging up words and writing them down even though my novel wasn't reading near enough like a real book to satisfy me. On top of that, I developed a toothache and had to have a tooth pulled. I was aggravated at first because the pain kept me from concentrating on writing during the week, but this wound up becoming a positive development. The dentist gave me a week or two worth of a narcotic pain pill. The pills killed the ache and the euphoria gave me lots of ideas I wouldn't have otherwise thought of. There was a downside, though. As I sat in my truck scribbling in a sort of dreamy state of mind, I wound up putting way too much sex into the book in places where it wasn't really warranted. I didn't realize it then, though, because I had yet to develop the habit of going back over my work, reading over what I'd written the previous day and making corrections. I just spent each evening typing in what I'd hand-written during the day without bothering. I wanted to by damn finally *finish* writing a book.

I became so involved in the book that I hated to see the weekends come despite that being the days of the week where we made most of our money. I fairly itched to have the season over with so I could concentrate on writing and nothing else. Time seemed to drag, especially on weekends. I had trouble paying attention to business, not only because my mind was elsewhere but also because working in the daytime and writing at night was beginning to catch up with me. I was always tired and way over in the deficit column so far as sleep was concerned. It would have gone much easier if, when I taught myself to type, I'd learned to do so without looking at the keyboard. Transcribing my handwriting involved reading a few words from my tablet, looking at the keyboard and typing them then repeating the process over and over. My mind was so dulled by the time I got to my computer that I couldn't memorize and hold more than a few words at a time in my mind between reading them and typing them. I stuck with it though, and of course eventually, the selling season ended and I could really get to work on *The Pet Plague*. I continued writing furiously, completely involved now. In fact, I did some of my first outlining at that stage, planning in advance what I'd be writing for the next few days. I did this not because I thought an outline would help make what I was writing a better book, but because by then my thoughts were coming so fast that I had to either write some of them down or lose them. However, I still had no idea how the last part of the book would go or how it would end and those were the very areas where I had bogged down so many times before.

The computer made the difference, mainly because the word processing program made correcting the manuscript so easy. That in turn, propped up my determination to, for once in my life, actually finish a novel. Also, I found that the more I thought about plotting the next few chapters, the easier plotting became. That created another problem, though. Now I found myself frequently having to go back and change some of what I'd already written. The little search program and the cut-and-paste program were both life savers. All I had to do was remember a couple of words or a key phrase and I could find the spot in the manuscript I wanted, and if necessary, move segments of the story around without having to retype. As I said, the computer made the difference.

There came a day a couple of months later when I typed "The End". I can still recall the immense satisfaction this gave me. At last, I had really and truly finished writing an entire novel! I'm sure I'm not the first person in history who wrote a book without asking for advice, belonging to a critique group, without knowing a thing about the technical aspects of fiction writing and all the other details that go into producing a decent work of fiction, those things I've since learned that beginning authors most often do. About the only thing I can say I did correctly (and that without knowing I was) involved following the writer's maxim that I read about later: Write what you know. I certainly did that, knowing a lot about science fiction and science both.

I'm also pretty sure I'm not the first person to complete a novel without wondering whether it was any good or not. I've always been sort of a loner and lived a lot inside my head and in the worlds of books. Many times this has caused me a lot of grief, going off and doing something without properly researching the idea first. The Christmas tree farm is a good example. My wife read an article about farming Christmas trees in our area and I promptly started a farm. See? But back to writing. I had finished a book. It *felt* like it was a good book to me but I really didn't know so I gave it to my wife to read.

Betty likes mysteries rather than science fiction but our tastes overlap to a certain extent. Anyway, she's the only person I would have let look at it so she was the one who read it first. A few days later she gave me her verdict: "It's a good book," she said. "Typos and all."

Great! I thought. *But typos?* I decided it might be best to go over the whole thing again. That's where some of the excessive sex got eliminated as well as some, but by no means all, of the typos. And *now* I had a book!

I won't go into the horrifying details of what happened to *The Pet Plague* and my writing career after that. If you're interested, you can find the story in my autobiography, *Darrell Bain's World of Books*. You can also find *The Pet Plague* still in print today as part of a trilogy, and in ebook versions at most of the ebook stores if you'd like to read it, because it did eventually get published.

One more note I might mention. After finally finding its way into print, *The Pet Plague* was well received and got good reviews. Not bad for a first novel, especially from someone so utterly lacking in knowledge of the techniques of fiction writing!

About the author

Darrell is the author of about two dozen books, in many genres, running the gamut from humor to mystery and science fiction to nonfiction and a few humorous works which are sort of fictional nonfiction, if that makes any sense. He has even written for children. For the last several years he has concentrated on humor and science fiction, both short fiction, non-fiction (sort of) and novels. He is currently writing the fourth novel in the series begun with *Medics Wild*. http://www.darrellbain.com

Recent release: The Cresperian Alliance, SF suspense with Stephanie Osborn

How I Came to Write *Bobby becomes Bob*

by Bob Boan

In order to tell you how I came to write *Bobby becomes Bob*, I must take you on a journey. It is a tale filled with history and philosophical viewpoints. My story may seem more complex and convoluted than most; however, it's more likely just the way we each tell our individual stories. With me, there is normally quite a tale to be told; it has been said that I successfully demand to be different. It may appear to have bumps in the roads and detours, but all of it addresses the topic. The short version would do you an injustice. I hope you enjoy the trip.

I have been an avid reader since I was about 11 or 12. Reading allowed me incredible freedoms. It allowed me-me the son of strong-principled, hard-working parents who were among those making up the backbone of America-to enjoy experiences my family could never have begun to afford to provide me. Reading allowed me to move outside the constraints of reality. I could, and I did, plant myself firmly in the middle of many a plot. With equal ease, I could become a king, a banker or a boy getting others to whitewash his fence. When I was immersed in a book, it was my world and I, its master. For the first time in my life, I was in charge. I alone had the option of deciding when the passage said the sky was blue that it was, regardless of whether the character was crying or whether the sky was actually blue. While I'm bound more by the conventions of today's society, I'm still in charge when diving imagination first into a book. Where, other than reading, can any of us have almost totally unbounded freedom at such an affordable price?

Bandwidth is a major issue in the entertainment world, albeit one a robust sixth grader was unconcerned about. It's as true today as it was in the 1950s. I didn't know what bandwidth was and I didn't care. I didn't know there was cause to care. However, thinking back on the situation, I realize now bandwidth had pronounced impact on my reading. I didn't think about it in these terms, but the written page with its limited bandwidth can display significantly less context and information with respect to a scene than is true of video. The unrealized bandwidth limitation as it turned out challenged me to fill in missing information relative to the story. I was empowered to decide the sky was gray and the grass was brown or the snow was drifting to 14 feet. The bandwidth limitation of the printed page turned out to be a great feature because it encouraged me to be creative in order to add an environment to the story which was pleasing to me. That feature is still available to me. You can take advantage of the feature as well.

I became enamored with the way Mark Twain so casually stated simple truths and with the elegant verbosity of Jane Austen. Mark Twain had a keener insight into life than most of us which allowed him to provide us precise glimpses of ourselves. His ability to do so has induced many a person to enjoy more than one laugh. Jane Austen was the all-time leading authority on the drama associated with getting daughters married. Other writers affected me but not to the same degree as those two.

Even at my young age, I briefly wondered before heading off to play basketball, baseball or some other sport or perhaps to work in the field if I could approximate the wonders of the stories told by my favorite authors. I soon put those thoughts behind me as maturity and responsibility took control of my life in spite of my concerted efforts to stave them off as long as possible.

My enthusiasm for reading was somewhat blunted when I took high school and college literature courses. Here were teachers who, while more experienced than me, could not understand my emotions and my dreams when I was reading. Yet, they were telling me how to interpret the real meaning of many of those books I had enjoyed. Their interpretations just did not jive well with what I had experienced as I read the author's words. I did not want their interpretations; I wanted to get from a book that which was personal to me. Maybe those teachers were doing me a great service, but I sure didn't see it then. By the way, I still don't.

However, as I reluctantly took on the trappings of adulthood and family life with all their accompanying commitments and constraints, I rekindled my old love for reading and took it with me. In the early days of marriage before children, I was a science teacher and coach, an occupation which allowed me reasonable degrees of latitude with respect to time during the off-season. I often picked up a book on Friday afternoon after work and read it to completion before putting it down. I often read into Saturday and even on occasion into Sunday. You see I was a notoriously slow reader when reading for pleasure. I was determined to get the most out of every word.

As my children and new career in industry played an ever-expanding role in my life, my reading habits shifted. I felt it necessary to read things which could be consumed quickly. I found myself infrequently reading for pleasure but instead exploring scientific and technical articles. Sometimes the material was selected for entertainment and edification, but most often, it was for some research relative to my profession.

Over time, I became involved in writing inputs for proposals to study or to build technical devices, the majority of which were intended for use in Department of Defense satellites. I was involved with systems for NASA and commercial spacecraft as well. We were fortunate enough to be successful and win some of those proposed efforts. I made modest contributions to some of the studies and to the design, development and fabrication of some of those systems. The results of company funded independent research and development was one of the factors which led me into writing articles for technical publications.

I also prepared a number of presentations for delivery at highly specialized scientific conferences and meetings. Many people will tell you they would rather die than make a presentation before an audience. It is truly frightening to give your first public presentation before a large audience consisting primarily of some of the world's leading authorities in a particular scientific field. Such was my fate. When I agreed to do my first presentation based on finding a solution to a corrosion problem, I found myself standing before an audience full of experts. Those people knew all there was to know about their field.

I was uncertain as I walked onto the stage following a brilliant paper if I knew anything about corrosion or anything else. My topic had seemed so important before I heard the previous presenter talk about saving an oil field. Negative thoughts flooded my mind. *They are going to think I'm wasting their time with this mundane stuff. Where's the bathroom?* I don't remember walking across the stage. The only reason I made it to the lectern because of a strong belief in honoring a commitment which was being sorely tested. I'm not sure which was louder, the riveting rhythm of the chattering of my teeth or the thunder of bone on bone as my knees shook violently, making frequent collisions.

I am consoled by knowing I don't have to struggle through making my first presentation again. The nervousness ameliorated with each subsequent presentation, but it was always there before taking the microphone. I reached a point where I became comfortable after starting to speak. If you make a mistake in front of a group of brilliant scientists, they are normally understanding but seldom subtle. They are always ready to take you to task in the event of an error. Scientists and engineers usually attack the mistake without attacking the person who made it. They do it in a blunt, matter-of-fact way out of respect and in an attempt to help you improve your work. I found it worked best for me to attempt to entertain those learned audiences while striving to educate them on the topic at hand. I brought the entertain-and-educate philosophy which I learned at the hands of those tough taskmasters to my novels.

I am back to reading for me. I typically enjoy two to four books per month. To my surprise, I've gone full circle. I'm back to predominately reading fiction as I did in my youth. I find time and desire to take on technical articles though far less of them than at the peak of my professional career. Those I pick to read are most often related to lasers, space or advances in medical technology.

During the last decade, I have frequently made long trips by car. Spending hour after hour behind the wheel reduces the amount of time available for reading. Modern technology came to my rescue leading me to become a fan of audio books. Listening to a book as I travel tends to heighten my alertness as I am entertained by the contents. I've reached the conclusion that the audio book reader is every bit as important as the writer. It is best when the reader is a good actor who adds dimension to the work. A good reader can significantly improve an average book. A weak performer can detract from a good book.

Regrettably, a number of books are abridged to make them ready for audio production. I am led to conclude that one of two things is at work. The first is that important information is denied the listener. Leaving out valuable details is an egregious disservice to the reader. The second possibility says the book is too long and filled with superfluous content as written. In this case, the abridgment is a service to the listener.

Listening to abridged audio books offered me one advantage. Comparing the shortened versions to the unabridged printed versions I read eventually influenced the length of my fiction work. Such books taught me the value of being concise-make the product as short as possible while conveying all the necessary information. While audio books are great, I recommend the printed copy. Read friends. Read!

You might ask me, "Who is your favorite author?" My initial response said in jest would be, "You mean other than the obvious-me?" Your legitimate, serious question deserves a well-considered answer. After taking on a more serious tone showing you the respect you deserve, I would tell you, "I don't have a single favorite author. However, I will try to provide deeper insight into the answer to your question."

While Mark Twain and Jane Austen still top my list, most of my favorite contemporary authors fall neatly into two categories. I read books of all genres but I tend to read more mystery and humor than anything else. I lean toward those types of books in part because of the authors to whom I have an affinity. I am drawn to writers whose characters are believable; there are already enough supermen out there to suit my taste. Stuart Woods and David Baldacci stand out among mystery writers. When looking for humorous works I prefer Joshilyn Jackson, Dorothea Benton Frank and Lewis Grizzard. By the way, I think Ms. Jackson is one of the most talented audio book readers to whom I have had the pleasure of listening.

While I am a fan of science fiction, I am inclined to pick up SCIFI less frequently than literary fiction. When I reach into the category, I look for the works of Travis S. Taylor and John Ringo. I don't know why but as a rule, I find science fiction less suited for audio books than most other fiction.

A revelation about my favorite contemporary authors came to me while writing this treatise. I realized all of them are Southerners like me. I accord Ms. Frank the honor despite the fact she lives part-time in New Jersey. She spends the rest of her time in her native state of

South Carolina. Mr. Ringo was born in Florida. After extensive traveling during his formative years, he has returned to the South to pursue his literary career. It is interesting that out of the seven, three are from Georgia. It is mere coincidence that they are from the South. However, perhaps as a moth is drawn to light, I am attracted by the ease and clarity with which Southerners spin tales.

I believe it's fair to tell you I pay attention to the style, technique and wordsmithing of every author with whom I come in contact. As I strive to educate and entertain with my writing, I hope to learn something from each while he or she distracts me from reality. The ancient Chinese taught we should always part from another by saying, "I have learned a lot from you." When read carefully, one finds the statement is very deep and profound. I can honestly repeat the wisdom of the Chinese to every author after completing his or her work.

An author might have one or both of two traits which might lead me to put down a book without finishing it. I avoid authors who are formula writers. Once you've read one or two of their offerings, you typically know approximately what is coming next and how it's going to turn out. The major events are normally repeated in their books step-by-step. The writer might skip a step now and then, but the basic story is the same from book to book. Only the characters and the environment are different. If a writer has a successful formula, he or she will be well rewarded after achieving some notoriety. My other reading pet peeve is I expect, no-I demand-authors get their science right. A writer should stick to the bounds of well-understood physics. I might cut a science fiction author a little more slack in such a case because they normally take the time to explain the physical anomaly. Please don't tell me one or more characters have the ability to violate the laws of physics and suspend the motion of spacecraft in a high-energy, highly elliptical orbit. Other aberrations of the natural laws are equally unwanted. Where are the editors when such problems arise?

Some years ago, I revisited my childhood question. Once again, I was haunted by a desire to know whether I, a mere meager mortal, could write stories on the level of the authors of my past let alone Mark Twain and Jane Austen. I sat down and started outlining several potential books, paying close attention to the well-known and well-worn advice to write about something you know. I tried writing several books with little success over the next few years. I found work was getting in the way. I needed extended uninterrupted periods of time to accomplish any writing; I was already using much of my available time to prepare technical articles and presentations.

My requirement for so much concentrated time resulted largely from my being an extremely poor typist. If I were reincarnated as a human, I think I would have such a strong subliminal memory of my struggles I would surely take typing at the earliest opportunity. I was not even an accomplished two-finger hunt and pecker, yet I was able to produce an astonishing 14 to 16 words per minute using the hunt-and-peck technique. Why, in an eight-hour day I could turn out a theoretical upper limit of about 7000 words if I sat at the computer nonstop. I'm sure you can do the math telling you quickly I would need over 14 days working eight hours each and every day in order to turn out a 100,000-word book. I did stop. I stopped regularly to think of how to say what I wanted to say next. Those stops put a significant dent in the theoretical limit of 7000 words. I forgot to mention to you there were mistakes which would have to be corrected, dramatically reducing my daily output even more.

The net effect was a significant reduction in productivity because most of my time was spent reviewing my previous effort and refreshing my thoughts on where the book was going. Working at my pace required going back over the previous output to refresh myself on the content before resuming added significantly to the previously mentioned 14 days. Fourteen days was merely a dream; it is a wish which is never going to come true. Not even close. Hence, there was little new output when I managed to filch time for writing. I think you're beginning to see why my approach was not working for me.

Despite being a severely typing-challenged adult, I was able to co-author a science text. Brown Walker Press published *An Introduction to Planetary Defense: A Study of Modern Warfare Applied to Extra-Terrestrial Invasion* in 2006. We needed four years to bring the finished product to the target community. We would probably have taken longer had we not been faced with the pressure of a publication date prior to completing edits of the book.

When I decided to retire, the decision was driven largely by my desire to pursue a career as a writer. I now had the time to write. You would think 14 days to turn out a novel was not bad. Anybody could write a book in 14 days. Just what I thought based on my mathematical analysis. However, two weeks turned out to be the theoretical lower limit. In practice, my output was only 30 to 40% of the theoretical 7000 words per day. Moreover, the statement only applied to times when I was able to sit for eight continuous hours which was unusual. I normally was able to work more like six hours on extended days. Oh my, how my shoulders ached at the end of a six-hour day hunting and pecking at the computer. A seemingly easy 14 days realistically was going to require well in excess of 60 full days to complete the first draft. As it turned out, I was constantly revising and correcting what I had already written. I was further slowed by having to stop and think how to best relay passages to the reader.

Before the turn of the century, technology promised to rescue me from my typing limitations. Speech recognition software had been around for a little while and was beginning to make significant strides in accuracy. Being a technologist at heart, I had to try it. It yielded far less than the radical, turbocharged increase in speed I had hoped to achieve. Fortunately, I found I could get more words on the page per hour. Unfortunately, it did not radically improve my overall output even after I spent hours training the program with the materials provided by the manufacturer. To my horror, I found my diction and spoken writing pace didn't match one required by the software to achieve a high degree of accuracy. The translation from my voice to the page was filled with errors. I was looking for 97 to 98% accuracy when in actual practice I was getting more like 70%.

I had to spend significantly more time proofreading and making corrections than I had in the past. Editing created a problem because I tend to read what's on the page the way I thought it as opposed to the way it actually appears. I would frequently miss an "at" which should have been a "that" or an "an" should have been an "and" among other small mistakes. To make matters worse, the speech recognition software would make mistakes such as "dear" instead of "deer." As you can see, running spellchecker stood no chance of finding either of those errors or other similar situations.

I continued to believe in the promise of the technology and upgraded to each new upgrade of the software as it came to market.

My faith in my fellow scientists has been rewarded by the latest version which is highly accurate. Their efforts and advancements have allowed me to write this discourse more efficiently than I would have been able to do otherwise. Thanks guys.

Though speech recognition software has improved dramatically in terms of accuracy, I still find it beneficial to work alone. I have been asked if I find working by myself demotivating or boring. I view working long hours in isolation as a benefit as opposed to a liability for a couple of reasons. I guess my thought has its roots in spending lots of time in the lab by myself and in attempting to solve technical problems solo. Let me assure you boredom is something I have yet to experience. I have too many things which I'm excited about doing to allow boredom to take over. To the contrary, working alone is motivating, not demotivating, because I can continually take stock of my progress. I am afforded the bonus of avoiding numerous interruptions. Second, working alone eliminates the potential of someone else's voice being transcribed to my word processing software. Such inclusions would expand the amount of time required for proofreading and removing those unintended intrusions.

As I'm sure, you realize by now, I have put *Bobby* down and come back to it on numerous occasions. I found it easier to come back each time than the one before because my excitement mounted as I continued to progress through the story. Doing something I had longed to do for years was enough to keep me motivated from day to day. I was driven by my desire to complete the book.

I strive to be a positive person. It is my philosophy to keep track of how much of a task is left before me. Seeing every day that I was closer to my goal made it easier. I would have only 90% left to do, later only 40%, and in time only 10% before eventually reaching my goal. It is much easier for me to have *only 20% left* than to be faced with having 20% left. The two scenarios sound essentially the same; however, that little word "*only*" was important to me. For me, looking it from that perspective reinforced what I had accomplished.

I was elated when I finished the first draft. Completing it was a major accomplishment by any standard I employ. When I came to grips with understanding there was still an enormous amount of effort facing me, my elation abated slightly. I quickly climbed out of the trough and went back to work. I forced myself to rein in my enthusiasm until the final version had been prepared and was ready for publication. I saved my celebration until I had prepublication copies in my hands in early August 2009.

I found publication means it is time to move to the next phase with the book. It was time for marketing. The prevailing economic environment made marketing more difficult than expected. Across America incomes had dropped so people were buying fewer discretionary items such as books. Newspapers were cutting back on the space they allotted to book reviews. A number of newspapers eliminated book reviews altogether or in a cost-cutting move released their book reviewer in favor of reviews coming from the Associated Press or other national and international media sources. The net result is sales have initially failed to meet expectations. Undaunted, the marketing efforts continue.

I had the original idea for what eventually became the *Bobby becomes Bob* in the late 1980s. In the book's incarnation, Bobby was going to be a spectacular hero. He was going to be so extraordinary that he exceeded all the bounds of his environment. My plan changed one day when one of my daughters said she would like to know more about how things were when I was growing up. I didn't know what to tell her about my environment so I told her to ask questions and I would answer. I can see now she didn't know what questions to ask because she had no understanding of my pre-adult life. So, I decided to provide her and others a glimpse at life as a poor boy in a rural southern town in the 1950s and 1960s through Bobby's eyes. I set about re-configuring the book. While I basically kept the original concept for the beginning and the ending, I changed the tone of the body. I made Bobby a vulnerable, naïve lad. I think my efforts to tell her about life in the 50s and 60s produced a far more realistic and likeable Bobby. I had to coax the final Bobby out of the corners of my mind where he was hiding, intimidated by the original concept. It was difficult to bring him to life after having had the original vision for my hero.

Bobby becomes Bob was my first novel. Some people might think I had finished writing it when progress was interrupted in 2007 in favor of producing another book. Actually, I had completed the original draft and about a half dozen rewrites. I was not finished! I was a long way from being finished. No one had told me so I had to learn for myself that once you've finished the original draft the work really begins.

The book which interrupted progress on *Bobby becomes Bob* revisits one of the touchstones of my life. Let me remind you I am known for being different. *Williams Lake Was Once the Center of the Universe* is consistent with the label. It is divided into two disparate parts. The first is a mix of fact, fiction, lies and legend. Some of the stories told are based on memories extracted from the dusty corners of friends' minds as attenuated by time and distance. The characters enjoyed high times and endured lows. The novel is followed by historical glimpses of people and items related to nights attempting to have fun at Williams Lake and other venues.

During my adolescence, my friends and I were fortunate enough to live close to Williams Lake in its heyday in the second half of the 1960s. We spent many fondly-remembered nights at the remote venue. We were drawn to the little pavilion on the lake by the opposite sex. Williams Lake provided bands, dancing and friends as the bait to lure the boys and girls.

Robert Honeycutt who had run Williams Lake during its peak of popularity was planning a 40-year reunion for August 2008. I had promised some friends 40 years earlier one day I would write a book centered on some of our exploits from the "The Lake" era. It was a very casual promise if promise is even the proper term; however, I and at least one of the other three members of the group present when I let my mouth overload me remembered the statement. Cornered, I decided to honor my loose commitment. What better time could there have been to write the book than to have its publication coincide with the reunion? I had started *Williams Lake* earlier as well. I put down everything else and spent a little over a year working on *Williams Lake Was Once the Center of the Universe* in order to have it published and available before the reunion.

While building a schedule for publication, it became obvious how daunting job lay before me even though I was committed to spending long hours on the project. As I was lamenting how tight the schedule was going to be, I remembered something I used to tell my other daughter. I would often tell her, "You don't have time to make all the mistakes yourself." I slapped my forehead when the thought materialized, *If that advice is so good for her, why isn't a little of it good for me too?* While she didn't know to do so, she would have had every right to repeat my admonition to me right there and then. Where was she when I needed her? I sought outside assistance. I found a friend and mentor in Rickey Pittman. Rickey is an author and editor in his spare time in addition to serving as a freshmen English composition teacher at Delta Community College in Monroe, Louisiana. His sage advice led me to a far better product. With his help, *Williams Lake* reached the market a little over a month before the reunion.

To my surprise, I found an even more challenging obstacle to becoming published than getting a book completed. As I talked to prospective book agents and publishers, the normal response was "Good luck with your technical writing." I guess they were saying stay away from literary fiction because you can't possibly make the transition. It would have been easy advice to follow had I been less determined to succeed. The other, kinder response I received from prospective agents was "I'm too busy to talk to you." I frequently received those responses more rapidly than an unchecked wildfire in a dry forest-faster I thought than potential agents could have possibly evaluated my work. I was stubborn enough to continue seeking publication. Maybe those agents and publishers felt they were incapable of producing technical output; therefore, members of the scientific and technical world find it equally impossible to complete a literary piece.

While *Williams Lake* was in progress, I renewed my search for an agent and/or a publisher for *Bobby becomes Bob*. My search was rapidly leading nowhere when I was fortunate enough to be encouraged to contact Lida Quillen. Lida is the owner and publisher of Twilight Times Books, http://www.twilighttimesbooks.com. She must have found some promise in my work. I am indebted to her for having enough faith in the story and in me to agree to publish it. I thank her for her courage which I am striving to prove was a stroke of genius.

I had already recognized some major differences between writing a science text and a novel. Rarely, if ever, does one use dialogue in writing a technical work. Second, scientists typically eschew the use of flowery language to paint a clever illusion. Scientists are much more likely to use math and higher-level language than the novelist. It is quite unusual to see mathematical expressions and equations interspersed within a novel. On the other hand, it seems to have become increasingly popular for novelists, especially mystery writers, to use the names of chemical compounds and drugs in telling their stories. Medical conditions are also commonplace in fiction today. The other difference has to do with point of view. Whereas novels are most often written from the first or third person point of view, a scientific article is rarely written in first person. An active voice is used meet the goal of clarity and understanding in a technical work. Despite these differences, the ability to tell a story in a fashion which allows the reader to follow is equally important in both domains. It was always my intent for *Bobby becomes Bob* to be given to the reader through Bobby's eyes. I wanted the reader to get to know Bobby and learn to think as Bobby thought. Last, members of the technical community practice strict adherence to the laws of physics as we understand them.

My first approach to writing *Bobby becomes Bob* underwent technical change as well. I was fortunate enough to get some valuable tips on writing from Dr. Bob Rich. He counseled me to use the power of the "Rule of Three." He indicated that I was expounding in lists of more than three items and beginning with the fourth they begin losing impact as the reader becomes disinterested or inpatient to be rewarded for reading the text. He admonished me to stick carefully to the point of view of the story. In this case, Bobby's point of view was important. As part of telling the story, he warned me to avoid author intrusion.

My original plan was to emphasize Bobby and the secondary characters while leaving people I considered incidental characters nameless. I wrote the first draft using Sergio Leone's man-with-no-name tactic. Having a man with no name worked in the spaghetti western because his nameless character was the star. I even carried those individuals without names through the next handful of drafts. Only after receiving guidance from more learned writers Carol Guy and Michael LaRocca did I decide to personalize those characters by giving them names. My initial thought was noteworthy nameless and faceless characters spared the reader spending time and emotion getting to know them. I accomplished my object; however, to my surprise I found people became more real and I knew them better after bestowing names on them. I concluded characters with names are just more interesting. I decided the favor I erroneously thought I was doing the reader in actuality was a disservice. The use of names allows the reader more freedom in how he or she interacts with the characters.

Carol Guy and Michael LaRocca provided other invaluable advice. Both were editors retained by Lida Quillen at Twilight Times Books. Each had enormous positive impact on the readability of the final product. Carol provided guidance on storyline, character development and point of view. Michael helped polish and clean up the language by attacking my wordiness. His suggestions, often colored by his North Carolina background, added levity and quickened the pace of the story.

I wanted to give the reader the best possible experience. My primary objective was to entertain the reader. It was also important to me to provide some level of education to the consumer. Those goals led me to rewrite the book something like 16 or 17 times before it was published. It took about 20 years to claw my way from initial concept to published book.

I spent many unrecorded hours by myself while producing the manuscript. My isolation was driven partially by the desire to avoid interruptions. It is something of a necessity when I am using my voice recognition software. I spend enough time proofreading without adding the confusion of other voices in the speech recognition environment.

"Would you do it again?" you ask. Yes, I would. It was demanding, time-consuming work but I intend to do it again and again. In fact, I have done the writing part again; look for *Don't tell Brenda* from Twilight Times Books in 2011. I have written my portion of *The Defense Affair*. The collaborative mystery is waiting for my co-author to pen the remainder of the text. I will continue to do it again as I write additional books. I have story lines for several others.

Most stories have to have characters. It's probably true of all I would want to read and definitely all I plan to write. Where does one get one's characters? Their origin varies from story to story based upon the author's desires. I chose to base the most prominent characters such as David, Tea and John on childhood friends. Mike, Joe and a few others fall into the same category. I tried to assign them proper size, demeanor and language with the greatest fidelity my imperfect memory would allow. As an example, in retrospect, I should have given David a ducktail haircut. A little detail I had forgotten until recently. Many of the characters are wholly my creations.

I based some of the episodes in Bobby's life loosely on events I had experienced or witnessed. Even those are fictitious. Other episodes are total fabrications. All of the dialogue is courtesy of my imagination.

Bobby becomes Bob is set in the fictitious town of St. Umblers, North Carolina. To the best of my knowledge, there is no place named St. Umblers in North Carolina. I took the liberty of placing St. Umblers in Johnston County near Raleigh. St. Umblers could just as easily have been located in almost any of the United States. In the 1950s and 1960s, thousands of small towns across the country shared the mores and values of St. Umblers. I suspect the real small communities were also nurturing environments, protecting their own.

Most of the citizens of those small towns were hard-working people who believed it was incumbent upon the individual to earn his way and to provide for his family. They were unaccustomed to welfare and wanted nothing to do with charity or "handouts" as I so frequently heard my elders call it. It was a fierce point of pride to be able to take care of one's family without being an imposition on anyone. It may appear we have lost that ethic particularly in some of our large cities; however, deep down in small town America, St. Umblers is wounded, but alive and kicking today.

Allow me to introduce you to Bobby Padgett. We first encounter him on the streets of St. Umblers in 1973. He is back as a man who has had a forced five-year absence from St. Umblers. He is back, hoping against hope to reunite with the love of his life-Sam. He knows success is a long shot. He also knows he must try. He and Samantha Ann Morris had almost been one since a magical afternoon on a street in St. Umblers when they were in the third grade. Nothing else matters to him now. As he searches for Sam, Bobby allows you brief glimpses into his past. He chronicles for you events from his earliest memory as a four-year-old along the path which led him to where he is as a man today. You'll experience the ups and downs Bobby experienced. You'll be privy to his thoughts as he reviews his life's journey.

Bobby moved to St. Umblers with his family when he was in the first grade. The Padgetts had come from a much smaller community in South Carolina. Though he had his share of low points growing up, the little town and its residents nourished and protected him on a day-to-day basis. It could not save him when his life was interrupted shortly after graduation from college. Between his departure and the present, he had endured five harsh years. Bobby left a boy. Bob returned. He was unquestionably a man to be respected. The boy Bobby was hardly recognizable in the man Bob.

About the author

Bob Boan has been a member of the space community for over twenty-five years developing RF and optical systems for communications and sensing satellites. He has multiple patents and publications in his field. Bob previously served in academia. He earned a B.S. from Campbell University, a master's from the University of Mississippi and a doctorate from Florida Institute of Technology.
http://bobboan.com

Ask for *Bobby Becomes Bob* from your favorite bookstore.

Upcoming release: Look for my next novel also from Twilight Times Books on shelves in 2011. *Don't tell Brenda* is a mystery centered in Johnston County, North Carolina. It is a story of crime and revenge. It teaches revenge more so than crime does not pay.

Tips on Writing Your First Novel

by Mayra Calvani

From the time I was about eleven, I loved writing stories. That was my special talent, what made me stand out among my peers. Later, in my mid-teens, I seriously began picturing myself as a published author. The possibility of holding my own book in my hands and seeing it on bookshelves was a thrilling fantasy to have. I remember being asked in class what we planned to do with our lives. We were supposed to stand up and answer and, of course, I answered 'I'm going to be an author.' Agatha Christie was a big influence back then. I think I had read all of her novels by the time I turned fifteen. In those days, I also read a lot of Barbara Cartland and Janet Daily. I gobbled up their books and dreamed of becoming a known author just like them some day.

I wrote my first novel when I was fifteen. It was a Harlequin-type romance. However, that isn't the book I'll be discussing here because, naturally, that one never got published! It just ended up being passed around the class (behind our teacher's back) and guiltily devoured in secret by my friends. I wrote many short stories and another novel during my early twenties, but it wasn't until I was twenty four, that I sat down to *really* write a book intended for publication. Back then, the novel was titled *At the Time of Dinosaurs*, and it was a parody/satire about the artistic scene in San Juan, Puerto Rico, where I grew up.

The conception of this book stemmed from two factors: my personal observations of Puerto Rican artists when I was a teen and my love for satiric writing, a taste I developed in college after discovering Tama Janowitz's *Slaves of New York*. My mother was-and still is-an artist, and although she's 'retired' now, back in the early eighties she was an active painter in San Juan, showing her works at art exhibits and galleries regularly. She took me everywhere with her, so I attended all these shows and activities and I *observed*.

Let me tell you something, the art scene can be extremely interesting and that is because so many artists are eccentric, unconventional people. There's so much competition, jealousy and gossip! Anyway, I guess all these experiences must have made an impression on me. When the time came to write my book, I knew these were the people and situations I wanted to write about. I decided I would make the book a parody, this way I could keep it upbeat and have the freedom to exaggerate to the point of being ridiculous. I was sure an upbeat, sharp, satiric, darkly humorous style would be perfect for my novel.

When I started writing this book, I had just arrived in Ankara, Turkey. Because of my husband's work, we would be living there for the next two years. I had the whole day to myself and my own cozy little office, so the environment for writing a book was perfect. As soon as my husband left for work, I'd sit at the computer and start working. As I look back, I remember writing until early afternoon (with just a small sandwich lunch break-I love eating lunch at the computer!), when I'd finally leave the manuscript to go shopping and prepare the evening meal. At the time my computer was a Tandy 2000 and my word processing program was called PW (for Professional Writer). I loved that little program! Of course, it wasn't as sophisticated as today's Word, but it had everything I needed at the time. So that was my schedule: 3-4 hours a day of writing during week days. It took me about six months to finish the complete manuscript.

Living in Ankara had few distractions, so I didn't have to deal with unexpected phone calls or nosy neighbors. This worked for me. I'm very self motivated by nature and being alone most of the day writing didn't bother me too much. I'm one of those crazy people who seldom feel lonely—how can I, with all those characters talking in my head, demanding me to write their stories? That said, I sometimes wondered if I was becoming a total hermit. I did wish I had known other authors, like minds to share my writing troubles with, but unfortunately that wasn't the case. The world didn't have the Internet yet!

Living in Turkey did have a tiny influence on my first novel: One of the characters in the book, a cat, is Turkish! However, the Turkish culture had a larger influence on my subsequent books. The vampire hero in my paranormal suspense, *Embraced by the Shadows*, is a

Turkish prince, and the villainess in my supernatural thriller, *Dark Lullaby*, is a Turkish jinn. Both novels are partially set in Turkey, too.

Though nowadays I usually plot my stories in advance, that wasn't the way I worked when I wrote *In the Time of Dinosaurs*. I had a general idea of what was going to happen and how I wanted the story to evolve, but other than that, everyday it was an adventure. In this sense, I wrote the novel in a stream-of-consciousness manner. I wouldn't do this today. I've found from experience that not plotting in advance can get me stuck in the middle and that's not a nice place to be, believe me. When you're stuck, you can get writer's block; when you get writer's block, you can become disconnected from your story; when that happens it can be difficult to return to your old momentum. On the other hand, when you write everyday for a sustained period of time, it's easier to get into 'the zone'-that state where you lose all sense of space and time because you're so immersed in the story. Let me tell you something: that's a damn fine place to be.

Then, eventually, the day comes when you type the words 'The End.' Finishing a novel feels absolutely wonderful. First, there's an immense feeling of validation because you feel like you have attained your goals. Many people start writing books but never finish them. I read somewhere that only about 10% of people actually finish writing a book. Finishing a book means you have completed what you started, and that takes determination and persistence. The key to being a writer isn't just creativity and knowing how to construct sentences. Being a writer also entails perseverance, discipline and hard work. If you want to succeed as a writer, you have to approach it like any other job, and that means getting up from bed each morning and writing your daily quota-be that one page or ten pages. You have to show up on the page.

So I thought, 'I did it!' I think I might have jumped up and down. For sure, I celebrated with my hubby with a glass of the bubbly. Of course, as all savvy writers know and as one famous author once said, "Greats books aren't written. They are rewritten." But that's another subject altogether.

So writing a book sounds easy, right?

Wrong.

The truth is, I encountered a few problems while writing my first book:

Procrastination
This is a big complaint with many writers and I was no exception. When I first started writing the book, full of passion and enthusiasm, all seemed easy. That's because as a rule those one to two chapters are easy to write. It's later that things begin to get increasingly difficult. And when things get difficult, it takes even more determination to get your butt on the chair and keep working on the story. All of a sudden a million distractions invade your mind: dust the furniture, wash the laundry, run errands, sharpen pencils, get something to eat... The list is endless. Your mind will come up with the most unexpected suggestions to keep you from writing. It's at times like this that you need an iron will.

Often, your prose won't seem like it comes from a masterpiece-at times you'll hate it, wondering 'What on earth made me think I could become an author? My writing stinks!' Listen: The easiest way to fight procrastination is to sit on that chair and start writing one word followed by another. Repeat this procedure until you have at least a few sentences and you will find that you will feel better. It's having to sit down, face the blank page and write those first few words that kill you. Then the rest gets easier.

One way to avoid procrastination is to write as often as possible and/or create a writing schedule. You have to make a habit of writing. You have to create a momentum. It's the same with exercise. The more you do it, the easiest it will be to create a habit and honor it. It's easier to exercise a little everyday than only once or twice a week. Also the more you write, the better your writing will get.

Writer's Block
When you have writer's block, you can't write. Your mind freezes. Words don't flow. You can't even type or if you do, you delete it immediately, believing it is the worst writing in the entire world. You become terrified. You hate yourself and the world-and family members beware, because you're definitely NOT a happy person!

Writer's block is an elusive and even controversial term. Some writers swear by it; others claim such a thing doesn't exist. I have suffered from writer's block in the past, but over time I've learned to control it. Every time I face the blank page, I experience a little of writer's block. I know because I'll immediately become nervous and feel the urge to get up and inspect the fridge. It's a bit like a dog turning this way, then that way, trying to find the perfect spot to sit down. I have learned that there's no such a thing as a perfect moment to write. I just have to dive into it, like closing my eyes and jumping off a cliff. I tell myself, "Jump and the net will appear." Most of the time, it's true. But you can't expect to feel the net right away, after only a sentence or two. You have to insist and persist and keep writing for a sustained period of time. That's when everything starts getting easier, when the waters start to calm down. It's like first diving in a feral sea, then, as you keep swimming, you reach a place where the waters are calm and peaceful. You just keep swimming, one lap after another.

It's at times like these when I reach the 'zone,' that marvelous place where you lose sense of place and time and you're totally immersed in the world of your characters. That's the best place to be as a writer.

Procrastination is often—not always—a result of writer's block. That's because when you feel you can't write, or when writing becomes a torture, it's only natural that you will try to avoid it.

For me, not having an outline in advance and not writing often are sure ways to get writer's block. I need to write often, everyday, ideally, but if you can't make it everyday, then as often as possible. You don't want to distance yourself from the story and the characters; you want to stay right there, so that when you face the screen every time you sit down to write you'll know exactly where to go. This is the best way to fight writer's block.

You also have to turn your inner critic off. You have to realize that all is accepted when you're working on that first draft. That the time to edit and polish it is not now but later, once you have finished the book. You have to allow yourself to write a crappy first draft because first drafts are supposed to be just that: crappy. The time to make your manuscript sparkle is later during the editing process.

When I wrote my first book I wanted each chapter to be perfect, so I kept editing and re-editing before moving on to the next chapter. The result was that my creative process was disrupted. First drafts are all about creativity and about writing the story-what *happens*-down. They're not about choosing the right synonym or adjective.

So learn to shut down your inner critic. When you hear it say, "And you call yourself a writer? Ha! Who do you think you are?" Tell it to shut up. Give it an obnoxious name. My inner critic is called Helga. I say, "Shut your damn mouth, Helga. I'm working." Most of the time, Helga goes and does her own thing and leaves me alone, but I have to be very assertive and persistent—as much as Helga is!

Not Having a Life

I get obsessed and intensely antisocial when I'm writing a book, and with my first novel it was no exception. I did mention I was afraid of becoming a hermit, didn't I? I may have been writing 3-4 hours a day, but I was thinking about the book 99% of my time-even in my dreams I thought about characters and scenes! It's so easy to become overwhelmed to the point of becoming a recluse. Telephone calls bother you; neighbors bother you; having to go out of the house to run errands bothers you. Before you know it, you can become quite a loner. It's important to take breaks, get out, go on a walk, meditate, breathe fresh air, talk with people, and have fun with friends. Taking these breaks will rejuvenate you. Don't let fun times like these make you feel guilty. Instead, use them as rewards *after* you've done your daily work. Rewarding yourself on a regular basis will keep your inner child-and the creative writer in you-happy and motivated.

Lack of Feedback and Critique Groups

I didn't know critique groups existed when I wrote my first book. I wish I had known about them; I wish I had looked for a supportive writing environment, but, as I already mentioned, there was no Internet back then and I was living very far from the States. So I just had myself as a writer. I didn't have any writer friends. I was a lone wolf, all by myself in my world of books.

Getting constructive feedback is essential for a writer and we're lucky that nowadays, thanks to the Internet, it's easy to find critique groups to help us hone our craft no matter where in the world we're located. The business of publishing is so competitive now, the best investment you can make, if you don't like joining a critique group, is to pay a professional editor to look over your manuscript before you start submitting. As writers, we get so close to our own words we become blind. We need a set of objective eyes to go over our words. If I could go back in time, that's one thing I would have done after finishing my novel. I would have joined a group or gotten professional feedback. My book would have been stronger because of that. I wouldn't dream of submitting a manuscript now before running it first through my critique group.

Remember as important as it is to seek criticism, it is also important to be able to take it. Some writers can't take criticism. They think their creation is sacred and their sentences and plot structures are perfect. If you're one of those writers, you won't be happy joining a critique group but you'll lose in the end. Don't be one of those arrogant writers. Writers can learn from other writers. That doesn't mean you have to accept everything negative they say, but you can certainly pay attention to repeated criticism. If several people comment on your protagonist being whiny, then chances are they have a point and you better revise your manuscript to make her or him more sympathetic.

Lack of a Submission Schedule
Besides a writing schedule, a writer needs a submission schedule. Again, I wish I had done this when I wrote my first novel. I submitted my manuscript to just three or four publishers, and when they rejected it, I lost hope and decided to self publish. Who in their right mind does that? Of course, I didn't know in those days that a writer first needs to gather rejections before getting to acceptances. You can't let rejections put you down. Dr. Seuss submitted his first manuscript 150 times before it got accepted. Now he's a household name. What does that tell you? You have to persist! As soon as you get a rejection, tell yourself, "I'll show them!" and submit again.

If you're lucky, and the editor or agent writes a comment on your manuscript or query, pay attention to what he or she has to say, BUT remember that many times their decision is subjective and doesn't necessarily mean there's something wrong with your writing.

So first write your novel. Then get feedback. Then, when you think your prose is positively shining, start sending it off to agents and publishers/small presses by following a steady submission schedule.

It doesn't matter how great a writer you are. If you don't submit, if you leave your manuscript hidden in a drawer, you will never become a published author. Sure, you might be afraid of rejection. Everybody is. But you can't let that stop you. Decide how often you can submit, make a plan, and stick to it. That may be three times a week; perhaps five a month. The decision is yours. You should know, however, that submitting only once a month is a drop in the bucket. You need to keep those queries and sample chapters or manuscripts around agents/editors' desks at all times until you hit jackpot. These days, most editors and agents don't mind simultaneous submissions as long as you specify this in your query.

Finally, writing a book without knowing how to do it is like driving in the dark with no headlights. I majored in Creative Writing in college, so I had at least some idea on how to go about it. But if you don't, take a class or an ecourse on novel writing, join a workshop or study books on the subject. Becoming a better writer and honing your craft is a never-ending process. Sure, some people are born naturally good writers, but, unfortunately, that's not the case with most of us.

Writing a first novel is an exciting, thrilling experience, and the more passion you feel for your story and characters, the more that will reflect on your finished manuscript. You may have heard the saying, "write about you know." That is important, but not as important as feeling enthusiasm for your project. After all, you can learn about everything by doing research. So write from the heart. Write the kind of story *you* would like to read. Write for your most important audience: yourself.

About the author

Mayra Calvani is the author of several books. Her stories, articles and reviews have appeared in many online and print publications in the States, England and Puerto Rico. In addition, she is assistant editor of Voice in the Dark newsletter, where she writes a monthly column. She has lived in America, Asia, the Middle East, and is now

settled in Brussels, Belgium, where she lives with her husband, two children and a variety of pets. Her hobbies include playing the violin and astronomy/sky observing.
http://www.mayracalvani.com

Recent release: How to Turn Your Book Club into a Spectacular Event, YA non-fiction. The novel Mayra mentions above, *In the Time of Dinosaurs*, is currently available under a new title, *Sunstruck*.

How I Wrote My First Book: Understanding Numerology

by D Jason Cooper

Once upon a time in 1975, I had a dream. A friend of mine at the time was sitting, leafing through a book. I stood to one side telling her about the book which I had written. The book was about numerology, it had some new features, and the author's name on the cover wasn't mine, but in the dream it was mine. As my friend flipped a page, a sudden thought came to me, "If this book has been published, I'd better hurry up and write it." The thought woke me up. That's how the idea for my first book, *Understanding Numerology*, came to me.

I'd like to say I bounded up and wrote the whole thing down, but, sadly, that is not the case. What the dream did do, though, was confirm that I wanted to write.

I'd had the notion for some time but, beyond the odd letter to an editor or poetry to a school journal, most of my attempts at writing aborted somewhere between a half and a half-a-dozen pages. Those I completed to the end, I tended to burn in lieu of firewood.

I would have given up: my life was full from moving from continent to continent, father dying, going to university, poverty, wife, graduation, panic, job, buying a house, and so on. But through all that, there was still the writing. Apart from papers at university (a couple of which I got published and one which had an article I wrote in the bibliography), I wrote because to think things out I increasingly had to write them out. Writing became an essential part of thinking about things, including numerology.

What would become the book began as a piecemeal investigation. I don't have any party tricks, but I can do your numeroscope. For example, I did one for G. M. Glaskin, author of books like *Windows of the Mind* and books-turned-into-movies like *A Waltz Through the Hills*, who was then authoring a work on the genealogy of European Royalty.

'I don't understand. According to this, you're a slob, but this place is as neat as a pin.' 'That's not me, that's Leo. He's the one who cleans.'

When I came to it, numerology was in a degraded state. The only way you could write a whole book about the subject was by padding. I remember one that belabored America's connection to the 'powerful' number 13 and its resolution of 4. It mentioned the thirteen original states, the thirteen stripes on the flag, the thirteen stars on the original flag, and the fourth of July as the date of Independence. Never mind that two of those numbers (the number of stars and stripes) were based on the third (the number of states), making the number of examples statistically worthless.

For that matter, any person's name was always reduced to a single digit number of one through nine; that's all you got. The letters in your name were converted one-by-one into a digit from one to nine, then individual numbers were added up and the total was reduced to a single digit number again. But when I read of the numerology of the ancient Hebrews and Greeks, they had letters with values in the tens or the hundreds. There was even a well-known technique by which you took the total value of a word and found another word with a matching value, and that meant the two words were connected. In the Biblical pesher studies of scholars like the Essenes who used it to try an illuminate what the holy writings meant, the technique was used quite often. But there would be an awful lot of connections if you only allow nine numbers for all words.

Perhaps it was my studies in medieval history at university, but I really thought that, just maybe, we were living with a past where they could do things better than we could.

It was the teachings of Pythagoras - who lived in the seventh century BC - who gave me the second clue. He described the numbers, but when he got to ten he described how the number 'resolved' into one. Really? But the decad (base ten) system wouldn't be invented for centuries - in fact it wouldn't be invented for centuries after the date of the earliest version of this writing. Historians tell us Pythagoras would have been using the Greek alphabet for his numbers, but if that was the case, the number nine (the letter theta) would have 'resolved' into the letter iota. If Pythagoras had been Roman, then IX would have resolved into X.

I also ran across a poem allegedly from the time of the emperor Domitian. Historians universally regarded it as a fake because it describes the planets as revolving around the sun when Domitian ruled in the fourth century AD. But Pythagoras lived in the seventh century BC, over a thousand years earlier, and he believed that nine planets revolved around the sun (not our nine but that's a whole different story). The poem does not counter any Pythagorean beliefs, so it might be genuine.

And nine resolves back into one, and the thing works exactly as it says it does. Nine resolves back into one, in another column. Take a number like 2413; there's a 3 in the ones column, a 1 in the tens column, a 4 in the hundreds column, and a 2 in the thousands column. Reduce that number by the usual method and it's a 1. That number doesn't go away, it's still there, but that number guides each of the others individually.

It was as if, after a lifetime of sun-sign astrology, somebody said, "I betcha all those other planets mean something, too."

Everything I'd gone over (and that was a lot), I went over again. A flood of new information came through and with it, explanations of mysteries and categories for the information I now had. It was like a drought breaking, not just with rain but with steady, heavy rain that soaks the soil and by run-off, creates brooks and streams. I was having a good time.

I went back to the traditional tools and looked at them again. Some I still reject as being useless, like putting the numbers of the date of birth on a tic-tac-toe board of the numbers from one to nine. Others, like using the vowels and consonants each on their own as well as all letters together were, though not much used since the nineteenth century, useful tools.

Once I had the theory of higher numbers, I was faced with one of the worst pieces of rubbish in numerological history, which is saying something. Back then, numerologists were split between those who used the Chaldean alphabet and those who used the Pythagorean alphabet. Neither Pythagoras nor the Chaldeans had anything to do with these alphabets: they were named for, not created by. Neither was an alphabet per se, they were tables for converting the letters of the Roman alphabet (the one this article's written in) into numbers.

Thing is, whichever 'alphabet' you use, you can get a completely different number for a word or name. Take the name Karl: by the Chaldean alphabet it would be an 8, but by the Pythagorean alphabet it would be a 6. So our choice of alphabet decides whether we tell Karl he's aggressive and career oriented or more concerned with harmony and the home. I could have asked the Bundesrepublik for a visa to study their Karls (that's people named Karl), but they'd probably say no and I probably couldn't have afforded the trip in any event. Besides, I could look around for Freds; the name Fred also comes out to an 8 or a 6 depending on the alphabet you use.

In the end, I went with history and the bulk of my studies. I would base the numerical value of the letter on its position in the Roman alphabet. And, by the way, no way was I going to call my method an alphabet. Apart from the sheer stupidity of it, it could get confusing. I was working with the Roman, Hebrew, Cyrillic, and Greek alphabets and the Japanese alphabet, the Hiragana. So if I translated from the Cyrillic to the Roman alphabet, should I use the Chaldean or Pythagorean alphabet? See what I mean? Two totally different things, there.

So an alphabet is the set of letters used to convey written messages by one people or another. For the conversion of those letters to numerical values for numerology I used a new word, taken from the Greek and meaning "to make stand with." I called this a systemata. It was the Chaldean systemata, the Pythagorean systemata, and my own Ulian systemata. And from the time my book was published, numerologists and skeptics alike have changed their use to the term system.

Rats.

Then again, if skeptics (or at least Australian Skeptics) use my methods exclusively when they argue against numerology (and they do in at least two of their references), then I can justly claim to be the preeminent numerologist of the late twentieth and early twenty-first centuries. But I digress and jump ahead in the story.

Anybody else would have thought, "hey, here's a gravy train." I could have just used what I'd found and kept repeating myself into some tiny corner of fame (and more money). The thing is, though, I wanted to know how it was that the sound r, when written in different alphabets, could have different numerical values. Why did Resh (Hebrew) and R have different values?

For that matter, there was a little problem with the calendar.

I had always thought that I was pursuing some kind of spiritual study. But what universals was I looking at that could be so affected by ... something? The ignorance (sorry, but that's what it was) of other numerologists was a great defense against problems like this. They never confronted hard questions, nor did they have any discoveries that were other than what you'd expect their customers to want. American numerologists were all-American, everything was up beat and better times were coming.

OK, there is a demographic of people who haven't had it so good and who would like a book to cheer themselves up. But if the book says to try one course rather than another, surely it would help if the suggested course had the best chance possible of working?

More than that, I looked at history. Calendars. They change from time to time. At one point, the English shifted the date 14 days forward to put the calendar date back in synch with the seasons. It's like today's the first and tomorrow's the fifteenth of the month. There were riots with people chanting 'give us back our fourteen days.' Although it hadn't yet come up when I was writing, the latest change in the calendar was 2000, when they added an extra day.

Technically, every fourth year is a leap year, with a February 29th, except a year which is evenly divisible by 400. So 1600 would have not been a leap year, except they didn't have the system in place then (the fourteen days fiasco was still in the future) so the first time would have been 2000. However, they added in the 29th leap-year day even though it shouldn't have been a leap year. The Earth had slowed down a bit and therefore they added the extra day.

For that matter, not everyone uses the same calendar. It is possible that someone born at the same time as you in a culture with a different calendar would have a different birth number. They might get a completely different numerological message from the calendar and their date of birth.

And then we're back with all the different alphabets and the systematas that interpret them.

At least with astrology, they can agree where the bloody planets are - except, no they can't. There's Western Astrology, Hindu Astrology,

Chinese Astrology, and some offshoots like putting the dates and signs back into alignment (most people have been born one sign from the one they think is theirs).

What I had to finally admit is, when you cut away all the gunk and all the things numerologists can't answer, what you're left with is not some mathematically precise spiritual science. It's a social science like psychology, sociology, economics, anthropology, and an exclusive bunch of other ologies who couldn't get a decent job.

I had a breakthrough, but it was the kind that no one would care about except the numerology geeks, whatever we called them back then. The fact was, a systemata is a social construct and so is a calendar. Despite this, they each provide information because they each must follow certain principles.

Once I had that under my belt, I continued to pursue numerology. I worked out how the Japanese alphabet, the Hirigana, only uses odd numbers and has negative numbers (the only alphabet to have both). I also worked out the same language in different alphabets will cause a people to split, but with Poland and the Ukraine on the one side and the Balkans on the other as my examples, that didn't seem too brilliant. Then again, maybe the split among the Chinese which numerology predicts will give some new data.

There were other things I studied, but I wrote only a fraction of that for the book. In fact I only wrote a fraction of the book. I wrote to Aquarian, then an independent publisher who would soon be swallowed up by HarperCollins. I sent a synopsis and sample chapters and got back a contract.

Since I'd already sold the book, I guessed I had better hurry up and write it. I told my wife that. Didn't tell her about the dream.

As far as all the planning ahead and such that writers tell you that you have to do, I really didn't do that. The five drafts you have to do to make every word perfect that someone wrote as advice for other writers, I didn't have to do that, either. My biggest problem was making my fingers move fast enough on a soon-to-be-obsolete typewriter.

The fact was I had gone through each bit of this stuff a thousand times. So I didn't have to think much as I wrote down a book in about a week. The only thing I had to do was keep everything at a level 101.

The readers weren't going to be experts in numerology, just people who wanted a step further than the drivel they'd had available for years.

So I typed and I posted and that was that. It only took ten years to get ready for a week's work, but then, as any painter will tell you, preparation is everything.

About the author

D Jason Cooper was born south of Toronto, Canada, grew up in Buffalo, New York, and now lives in Perth, Australia. He has a wife and two children, a girl, Shadra (aged twelve) a boy, Darius (aged eight), and two cats.

Current release: Slums of Paradise, Futuristic vampire

Two Beginnings

by Lee Denning

I should start at the beginning, my friends. Actually, there were two of them.

In late 2002, I'm approaching a decade birthday. Those are tough birthdays; they raise existential questions. Mine was 'what do I really want to do when I grow up?' To make it more difficult, that question itself is questioned by the Peter Pan reflex—'do I really want to grow up'? So here I am, sliding toward sixty. I've been a construction worker, student, soldier, mathematician, scientist, engineer, corporate type, entrepreneur. I've helped build some nuclear plants, solved some environment problems, started and built a successful consulting company. Satisfying work. Not a bad run. But a lot of the fun has gone out of the environmental business lately. The government has gotten prescriptive in its solutions; creativity has been shoved to the back of the bus. Politicians make crazy noises at each other and some of those noises even get turned into environmental regulations. Ycchh. "Thank God we don't get all the government we pay for," Mark Twain said. The work has become boring; I'm getting fidgety. There's more to life, *n'est-ce pas?*

Now, let's flash back to the previous beginning. In mid-1970, I'm an Air Force officer, doing a staff job at Tan Son Nhut airbase in Saigon, during the Vietnam war. The job is neither demanding nor dangerous, and the temptation is to while away the off-duty time chasing nubile young mama-sans and drinking the native beer. The downside of the mama-sans was that a fair percentage were contagious. The downside of the native beer (called "33" or Ba Muoi Ba in Vietnamese) was that you really didn't know what was in it, although it was generally conceded to have a high formaldehyde content. I'm no saint—did a little of both. But mostly I wrote—got about a hundred handwritten pages into a sci-fi novel. Then, after a couple of months in Saigon, I got an opportunity to go upcountry with the Army Special Forces. At this point life got a lot more interesting and I put aside those hundred pages.

So I guess you could say that—one way or another, in one decade or another—boredom gave birth to the book.

After Vietnam, the handwritten draft stayed put for thirty-some years, migrating progressively further downward in the attic underneath the boxes of accoutrements that time-stamp the progress of an upwardly mobile yuppie: grad school, corporate life, small business owner. Yeah, I thought about the story periodically during those years, because it was a really good one: *aliens invade the minds of two lovers, distort their realities and pit them against each other in a struggle to the death... while the fate of humanity hangs in the balance.* But I had a life to lead... hard worker, decent spouse, good father. And though a few little karmic reminders (mostly movies—*War of the Roses, Terminator 2, Mr. and Mrs. Smith*—probably because the story was very visual to me) would pester me from time to time, I ignored them. No time for a novel. Too busy. *[Insight #1].*

(So what's this 'Insight', you ask? The basic purpose of this book is to share the creative process and experiences with prospective writers. So when it occurs to me, I'm explicitly writing down what I've learned writing this first book that I think may be useful to you. Some of it may not; I make no claim to represent a typical writer. These are a few brief words of useful information. Or to some folks they may just be turds. I don't have a problem with either perception, everybody is different and vive la difference. In the absence of magazine-style formatting that would put these 'Insights' in little boxes embedded in the text, I've placed them all at the end of the narrative. Take what's useful and forget the rest.)

Back to 2002, to the squishy decade-birthday question: what do I want to do when I grow up. *The time has come, the walrus said, to speak of many things...*I could do a lot of stuff, I tell myself. I have an open mind. But there are two important criteria: (1) the undertaking has to be highly creative; and (2) I have to be able to go to work naked. Yes, there are jobs besides writing that you can go to naked, but history has proven I'm a lousy stock-picker... and the other obvious alternative I'm getting too old and ugly for. *[Insight #2]*

Now, I suppose I have a reasonable allocation of intuition or gut-sense (mama's genes), but I'm also (as mathematician/scientist/engineer) pretty far into the rationalist camp (papa's genes). So I ponder my existential question both emotionally and with decision-analysis tools straight out of Harvard Business School. Narrow it down to two options: (1) write sci-fi, or (2) build gaming software that uses environmental issues to teach fundamental logic and critical thinking at the middle school level. Then I evaluate the options on a decision grid—weighted criteria, the typical nerd approach. This results in an outcome of 659 points to 613, basically a tie given the subjective nature of the process. What follows then is a little more thought but essentially a mental coin flip, and I'm suddenly a novelist. Whoopee! Time to dig that sucker out of the attic!

I do, sneezing out a lot of dust until I find it. After thirty-some years, the writing is past bad and heading into horrendous. It must have decayed in the attic; I know I'm a better writer than that. The other possibility is that the formaldehyde in Ba Muoi Ba nailed too many of my brain cells in Nam. So what now? Go back to the software development option? I thumb through the manuscript's brittle pages. It's that funny old government paper, smaller than the standard 8.5 by 11. The paper's old, the writing's crummy... but by God the idea is still great, and the plot ain't bad either. *[Insight #3]* And as far as I know, nobody has written anything close. *[Insight #4]*

At this point, enter the nay-sayers and devil's advocates, both internal and external. A piece of conventional wisdom for aspiring writers is that the first million words is practice. This is not unreasonable, I think at the time. After all, practice is usually what gets you to a goal. *[Insight #5]* How many notes did Stern play before doing Carnegie Hall? How many tennis strokes did Federer hit before getting to Wimbledon? But a million words is between six and eight good-length novels, I figure. Jeesh!

Fortunately there's a handy rationalization. I carefully calculate that in the course of a long professional career I've written between five million and eight million words in technical documents. They ranged from dispassionate disclosure of research results to advocacy legal briefs that—haha—sometimes verged on fiction. Sure, technical writing is different than fiction, but you've still got to assemble words into sentences, sentences into paragraphs, organize ideas to tell a coherent story. I figure five to eight million technical is more than equivalent to one million fictional. *[Insight #6]*

So I'm golden... back on track... gonna be a sci-fi novelist, mama! And here we've come to the end of my two beginnings: I trash the old manuscript but keep the idea.

Now... here's the middle of 'my first novel' story...

Monkey Trap is a sci-fi thriller, but it's underpinned with a number of philosophical and moral issues. Chief among these is the observation from Jimi Hendricks that only "when the power of love overcomes the love of power, will the world know peace". So, how to wrap a story around that?

In India, villagers used to trap monkeys by hollowing out a gourd. The hole in one end held a rope that was attached to a distant tree. The hole in the other end was just big enough for a monkey to work his hand into. The monkey's favorite nuts were dropped in the gourd as bait. The monkey worked his hand in to grab them, but with his fist closed couldn't pull his hand out. So he dances around at the end of a tether, madder than hell. He wants what he wants, and won't let go of the bait to pull his hand out. Thus he becomes monkey soup for the village.

There is an answer, of course: let go and save your sorry ass, my monkey friend. Or better yet, shake the nuts out of the gourd into your hand and run away laughing. But monkeys know what monkeys know... just as in us humans, it's a complex mix of genetics and learning. In the heat of the moment most monkeys get trapped. So the metaphorical question is... if you wanted to test a human, what would you use for bait?

Power.

And what would cause your trapped human to release that bait?

Love.

An interesting premise. *[Insight #7]* Worthy of a decade birthday. Worthy of some serious effort. So the project is off and running, late 2002.

I may be crazy, but I'm not stupid, so before I even start writing, I want to see if there's a template to make the writing easier. Because the story—plot-wise—is a series of chase scenes (and maybe also because I'm so visually-oriented), I watch Terminator 2 six times to get a sense of structure and pacing. I take copious notes. After that sinks in enough, I begin to outline. That was my only specific preparation. No writing classes, no groups, no on-line research on how to go about writing a novel—just jump in, and like Nike says, "just do it". *[Insight #8]*

I have a co-author in this writing business, my daughter, Leanne. (Thus the pen name Lee Denning.) It was sort of an accident. In early 2003, she's in college in sunny southern California while I'm shoveling snow in Connecticut, drafting chapter 8 of *Monkey Trap* when I happen to mention it to Lee in our weekly phone chat. She gets very excited, wants to read installments as they come off my computer (a chapter per week, roughly). I say sure, just send me back your comments and ideas. She does. They're pretty good. And they get better. I tell her to write some stuff if she wants. She does. By the time we get done, I figure she's written maybe a fifth of the book. Didn't help her grades much, but it's her senior year and she's graduating, so what the hell.

Here's my time breakdown for *Monkey Trap*: structure and outline—173 hours; write first draft—973 hours; edit and rewrite to final manuscript—1173 hours. I'm not really anal-retentive, I just was curious as to how long the process actually would take, so I kept track. Add maybe twenty percent more for Lee's time. *[Insight #9]*

We did six edits, total. I thought that was overmuch until I discovered Mark Twain edited *Huckleberry Finn* seventeen times without benefit of a computer and word processor, ouch! So I spend a lot of upfront time. However, I'm <u>not</u> suggesting any particular writing methodology here. *[Insight #10]*

Now, while all this novel writing is going on in 2003, mind you, I'm still running a small business. And as any small business owner will be happy to tell you, that means a *lot* of time and energy. So I tell my junior partners the plan: I'll show up two or three hours late most mornings and you guys can suck up the slack. Those lads are great partners and great friends and don't even blink... not sure what I did to deserve them, but I'm blessed. So, the writing program becomes: up early, write two to three hours, go to my day job. On the way home, hit the gym or tennis court. Late dinner. Sleep like a baby. Get up and do the same the next day. Spousal encouragement, no bitching... I'm blessed again; possibly I got something right in a prior incarnation. Weekends—more writing, fix problems. Make time for a little fun, sex and surprise dates. Which, by the way, is important. *[Insight #11]*

So that's how *Monkey Trap* got written, my friends. And here we've come to the end of the middle: the manuscript is written, edited, polished, even has cover art that reflects the nature of the story, so we're ready to go. (I won't trouble you with the details of finding a publisher and promoting a book, that's a whole different ballgame.)

Now, there is an end to the novel-writing saga, but completing the first book wasn't it. So here's the end... so far, that is...

About halfway through the first draft of *Monkey Trap*, Lee and I begin to realize that—although the tale itself comes to a clear and satisfying conclusion—it also begs the question of what happens next. I mean, this is about the evolution of a new human species, so something has to happen next. Right? We kick it around, and suddenly we've got a trilogy. *[Insight #12]* In our *Nova sapiens* trilogy (of which *Monkey Trap* is Book I), a long-suppressed gene is activated when our two lovers pass their monkey trap test... but the new path of human evolution is fraught with peril for the first of the new species, with only the slimmest hope of redemption for the rest of us...

In *Hiding Hand*, the eighteen-year-old boy, Joshua, comes of age in a blistering conflict between the love of power and the power of love... and must confront his own dark side as human evolution explodes around him (Book II).

In *Splintered Light*, the fifteen-year-old biracial girl, Eva, evolves into the first of the new human species and the reluctant Second Coming of Christ... in a world imploding around her (Book III).

The entire trilogy is strongly mythological, and draws on a variety of spiritual and religious traditions, turning some of them upside down or inside out. *[Insight 13]* By design, the books become progressively more character-driven as the trilogy progresses. *[Insight 14]*

Creativity is a wonderful thing to find inside yourself, but it's especially fun to watch it bubbling up in your own child. I'd had some inkling of it watching Lee grow up, of course, but I don't remember it being such a wellspring. Sharing a creative process with her as an adult, I just love it. Here's a bit of anecdotal history... and yes, it does have a point for you, my friends...

The four of us are sitting around the dinner table on Lee's 15th birthday. This was well before we started writing together. She announces, "When I'm 18, Dad, I wanna jump out of an airplane."

Her older sister, Meg, starts giggling. "Skydiving? Leanne!"

I savor a spoonful of Carvel ice cream cake, studying Lee. *Oh, oh. The kid is serious.*

Her mother looks at me. Gives me the eyebrow, the one that says *do not encourage her, dummy.*

I mentally calibrate the mother eyebrow elevation. *Way up. That's a bad sign.*

I mentally calibrate the daughter hopeful half-smile. *She's always been a determined kid. And this one is clear in her eyes.*

I swallow the ice cream.

"Lee, honeybunch," I speak as my mind balances the calibrations off against each other, "you're never going to jump out of an airplane..."

The smile runs away from my daughter's face.

Her mother's eyebrow drops down to its equilibrium position.

"...without me," I add.

The eyebrow shoots up at Warp 8.

Both daughters burst into laughter. They had the eyebrow calibrated, too.

Three years pass without another word on the subject. Then it's the morning of Lee's 18th birthday...

"C'mon, kiddo, we gotta go get your birthday present."

She's a little sleepy, not enough coffee yet. "Go? Present? Where, Dad?"

"Northampton."

"Massachusetts?"

"Yup."

"What's there?"

"Airport."

"Airport?" She's still a little sleepy.
"Yeah. With airplanes... and, you know... parachutes..."
She comes fully awake.
"Dad! You remembered!" That hopeful half-smile of three years past blossoms into a huge grin.
"Dads don't forget," I chide her.
We laugh all the way to the airport.

I tell this story to you, my friends, because jumping out of an airplane is—like writing a novel—an act of faith. *[Insight 15]* The jump is on the website, along with other stuff about the book and the trilogy, http://www.monkeytrap.us

I hope this is helpful. Best of luck with your writing, my friends...

Denning Powell
May 5, 2010

Insight #1: Ecclesiastes got it right. "... a time to every purpose under heaven". You'll know when that is.

Insight #2: Figure out what you really want. Of course you want your debut Great American Novel to get rave reviews in the New York Times and sell a bazillion copies in its first week out. That's fun to dream about. But you'll probably be happier and healthier if you focus on the creative journey and enjoy it, rather than focus on the outcome. Either Yoda or some other Zen master pointed that out. So... think about why you're really writing, and let that guide you, and be patient with the process. And with yourself.

Insight #3: Write the kind of stuff that really turns you on. What you enjoy reading is what you'll enjoy writing. And it will show. Do what you love. Even small niches have faithful readerships.

Insight #4: Originality goes a long way. Yeah, I know, all the plots have been done, etc., etc., all stories today are derivative, etc., etc. But that's the tune a lot of physicists sang at the end of the nineteenth century—'everything has already been invented'—but of course it hadn't. I like what Niels Bohr said: "Your theory is crazy, but not crazy enough to be true." And of course there always are interesting variations on any theme. So give it your best shot.

Insight #5: Persistence. I like what Woodrow Wilson said: "Nothing in this world can take the place of persistence. Talent will not; nothing is more common than unsuccessful people with talent. Genius will not; unrewarded genius is almost a proverb. Education will not; the world is full of educated derelicts. Persistence and determination alone are omnipotent. The slogan 'press on' has solved and always will solve the problems of the human race." Writing is tough. Getting published is tougher. The traditional market is terrible for new writers, partly because there's so much good stuff out there, and partly because the bigger publishing houses only want to bet on sure things (i.e., established names). But that's the reality, and you have to live with it, so persistence is essential; you just keep trying. And these days the industry is being turned on its ear, so you can persist along alternative pathways simultaneously.

Insight #6: Dismiss all nattering nabobs of negativity. The digital world is opening up non-traditional, imaginative paths to publication that weren't even envisioned ten years ago. Artists of all sorts now have the ability to sidestep traditional routes and go directly to the consumer. Novels, paintings, music, videos, animations... they're all finding more direct expression on the internet. Sometimes there's even serious money involved. Don't let the odds stop you. Also see Insight #5.

Insight #7: Feel the premise and promise, deep inside. All good stories are about conflict. And archetypes exist for a reason: they strike a deep emotional chord. (I'm speaking about fiction here, not non-fiction.)

Insight #8: Houston, we have lift-off. The hardest thing is beginning. The natural thing—at least for me—is to dither around... I look out the window, clean under my fingernails, scratch my butt, meow at the cat. You wait for something to happen, the light to dawn, the muse to strike. Some of that may actually be okay, because your brain may be working on things at a lower level. But at some point, you gotta get disgusted with nothing happening and boot the muse. After all, a kick in the ass is a step forward.

Insight #9: It always takes more time than you think it will. My years of experience say the factor is 2.6. Possibly the factor is some natural function or resonant frequency of the universe that's close to that—such as e, the base of natural logarithms—but 2.6 plus or minus a few tenths has generally worked well for me.

Insight #10: Your best style is the one that works for you. I freely admit all writers are different. Some can keep a story in their head—not outline at all, just start writing and work straight through to the end and have it all come out perfectly. Wish I were that fortunate. But I'm not. And I'm an engineer, I like to figure things out on paper before turning them into physical reality... erasers are cheap, especially the computer kind.

Insight #11: Total immersion is good, as long as you don't drown. It's good to be really absorbed in a story, but there are the occasional roses to be smelled, backs to be stretched, bodies to be stroked, perspectives to be retained. You know what I mean.

Insight #12: Think big. What the hell, it doesn't cost any more.

Insight #13: Have fun with traditions. Sex, politics, religion—all sure subjects that can get people edgy. So stir the pot. When the Pope got mad at Dan Brown's version of biblical history, sales of *The Da Vinci Code* spiked up. (And, by the way, the use of a noetic science backdrop such as what's in *The Lost Symbol?* I beat Dan Brown to it by a good five years. It's really fascinating stuff, and real science too.) Never let facts or traditions or other opinions get in the way of a good story. As a fiction writer, you're entitled.

Insight #14: Have fun with your characters. I relate to the character I'm writing about at the time—I do tend to get immersed. But I especially relate to certain qualities of some of the characters in the trilogy: Joshua for his moral dilemma; Eva for her innocence; Hessa for her mystery; Elia for her complexity; Zurvan for his unbridled evil. Qualities are really fun for a writer to play with. Most characters have good points (rooting interests) and bad points (flaws or emotional wounds or scars or other defects). Slam those bad points until they bleed.

Insight #15: Faith. When you're sitting in an airplane hatch with ten thousand feet of emptiness below your dangling feet, you're hoping that the expert you're strapped onto doesn't have a death wish, that he's packed his chute carefully, that he doesn't have a brain aneurism that's going to rupture with sudden elevation change or that if he does, that the backup chute popout is set for a high enough altitude above ground. All sorts of reasons not to launch, but... Faith, baby, faith.

About the author

Lee Denning is the pen name of a father-daughter writing team. Denning Powell has been a soldier, scientist, engineer and entrepreneur.

Leanne Powell Myasnik is a psychologist, poet and mystic.

He lives on the East Coast, she on the West. They correspond. With love. And hilarity.

http://www.monkeytrap.us

Latest release: Hiding Hand, SF suspense

How I wrote *Abithica*

by Susan Goldsmith

Making up stories is what got me through my childhood. When things got tough, I'd crawl right into my imagination, where sick mothers could be made better if you found the right star to wish upon, or crazy fathers weren't *really* crazy. They were just more evolved than the rest of us, able to see whole worlds and realities the rest of us couldn't. Mean teachers? They became witches - the whole lot of them.

Me? Oh, I was the main character in everything, of course!

While attending Rincon High School in Tucson, Arizona, I secretly loved the writing assignments. No way would I admit that fact to my friends or anybody else, especially myself, but no matter what the subject was, I'd search for the most obscure, "out there" idea and write an entire paper around it. Boy, was that fun! My teachers were usually so thrown off that I most always got an A. If not, I'd write a paper backing-up my paper. That usually did the trick.

Yup, loved to write, but when it came time to picking a college major in 1987, I decided I'd better pick a career path with a guaranteed income, no matter how miniscule that income happened to be. I proudly declared Journalism as my major at the University of Arizona, with a Political Science minor. Never mind that I'd rarely picked up a newspaper, or that if I did, it was to find the comics section or the movie schedule. Nope, I'd made my decision. Journalism was perfect. I could write, get paid and even use the skill later on, if I so desired, to help me get into the FBI. Yeah, *that* FBI. (I blame a combination of my imagination, *The Karate Kid*, *Indiana Jones* and *Beverly Hills Cop* for lighting *that* particular fire. God help me if Mulder from the *X-Files* had made an earlier appearance.) I did no research on the FBI stuff whatsoever - it simply sounded good - but more importantly, I visualized the outcome. It was a slam dunk. How could I possibly go wrong?

How I Wrote *Abithica*

Journalism and creativity are two words that don't belong in the same sentence, forget imagination! I learned quickly that I wasn't allowed to "spice up" my stories nor was anyone interested in obscure, "out there" ideas. For example, a councilman shows up at a meeting in a red and green plaid jacket, sporting a man-bag and a flip-over hairdo. Did it really matter what drivel he gushed forth, trying to sound important? Come on - *he* was the story! At least, in my mind he was.

What really pushed the wrong buttons was being told to write about things *other* people did, events *other* people experienced and ideas they'd come up with. I was to be a watcher and recorder, rather than a participant, and what I was watching was mind-numbing, to say the least. Planning and Zoning meetings, Tucson City Council meetings? This was my life, my future? Ah... hell! But I'd started it and, by God, I was going to finish it.

I was selected in 1991 to represent the University of Arizona as the Assistant Press Secretary for Congressman Morris K. Udall in Washington, D.C. To this day, I'm convinced it was my spunk rather than any journalistic prowess that landed me the gig, so I grabbed it before they had time to renege their offer. *Move over Washington, here I come!*

Impressive? Living in Washington, D.C, and rubbing elbows with powerful senators and representatives? Wrong! I never even met Mo Udall. Bummer, because I heard he was really funny. How could he not be? After all, he'd written a book titled *Too Funny to Be President*. Anyway, he ended up retiring a couple weeks after I arrived, but my time in D.C. wasn't a complete wash. I did get to shake hands with former President George Bush (the dad) and no, I was not compelled to save the dress I'd been wearing at the time. Wrong president, wrong time, wrong girl!

During my U of A graduation ceremony, right after they handed me my degree, I began working on Plan B, because for me a career in journalism meant a long, slow, painful death. What now, the FBI? Nope, not hiring. I'd have known that little tidbit if I'd bothered to research, but Pinkerton Investigative Services *were* hiring and their advertisement in the paper said they were looking for an *experienced* undercover investigator. Finally, my four years of journalism were paying off. I was now reading the want ads in addition to the comics and the movie schedule.

Somehow I convinced the regional vice president that he didn't want some stuffy old guy who looked like a cop. Nope, they wanted me. Who'd ever suspect I was undercover?

He bought it.

What was supposed to be a four-to-ten-week temporary situation spread into an eight-month job, where I was planted inside a company. I even received a bi-weekly paycheck like the other employees. Pinkerton paid me as well for blending in, keeping my eyes and ears open, and maintaining a daily log. Once again I had a captive audience, but couldn't embellish what I was seeing on a daily basis, and boy, was my imagination coming up with some really good stuff. In reality, I was bored silly. Eventually that boredom had me shaking things up... but that's another story entirely. I was glad when it was over. I didn't enjoy being part of the action as much as I'd thought I would.

Right about there, I married my high school sweetheart, Bryan, who was way hotter than Mulder and didn't mind - still doesn't - that I love to embellish my stories. Actually, he thinks it's kinda cute, God bless him! And, because he grew up with me and knew all about where my imagination came from, he'd sit and listen to my stories with that huge, all encompassing *I-adore-you* smile that still makes my knees go weak.

On his insistence, I started a journal of random thoughts with such gems as "Life is what you make it; the hard part is knowing what you want." Or, "Without the dark, how can you truly appreciate sunshine?" My father-in-law, otherwise known as Poppy, had one so good, I just had to add it, "Who has more fun than people?" Enough said, right? Yikes! But at least I was writing, and loving it. I'd officially become a "closet writer" - a habit that would take me years to rectify.

My love for reading... well, that I never hid. My passion started when I was five and came at me in the form of a record. Every single night, for years, I fell asleep listening to Richard Bach's *Jonathan Livingston Seagull*, told and performed by Neil Diamond. What I wouldn't give to find a copy of that today! Awestruck, that's what I was. I was also hooked on reading. The first book I was able to read by myself was *Amityville Horror* by Jay Anson, followed by every Stephen King and Ray Bradbury story I could get my hands on. I also liked C.S. Lewis, V.C. Andrews and Judy Blume, to name a few.

Basically, if it was a unique story, I'd read it. The genre had little to do with my choices.

I spent the next three years in sales, working for Dun & Bradstreet in California and Indiana. I sold information. Yeah, me! For the first time, I was getting paid to use my imagination to help companies improve their profit line. Oh, I was good too! Best proposal writer on the block, but I was getting antsy. Pharmaceutical sales seemed to be the answer. Good pay, fun people, lots and lots of brain exercise. In five years I had to learn thirteen different drugs from A to Z, the good, the bad, the hidden, the competition and the FDA's take on everything. (I learned quickly not to study at night because I kept falling asleep.) By then I had two daughters. I didn't have time to think, let alone write.

Fate soon intervened and I found myself home, being a full-time mother and wife.

Suddenly my writer's brain turned back on and I found myself staring at the blank computer screen. I'd make a point to walk by it on my way to the bathroom, in between Barney episodes, or during those times when my children actually *did* fall asleep during nap time, usually out of pure exhaustion. (My daughters were like puppies: they'd play until they dropped and it didn't matter where it was, the floor, their car seats, even the dinner table.) Anyway, there it was, that black square eye, beckoning to me, daring me to turn it on. It was the vacuum, Thomas Moore and my very persistent imagination that eventually got me to do so.

Wait, I better back up here and explain the vacuum thing. When I was a kid and my mom was still alive, her answer for every problem was "Clean your room, Susie, it will make you feel better." What? Clean my room and that behemoth of a girl, Carla, will no longer want to rearrange my face? Math will suddenly make sense? David will finally notice I exist? I rebelled, as you can imagine. My room became a place even I felt less than safe entering. My closet was the worst. Clothes were piled so high I didn't dare open it too wide for fear of being buried alive and, yes, I'd been known to wear the same pants two or three times before chucking them into the wash basket. Alright, maybe even four. They were off the floor, though. There, mom! My room is clean.

But over the years something happened. (I call stuff like this God's humor.) I'm not even sure when it occurred, but nowadays cleaning does indeed make me feel better, and, yes, the same advice I once balked at actually started to pop out of my own mouth on occasion or two. My poor, poor girls! But it made sense - a clean environment really was the first step to a clean life. It was sort of a Zen thing I guess, but it worked for me. All my best thoughts have come while tugging a vacuum cleaner. If asked, my family would say I'm borderline OCD when it comes to straightening up.

Mom's laughing. I can hear her!

Enter Thomas Moore. He wrote a book called *Care of the Soul.* In it, he asked a very profound question: what is your worst fear? Hmmm, what *was* my worst fear, I wondered? Naturally, I grabbed the vacuum and unleashed my imagination.

Losing my husband and children was my answer. Oh, but what if I was taken from them without their knowledge and they didn't even know I was gone? Ouch! That would definitely suck. But what would suck even more is if another soul took my place and I was there, unseen, invisible, watching their lives continue as if I'd never existed.

I was getting closer to my worst nightmare, but I wasn't quite there yet. It needed a little something more. Got it! What if the body I was in had never really belonged to me in the first place? What if I had been the intruder all along? I'd been "borrowing" the woman's life... and now... she wanted it back.

The question became an obsession, and my vacuum and I spent a lot of time together. Soon, the idea of "switching" was born. It grew legs and arms and even acquired a face, a woman's face. I started thinking of her as Abithica, for no reason I could state. The name simply came to me. She had no memory of how it all began, but she had a healthy sense of humor and a really big heart. Her one wish was to be normal. Her worst fear was finding out what she was. How in the world does a girl lose her body, and what if she never had a body to begin with?

When I started to dream about her, I knew it was time to turn on the computer. This was going to be easy-peasy. All I had to do was tell her story, right? Transfer it from my mental screen to the computer screen? How hard could that be? By the way, a white screen is much more daunting than a dark screen, but I soon filled it with lots of black letters. I wrote and I wrote and I wrote, for two whole months, but the words weren't matching the woman in my head. The tone was wrong. The voice was wrong. The action was wrong. The whole darn story was wrong. It wasn't Abithica, not even close.

If I can sit through four years of journalism courses, I can certainly do this!

I tried again. Abithica went from being a ghost to an unexplained genetic anomaly to a human Jonathan Livingston Seagull. Yuck! None of it worked, so in true go-getter fashion I threw a major tantrum, quit writing and began reading instead, lots of reading, everything and anything I could get my hands on, Diana Gabaldon, Stephenie Meyer, Anne Rice, Dan Brown. It was *The Time Traveler's Wife* by Audrey Niffenegger that put the "sp" back in my "unk." It was the first book I read that combined paranormal and romance and she made it look so darned easy. I absolutely loved it. Couldn't put it down. I can do the same thing, I said to myself. Besides, Stephenie Meyer's *Host* had really freaked me out. Her story was not "switching," but it came close enough to get me worried. The sooner I wrote *Abithica*, the better.

A day later, I was back in front of the computer and there was Abithica, waiting patiently for her story to be told, but once again I fumbled. Didn't even come close to doing her story justice. It was all wrong, all of it, and I was beginning to suspect what the problem was. My writing skills weren't up to the task at hand. Believe me, that was not an easy thing to admit, especially when I could so thoroughly "visualize" the end product. *You mean I have to actually work for this? It's not just going to come to me?* Ah... hell!

After a couple more tantrums and a really long, really good pep talk from hubby, I decided I better not start with *Abithica*. I was too attached to her. I needed a story I could flub up, and boy did I flub it.

Bryan had made up a series of bedtime stories for our girls. It was about a group of Madera Canyon fairies who disguised themselves as hummingbirds. The story never had a beginning. I decided to change that. For the next year, this became my writing exercise. I'd write four to six pages a day. At night, my husband would read those pages to our girls, who then made requests that I'd implement the next day. It was a family affair. To make it more fun, I made my husband, children and myself the main characters, even to using our real names. Every one of us was perfect in every way imaginable - beautiful beyond words, highly talented and unusually bright. Bryan and I were the best parents on the planet. Our daughters? Well, one ended up saving the world, the other ruled it and we all lived happily ever after. The End.

Hurray! I did it. I finished 161 pages. Never mind that the two or three agents who showed interest eventually passed on the project. "The story didn't capture me like I'd hoped," they explained. I re-read my work, this time with a critical eye. Boring didn't even come close to describing it. Stephen King would have puked after the first page! No worries though, there was a marked improvement in the last chapters from the first chapters. I'd learned what not to do, and knowing what not to do was a start, right? So, yes, even though it wasn't very good and I'd spent a lot of time working on it, I had no regrets writing it.

At least that's the story I told my gung-ho family. Truthfully, I was furious and more than a little humiliated. If my kids didn't mimic my every move, I would have taken a sledge hammer to the freaking computer. No, I decided, I'm done. It's over. Both girls were now in school anyway. Back to pharmaceuticals I go.

Enter more of God's humor. That very day my youngest came home and proudly presented me with a paper she'd written at school. A paper about me! There it was in black and white, written in her determined little handwriting: My Mom is My Hero. In summary, I was The Little Train Who Could. One day her mommy was going to be a published writer and when she grew up, *she* was going to be a writer too. Ah... hell! (Repeat twice for emphasis as you read this.) Where in the world had that idea come from? How many people had she told this to? More importantly, how had I managed to become *that* woman, the one I vowed I'd never be. I could "talk the talk," yeah, but my walk-the-walk walk was non-existent.

Well, I had two choices. Figure out how to walk the walk and talk the talk, or spend the rest of my life hiding from my daughter and her friends. So, with renewed vigor and determination, I returned to *The Fairies of Madera Canyon* and spent the next year creating a masterpiece, an American classic, the next breakout novel.

The Fairies of Madera Canyon morphed into *To Forever and Back*. The story improved dramatically and the writing along with it, but it still failed to capture the imagination of any agent I sent it to. By then, anything smacking of "fairy," including Tinkerbelle, made me retch. Those stories became my mind's own "vacuum cleaner," something I returned to from time to time when I had a writing kink to work out... or at least that's the story I was telling myself to ease my torment.

I spent the next couple of months doing anything *but* writing. My house was spotless. I made elaborate meals that took hours, and spent a lot of time volunteering in my girls' classrooms, but Abithica was always in the back of my mind. I should have known I couldn't stay away for long.

When I finally returned, I came to the computer armed with an open mind and a rock solid "no way out" clause. Close behind that was a one-page summary, some really kickin' music, a writing schedule and a whole lot of "Magic."

Leaving myself no choice but to write *Abithica* was by far the most important step I'd taken to date. I am a writer, I told anybody and everybody who was willing to listen, and one day soon I'm going to be published. No fanfare, no cheering section, but it no longer mattered. My ego was thoroughly and irrevocably engaged. It's amazing how motivating it can be when you're asked, on a daily basis, how the book is coming along. Some of those asking actually wanted to see me fail, but I didn't care. They were helping me with their pesterings.

Now that I was committed, I needed a map. I was tired of being lost. By the way, admitting that to myself was as hard for me to swallow as that nasty cherry cough syrup that I'm convinced exists for the sole purpose of torturing sick children.

I should probably back up for a moment and explain.

I didn't have an outline the first time I sat down to write *Abithica* and I ended up re-writing the first chapter thirty different ways, every one of which was the beginning of a completely different story. I was starting to suspect it was because I had no idea what Abithica was or how she was going to fix her problem, or how the story was going to end. I was like an artist standing over an empty canvas. Was I going to use pastels, pencil or paint? Was it going to be a nature scene or a portrait? Why not an elephant? Did it even have to be on a canvas? Why not the side of a building or a sidewalk? I had no idea so I kept trying a little of everything, until eventually, nothing worked and I found myself pinned to the ground, screaming "uncle."

At the same time, I was well aware that some of my best writing had come about by accident when I had unwittingly allowed the characters to tell their own story. They were the writers, I was the channel. Every single writing session after that, it's what I strove to duplicate. I'd sit down at the keyboard, clear my mind and relax enough to set the characters free. On a really good day, they'd talk for eight hours straight and take me places I'd never even imagined. Eventually, as I got better at it, I started to set an alarm to remind me to eat. I'd then set it to remind me to start dinner and then again to remind me to pick up the kids. This was the reason I wrote, and the reason I kept coming back for more.

I had a problem though. What I needed was something to keep Abithica on task, without constricting the creative flow I craved. The answer: a plot summary. Hmph! Easier said than done.

I turned to three specific writers for help. Their plots were unique, yet simple. Michael Crichton's *Juraissic Park* was about genetically engineered dinosaurs that ran amuck. William P. Young's *The Shack* was about a heartsick father who met God in the flesh after his daughter was brutally murdered, and Markus Zusak's *The Book Thief* was the story of a young girl trying to survive in Nazi Germany, as told from Death's point of view.

Hey, I thought, I can do this. Susan Goldsmith's *Abithica* - An angel learns the hard way that there was a price for meddling with humans. *Are you kidding me? Suddenly Abithica is an angel?* No wonder the first thirty tries failed. I took the next couple of days building on that concept until I had a sketchy beginning, middle and end. I now had a direction, but Abithica still had plenty of wiggle room to be creative and I was still willing to follow her on whatever tangents she chose to take me on.

Now that I knew her a little better, I started to hear her voice in certain songs. It was crazy, but music did amazing things for my writing. I was immediately transported smack into the middle of her world, where I found it much easier to step aside and let her take over. Somehow it connected us. I ended up creating a playlist on my iPod with sixteen songs, including U2, Evanescence, Neil Diamond (of course), Live, Muse, Godsmack, Stabbing Westward, Depeche Mode, Rob Zombie and Flypsyde.

The next trick was staying motivated. A regular writing schedule was the answer. Mornings worked best for me. After dropping off the kids at school, I'd crank that playlist up full blast and meditate (don't know what else to call it.) I usually did this while I vacuumed, folded clothes, unloaded the dishwasher, washed the windows... because... here it goes... organizing my surroundings helped me to organize my thoughts.

Thanks mom! You can quit laughing now.

Two thousand words a day was my goal. Once I'd set the alarm, placed my mug of green tea and Pepperidge Farm goldfish within arm's reach, I'd take a deep breath and promise myself to spend no more than an hour reviewing yesterday's work. I had to. It wasn't uncommon for me to spend a month rewriting one scene, only to end up deleting it a year later. I'd remind myself that it didn't have to be a masterpiece, that there'd be plenty of time to fix it later. Just get the story out.

Writing was starting to remind me of labor during childbirth. I'd push and push, all the while telling myself it's almost over. Come on girl, you can do it! The closer I got to the end, the more frantic my writing became. I no longer spent time editing past work, nor did I pause to look something up. No time. Had to get it out. Push!

In a flurry of activity, *Abithica* was finally born.

There, I'm done! The little brat's on her own from here on out. She's either going to fly or land smack on her face and I'm okay with that because I've done what I can. Whew! It's finally over.

All that was left was a tiny bit of editing. Maybe fix a word here and there, some typos. Used "if" twice in a row, that kind of thing. No big deal. It happens when you're willing to let the characters go on tangents. I'd follow behind with a broom, tidy up a bit, and see what I had when the dust settled.

Oh, holy hell! The story was good, no it was excellent, but my characters were flat, like pictures in a book. I needed them to walk and talk, cry and laugh, not just lay there like deflated balloons.

Another tantrum later, it hit me. Like any newborn, Abithica had to be taught how to do these things. I wasn't done; not even close. I needed to feed her, change her diaper, teach her to crawl, tie her shoes. In short, I had a lot of work ahead of me.

I spent the next four months doing just that and yes, the story was much improved, but still not where I wanted it to be. I had no idea how to fix it and was way too invested to leave it as it was, not to mention terrified of facing more rejection letters.

I needed a little "Magic" and his name was Gerry Mills. He even wrote a book to that effect, among many - *Magic for Your Writing*. Finally, I'd found somebody who could show me how to fix my masterpiece. The Abithica in my head became the Abithica in the story, and now she's in 3-D and glorious Technicolor. Hallelujah! It will be published a year from now.

How did he do it? He taught me how to inflate Abithica by hiding my "author voice." You, he said, are similar to a puppet master, so if you're looking to create magic, the audience should never see your hands, or the strings. For example, (Gerry would like this one!), he'd suggest that Abithica say the word "Ducky!" instead of my telling my reader that she was frustrated. I would then promptly change it to "Ah... hell!" so as to make his suggestion align with what I thought she would actually say. *Thank you, Gerry. Couldn't have done it without you!*

Is *Abithica* the end for this new writer? Is a mother ever done being a mother? I will probably always itch to fuss with her, polish her and make her better, but I've started on a sequel and you'd better believe that this time I spent a good month coming up with a strong plot summary. More than likely it will change, but at least I have a starting point. I've nailed the first chapter on the first try and have moved into the second chapter without looking back!

I'm still working on a playlist for my new inspirational environment. So far, Garbage, Creed and Silversun Pickups have made the list. My goal is to be finished with the "birthing process" by May. The "Magic" will promptly follow.

About the athor:
Presently a stay-at-home mom, she stumbled across a pondering personal question after reading Thomas Moore's Care of the Soul, that being her own worst fear. Losing her husband and children was the answer, arriving while she vacuumed the living room. What if she were to be taken from them without their knowledge? What if another soul was inserted in her place? She'd look the same, but oh, what would happen then?

The question soon became an obsession, the idea of 'soul switching' was born, and the result was her first novel, *Abithica*.

Upcoming release: *Abithica*, urban fantasy

Ten Lessons I Learned from Writing *Quest for Vengeance*

by Ginger Hanson

It was called *Quest for Vengeance*. It took two years to research and write and earned its first rejection in August, 1980 from Doubleday. It was my first novel, a historical set in 60 A.D. Roman Britain and told the story of Boudica, Queen of the Iceni, who led a rebellion against Rome. It was written so long ago, it was typed on a portable Smith Corona typewriter and there are no files of it in my computer. I have a notebook crammed with research notes, character studies, plot and scene ideas and a 4 1/2 x 8 x 11 inch box filled with manuscript pages.

As I gathered information for this essay, I realized that writing a first novel has provided me with valuable lessons about writing as well as life. As is often the case, I discovered it was the journey rather than the destination that changed my life. But let us begin at the beginning.

Why on earth did I tackle a historical novel set in Roman Britain as a first novel?

I vote for sheer ignorance and stunning naïveté.

The idea to write a book stemmed from my inability to get any of my short stories published. Obviously, I needed a larger canvas on which to explore plots and characters.

This revelation neatly tied together my unmarketable degree in history and my love of writing. It led to the writing of *Quest* and the commitment to getting a novel published.

Why did I choose to tell Queen Boudica's story? I don't think I choose a story to tell, I think the story chooses me. In this instance, I was introduced to the historical account in a survey class on British history. Intrigued, I read a more detailed account in Tacitus' *The Annals*. As I wrote in that long ago query letter:

For seventeen years the potential for conflict has been brewing in Rome's province at the edge of the world. Roman mismanagement of the province, increasing taxation for unwanted legions and buildings, seizure of prime farmland for Roman veterans, and persecution of the Druid priests all contribute to the growing discontent. The scene is set for a clash between the two cultures, but the diverse tribes of Britain need a unifying force.

Boudica, Queen of the Iceni, provides that unification. Prior to 60 A.D. the Iceni had existed peacefully under Roman rule and enjoyed special status as a client kingdom. That year, their king dies. His will names his two daughters as co-heirs with Emperor Nero, but the emperor ignores the will. He sends a force of tax collectors to inventory his new property. When Boudica refuses the tax collector's demands, she is publicly whipped and her daughters raped. The tax collectors pillage the capital city and strip the tribal leaders of their possessions.

The story of Roman mistreatment of these Britons reached out of the history book and grabbed me by the throat and said "this is a story that needs telling." I think I was drawn to the fact that a woman unified the unruly tribes of Britain long enough to hand the Romans some major military defeats. Women's history, long neglected by male historians, was just beginning to be told and there were few strong historical female role models available. I think Boudica's story resonated with me because she fought back. She was a feisty female and feisty is my favorite type of heroine.

I think a story not only chooses me, it nags me to death until I at least try to write about it. This was true about *Quest for Vengeance* and has remained true for every other manuscript, be it a novel, a short story or an essay. The writing may only entail a page of scribbled notes, but something about the story must be written.

Quest for Vengeance grew out of a historical footnote, but story sources are everywhere. "How do you think up your stories" is a question asked by countless readers of countless writers. It's such an easy question for writers, we are unable to comprehend why everyone can't see the stories that surround us. For example, I can be driving down the road, see a plastic garbage bag on the side of the road and immediately wonder, what's in that bag! My imagination churns out possible scenarios. A body? An undelivered love letter? A disreputable, but beloved pair of shoes? An engagement ring? Lost in my imagination, muscle memory takes over the act of driving while I work out various scenarios, somehow arriving at my destination with little remembrance of the actual trip.

It's impossible to list all the ways the imagination is triggered. Song lyrics, historical events, a sentence in a book or magazine, a casual conversation, a new food or even the smell of a favorite cologne. To me, stories are everywhere waiting to be told.

Although I've always loved to write, novelist was not my first career choice. As a high school student, my dream career was journalist. To reach that goal, I took journalism classes in high school and college. Then life got in the way. Financial resources for completing my degree program were slim to none so I went to work. While working to earn money for college, I met the man who became my husband. Marriage and our vagabond life in the military derailed my journalism career.

When the opportunity to complete my college education arose, I needed to finish my degree quickly. I had always taken history courses because I love the subject and a history degree ended up being the best choice at the small college I finally attended. Since I had always read historical novels, choosing to write a historical novel seemed a natural choice for a longer writing project.

I was not an inexperienced writer when I started *Quest*. I'd been writing short stories and newspaper articles for many years. I still have a copy of my first short story *The Magic Tea Tray* that I wrote when I was nine years old. I had also won a national children's short story contest when I was twelve. My schoolmates frequently complimented me on the articles I wrote for various school newspapers and my teachers enjoyed my essays. In fact, my essay on moiré patterns earned me an A in a college introductory physics class. I think the science teacher was so excited to have an interesting paper to read that his goodwill extended beyond that single score and influenced my overall grade.

In addition to that encouragement, my aunt told me how much she enjoyed my chatty letters. Was there any reason not to be a writer?

As a teenager, I submitted to *Seventeen* magazine and then, in my early 20s, to *Redbook*. Looking back, I realize now that I had a lot of confidence in my writing ability. I was submitting stories to two of the highest paying short story markets in existence at that time. Not that I knew this. I submitted to them because I read the magazines and loved their short stories. Ergo, it made sense to want my short stories printed there.

Not that any of my short stories were ever printed in either venue. No, I came to know rejection early in my career. Fiction writing for publication is not a career path for the faint of heart and belief in your writing ability can help a writer weather rejection. Few writers sell the first book they write to the first publishing house on their submission list. Rejection is part of the book writing process. Nor does rejection end with an editor's offer of a contract and publication. Rejection continues to dog writers. It comes in many forms, from strangers who write a negative review of your book to friends who "don't like to read your type of book."

Confidence in my own writing skill was a good thing, because I endured a lot of rejection once I started concentrating on novels. It was to take me over 20 years to get an offer to publish my first novel. Those years were not without personal writing achievements. Contest wins, encouraging phone calls and letters from editors, fantastic moral support from my family and friends, and dozens of readers who read my manuscripts and then asked if their mom or daughter or friend could read the manuscript, too.

During those years I penned novels for every age and in several genres. I also wrote nonfiction. My young adult book about the history of corporal punishment was published by a small press. I wrote and edited newsletters of every size and shape-personal, volunteer and professional. For several years, I wrote a humor column for the local newspaper.

If all these people believed in me and my storytelling, there must be someone in the publishing field who would also believe and want to publish my work. Perseverance became my byword as I continued writing and submitting manuscripts. I remember how much the chorus to Smash Mouth's *I Get Knocked Down* resonated with me when it was released. I kept getting knocked down by rejection letters, but I kept getting up. I refused to let anything keep me down. I'd sing these words aloud whenever I received a rejection letter, promising myself I would get published.

Of course, that was the future. The early rejection of *Quest for Vengeance* was met with tears.

Here's where the support of people who have confidence in your writing skills comes in handy. From my first attempts to get a short story published to today's modest success, my husband and daughter have always encouraged my writing efforts. My husband's support began in the early years of our marriage. His moral support kept me writing while his financial support kept a roof over my head and food in my stomach. He can only be described as a Renaissance prince, a true patron of the arts.

In those days, I can remember him letting me mope around the house for a few days after I received a rejection letter. There was much gnashing of teeth as I loudly despaired of ever selling a single word. Then he'd say, "You better write another story and submit it or you'll never sell." As I continued to write and the book manuscripts continued to mount, he told me to stack them in a closet because one day an editor would want everything I'd written. Well, I'm wise enough now to know no editor would want everything I've written, but I recently sold a manuscript I wrote over 25 years ago!

If that particular manuscript hadn't received such a positive early response, I may not have dragged it out periodically and revised it, but it almost sold on its first submission. It also garnered my first phone call from an editor. Imagine my happiness! An editor who loved my writing. She wanted to buy the manuscript, but it needed revisions in order for her to convince a review committee to say yes. What a joy to talk to an editor about the characters I'd created. I still have her letter outlining our discussion, but by the time I did the requested revisions and resubmitted the manuscript, she had resigned. A form rejection accompanied the returned manuscript.

I didn't give up on that manuscript. Remember, perseverance has been my constant companion. During its submission life, that manuscript was requested by half a dozen other editors and won or finaled in several writing contests. Every so many years, I'd revisit the story to update it and then submit it again. Here's a little hint from a longtime player, editors move to other houses, get married, get pregnant, resign, etc. I'd give the manuscript a new title, make some revisions and off it would go. I'm happy to report that manuscript will be published as *Ellie's Song* in 2011.

As I said, I was fortunate to receive encouragement from editors and agents early in my career. I was so naïve I didn't know they didn't usually write extensive letters to aspiring novelists. While frustrating on one level-I couldn't get a book offer-their encouragement kept me in the game.

I mentioned earlier that my daughter is my personal cheerleader. Her tenure as cheerleader began when I decided to write a young adult romance and I asked her to read the manuscript. She asked her teacher if she could write a book report on my first YA attempt. Her teacher granted permission, intrigued at the thought of one of her student's parents being a writer. My daughter even designed a cover for the book to go with the book report. Her initiative and creativity, as well as her well-written evaluation of the story, earned her an A+.

I'm glad the YA manuscript received a high grade from her teacher, because it never sold. The YA market collapsed and I abandoned YA and went on to write my first historical romance. What I didn't know was that my experience with rejection would deeply register on our daughter.

Years later, after completing a graduate program, she experienced rejection while job hunting. Too often she was told she had excellent educational credentials, but lacked experience. As she slogged through job interview after job interview that ended in rejection, she told me she couldn't give up on looking for a job until she'd accumulated as many rejections as I had! It seems she admired that I continued to chase my dream in the face of repeated rejection. Little did I know that my perseverance would help her through a difficult time. To my relief, she found a wonderful career path within a few months. She continues to be a first reader and I cherish her interest in my writing and willingness to give me honest opinions.

Without my family's love and understanding, the road to publication would have been an even rockier path to follow.

Quest was not rejected as many times as *Ellie's Song* because I only submitted it to two publishing houses. I can find the Doubleday rejection slip and I have copies of two panicked letters concerning my submission to Avon. Why the panic? We'd received military orders to the Washington, D.C. area and I panicked because my proposal package contained only our current address. Once we moved, how would the Avon editor know where find me to offer me a contract?

It turned out the Avon editor wasn't too concerned about finding me.

I was actually glad we were moving to another city due to the "rape scene" incident.

Let me explain.

Quest was typed on a typewriter. Personal home computers and printers and copiers didn't exist yet. Once I typed up an original, I had to trundle down to the local office supply store and copy the manuscript. Somehow, I left one page in the copier machine.

Remember my cover letter excerpt? Where Boudica's daughters are raped by the tax collectors? Yeah, the page depicting that scene was left behind.

It was my original. I couldn't press print on the computer and make another copy. Off I went, back to the store to pick it up. Of course, the proprietor and probably all his employees had read it. Thus, I was ready to leave town for a while. What I didn't know, was that the move to D.C. would prove career altering when a new friend introduced me to the romance genre.

As for the actual *Quest* manuscript, the folks at the office supply store probably read more of the manuscript than the Doubleday and Avon editors. If those editors read anything, they probably didn't get past the first few paragraphs of a very lengthy, single-spaced cover letter. Not that I blame them. *Quest* would have benefited from an objective reader's review. In today's climate of critique groups, it is hard to imagine someone submitting a manuscript unread by any eyes except those of the writer. Not that every writer needs to belong to a critique group, but it's a good idea to find at least one person whose opinion you value and ask them to read your manuscript. By the way, mothers and fathers don't count. They thought your first grade spelling test showed signs of early genius!

Looking back, I have no real idea why I tackled writing a novel when my knowledge of novel writing was as negligible as my knowledge of Roman Britain. I'd taken one class on creative writing and one class in British history. The creative writing class covered all kinds of creative writing from the poem to the novel, while the British history class spanned centuries.

The creative writing class gifted me with the first book in my how-to-write-a-novel collection. The textbook was a little paperback book on the basics of writing fiction. I don't remember the title, but I used that book until it fell apart. That class also introduced me to two writers magazines: *Writers' Digest* and *The Writer* which became my major source of information on the craft and business of writing. Over the years, the Writers' Digest Book Club would supply me with shelves of books on the craft of writing. Writers' conferences, getaways and workshops were part of the future. And there was no Internet or Yahoo groups to fill my brain with writing how-to. No, writing a novel or a poem or short story was a much lonelier path to follow in those days.

These avenues of learning may not have been available when I wrote *Quest*, but that didn't stop me from diligently studying the craft of writing. The ability to write well is a gift and while that first novel is the best you can write at that point, it shouldn't be your best book ever. Writing, like anything else, continues to improve the more you do it. For example, about fifteen years ago an agent who was reviewing a book proposal told me I wrote beautiful narrative, but my story's pace would flow better with more dialogue. (An example of an extensive critique from a very busy person!) He was right and I knew he was right because dialogue was not my strong suit.

I was working on the manuscript that would become *Tennessee Waltz*, my first published novel. I decided this would be my practice manuscript for increasing the use of dialogue. With that in mind, I read everything I could on how to write dialogue. I don't know if this effort paid off in publication, but I went from avoiding dialogue to being comfortable writing it. I continue to study the art of writing dialogue because dialogue plays such an important role in novels. Not only should a character's conversation seem natural, it also needs to enhance the story.

Since I couldn't miss what I didn't have (writers' conferences, the Internet, etc.), off I merrily went into the wonderful world of novel writing. Although I had no idea how to write a novel, I figured I'd read plenty of them. It couldn't be that hard to write one. So what if I'd never sold a short story,that was probably due to a lack of word length. A novel gave me plenty of room to round out my characters and plot.

I couldn't wait to get started. And I wasn't going to let a little thing like writing advice get in the way. Especially, not the sage advice I read in the how-to-write-a-novel paperback from that long ago creative writing course. The author had written: "Never write a historical novel as your first book." Naturally, that advice wasn't directed at me so I immediately discarded it. I had set my mind on writing a novel about 60 A.D. Roman Britain.

With several historical novels under my belt now, I think I ignored this pearl of writing wisdom for several reasons. One had to do with the sheer ignorance factor I mentioned earlier. Since I was incapable of truly understanding the complexity of what I had chosen to undertake, the advice was meaningless. Another reason I brushed it aside was its restrictive quality. Writers are blessed with an active imagination and insatiable curiosity. To me, "Never write a historical novel as your first book" squashed my imagination and curiosity. If Kathleen Winsor had read the advice about never writing a historical novel as a first book, she would have never written *Forever Amber*.

That analogy did not pop into my head way back when I started *Quest*, and I'm glad Kathleen Winsor never heard that guy's advice, but I realize now it is a valid observation for anyone tackling the historical novel as a first book. Why? Because choosing to write a historical novel as a first book meant I would have to deal with learning how to write a novel while mired in learning the historical period. I further compounded this challenge by setting *Quest* in a conquered country involving two separate cultures.

Sure, I have a degree in history, but my area of concentration is 19th century America, a far cry from 1st century Roman Britain. Thus, as I struggled to write the story, I also struggled to learn the history. The research aspect was daunting when you realize I lived in a rural area of southeastern Alabama. Information about Roman Britain was not easy to access, but there was one factor in my favor. We lived near an Army post. The military has great libraries and in those days offered free interlibrary loan services.

Slowly, I built my writing and historical resources. I bought some books and took copious notes from many library books. I still have a small metal file of 4 x 6 notecards filled with information about Roman Britain.

Slowly, I learned about Roman Britain. Slowly, I wrote the story. Why so slow?

Ignorance of Roman Britain history hindered the creation of my story world. Characters play out a story in scenes that connect to form an imaginary world. To build a scene, the writer needs points of reference to convey the setting. Without points of reference, the characters move in a vacuum. I had no reference points for this time period so I had no reference points for the setting. Not only was I learning how to move characters within a scene or from one scene to the next, I was also learning what existed around them, what could be used to set the reader into the scene with the character. For example, a character enters a room. If it is a British character in a British settlement, the housing is quite different from a Roman built room. The materials used, the interior design, and items found within the interior will differ.

My problem could be as simple as "Tamora looked in the mirror." Oh my, do they have mirrors, yet? If they have them, what are they made from? Was a pool of water the only source of a reflection?

Needless to say, I spent a lot of time doing research. The choice to write a historical as a first novel created obstacles that lengthened my how-to-write-a-novel learning curve.

I don't regret writing a historical as my first novel because it taught me how to write a novel and how to research a time period. What I didn't know then, but can do now, is write beyond the basic historical information. This technique better places the reader into the time period. How do I do this? I've learned to weave what I call "timeless sensory details" into the story to help the period come alive for the reader.

What are timeless sensory details? Timeless sensory details incorporate the five senses by using sights, smells, tastes, sounds and textures that have existed throughout time. The burble of water flowing over stones. The smell of burning wood. The taste of strawberries. The buildup of clouds in the sky before a storm. The texture of greasy hair. While all writers should use the five senses to bring a scene alive, the writer of historical novels must choose sensory details contemporary to the time period. This simple technique enhances the historical story experience for the reader.

While ignorance of the historical period hinders the world building process, spending too much time gathering data can create problems, too. It is important to know when to research and when to write. I love digging up facts, but research can get in the way of the actual writing. In fact, the Internet has made it even easier for writers to get sidetracked and spend too much time researching rather than writing the next chapter. This holds true for any type of research for any type of book. Once you have a good grasp of the subject matter, concentrate on writing. Don't let research bog down the writing. Rather than stop to find out about mirrors, put asterisks in the sentence as a reminder to do further research and continue writing the story.

Set aside time for research that doesn't interfere with writing the story. Continued research during the writing process adds to your store of knowledge about the time period and often offers unexpected details that add more texture to your work in progress.

As I struggled to balance writing time with research time, I learned the value of having a writing schedule as well as a writing space. With a regular writing schedule, the story stays in your mind. Sitting down in your special writing space triggers your brain into "write mode." You are telling yourself that you are there to work on your novel.

Although I can write at any time during the day, while writing *Quest* I discovered I produce more and write better in the morning. Afternoons are reserved for routine tasks that require the least amount of mental energy. It fascinates me how my brain continues to wrestle with story problems when I'm not writing, often solving them by the next morning. I've read many interviews with writers and have yet to find one who says "I write when the whim strikes" which leads me to believe establishing a regular routine contributes to completing a novel.

Where writers write is as varied as the writers themselves. Most have a preferred writing space. It can be as simple as a favorite chair and laptop computer. I was fortunate because we only had one child which meant there was often a spare room for me to use as an office.

I may have shared it with an ironing board, a sewing machine and a spare bed, but I always had room for a desk and file cabinet.

Although I established a writing schedule and writing space when I wrote *Quest*, I failed to develop any plan for how I would write the story. This meant my writing sessions were not as productive as they could have been.

What is a writing plan? For me, it is a synopsis, a writing tool many writers avoid like the plague. But I wish I had known how to make some type of plan when I was writing *Quest* because that story is a series of sidetracks and dead ends. Now I know there are plenty of writers who prefer not to know what's going to happen in their novels and I can always spot them because their stories trail off into nothing. They didn't know where they were going which means they don't reach a satisfying conclusion. And I mean satisfying in the sense that the conclusion satisfies the needs of the story.

A little planning can keep a writer on track. The writing plan can be vague or detailed, depending on the writer's comfort zone. Writer A may feel a short list of phrases for scenes is sufficient while Writer B prefers to have a detailed summary of every scene. Most writers have a general idea of the story they want to tell and getting it down on paper helps solidify their ideas.

To me, the greatest value of planning the story is the eradication of the dreaded blank page. Now there's something to look forward to, something waiting for you to write, something to trigger the next scene. This can be a word, a sentence or a paragraph but it's a scene awaiting development instead of the dreaded blank page. Since the outline/synopsis isn't written in stone, it can be adjusted as the story takes new directions.

I know I completed *Quest* and I know I made a lot revisions, but I'm pretty sure I was so new I didn't edit the manuscript. After all, that's what an editor does, right? I write a compelling novel and the editor edits it for publication.

Not so much then, and definitely not now. Today's editors and agents are overworked, without the time to polish a roughly hewn precious stone into a sparkling gem. It's up to the writer to submit a well-crafted, well-edited story.

In the rush to write a well-crafted story, some writers get bogged down in revisions. The story doesn't get told because the writer lacks confidence in their storytelling skill. Membership in an overzealous critique group can also influence a writer to make numerous revisions until the manuscript is headed nowhere. This further undermines the writer's self-confidence. It behooves any writer to choose a critique or writer's group with care. The writer should leave a session invigorated, eager to get back to work, not sad and dejected about their writing.

Editing is the last step in writing a story. It comes after the story is written because it involves a different skill set. It's important to remember that creative writing and editing are two different types of writing. The editor or internal critic must be shut down when writing the story because if the creative flow is hampered, there will be nothing to edit. On the other hand, the creative writer must take a second seat when it is time to edit.

Experience as a copy editor gave me a new appreciation for editors. Editing takes a clear eye, knowledge of grammar, knowledge of story structure and an overall feel for telling a story in the right sequence. Copy editing also taught me how to compartmentalize the writing and editing processes.

Once the story is told and it's time to edit, I switch into copy editor mode and read my manuscript with an entirely different mindset. If possible, I set aside a manuscript for two or three weeks. The time apart gives me a little distance from the manuscript. Then I pull it out, grab a red pen, get in a comfortable chair and start reading the manuscript aloud. Reading a manuscript aloud tells my brain I'm now editing. It keeps me from filling in missing letters and words, which our brains have a tendency to do when we read silently. Reading a manuscript aloud is one of the best ways to find all types of writing errors. It lets you hear the dialogue, experience the pacing, and trip over awkward sentence construction.

The title of this rambling narrative about my experience writing my first book promises the reader "Ten Lessons I Learned from Writing *Quest.*" Let's see if I can distill them for you:

1. Write what you feel passionate about because writing a book is a lengthy process.
2. Rejection is part of the process. Use it wisely.

3. Find someone who believes in you.
4. Perseverance is a good trait for a writer.
5. Beware of the pitfall of spending too much time on research.
6. Find and join a supportive writing group.
7. Have at least one objective reader read your work before submission.
8. If possible, establish a writing schedule and a writing space.
9. Make some type of outline of your story to ensure you never face a blank page.
10. Write the story first, but don't forget to edit.

That pretty much wraps up my advice about writing a first book. I don't regret writing *Quest for Vengeance*. It will probably never see print, but Boudica's story of going against great odds still captivates me. *Quest* ended up being a prophetic first book because, like countless other writers, I battled great odds in the quest of writing a first book as well as the quest of getting a book published. Unlike Boudica, I wasn't killed for my efforts. For which, I am thankful.

About the author

Ginger Hanson writes contemporary and historical novels. Her articles have appeared in newspapers, magazines, newsletters, blogs and ezines. An experienced workshop presenter, her audiences have run the gamut from kindergardeners to grandparents. Her stint as a copy editor of Federal Aviation Administration handbooks included updating and rewriting the *Aviation Instructor Handbook*.

http://www.gingerhanson.com

Ask for *Lady Runaway* at your favorite book store.

Upcoming release: Ellie's Song (The Wild Rose Press), a contemporary romance set in small town Tassanoxie, AL will be released January 2011.

The Manuscript from a Mystifying Source

by Toby Fesler Heathcotte

An unseen source dictated my first book through automatic writing, a process where the practitioner enters a meditative or light trance state and writes without conscious thought of what words will be produced. I hadn't a clue how to go about it or what it might mean in my life. Even now I can't explain with any kind of certainty what happened, where the material came from, but maybe why. Confusion reigned in my mind despite the fact that I held a degree in English and hoped to become an author, so I should have understood writing techniques.

The year was 1983 in Arizona. I taught speech, drama, and English in a Phoenix high school. My older son had enrolled in college in Tucson and moved away from home. The younger graduated from high school and worked at a fast food restaurant, saving money to join his brother. A difficult divorce lay two years behind me. My main emotional support came from my women friends, fellow teachers who had gone through divorces themselves. My friends encouraged me as I cast around for new ways to add meaning to my life.

Some odd dreams and intuitions began occurring to me, experiences for which I had no spiritual framework. I had always remembered occasional dreams. Now I became serious about writing them down, analyzing them, and trying to know myself better. These dreams proved significant both in my personal growth and as seed material for my writing.

One episode especially provoked me to search for answers. We had a gorgeous white cat that stayed outside at night. One morning I opened the door for him but didn't see him on the patio. I lay down on the couch to wait for the coffee to perk, accidentally fell back to sleep, and dreamed I saw the cat in a plastic bag sitting on green grass. The cat did not come home all day. The next morning I found the caretaker for the condo complex, and he told me that he had found a white cat dead on the grounds, placed it in a plastic bag, and dropped it in the dumpster. By comparing times, we discovered that he had found the cat within a half hour of my dream. Needless to say, the cat never returned.

Although I did not understand the how and why of things like dreams that came true, a voice in my head, or intuitive knowing, they began to happen to me more frequently. I felt alternately afraid and titillated by these experiences. I felt a spiritual lack that was difficult to define. I had learned Christianity in a Methodist Church as a kid but abandoned the belief for agnosticism during my college years. After my divorce I attended a Fundamentalist Christian Church for a while.

One night I didn't want to attend a Bible study, but a voice in my head said, "Toby, go to the Bible study." I went without hesitation. That could have been Jesus or an angel speaking. Who knew? The subject for discussion at the Bible study turned out to be people who heard voices in Biblical days, like Daniel did in the lions' den. The bizarre coincidence of subject matter with my experience of a few hours earlier awed me. I asked whether people heard voices in modern times. The answer? No, only in Biblical times.

Disappointed, I left that fellowship and enrolled in New Age classes for developing psychic abilities. I also read books on those subjects, including and most importantly the Jane Roberts books on the Seth phenomenon. Roberts, a medium, spoke in trance for a spirit entity named Seth, who dictated several books on metaphysics. I read the Seth books and found the material fascinating because it explained our reality in esoteric but believable ways.

During this time I had some dreams where someone called Emmons gave me instructions for doing automatic writing: relax with a pen and paper, allow a meditative state, listen, and write the words that occurred to my mind without judging their meaning.

When I talked with a medium from the local Spiritualist Church about my experience, she encouraged me to give it a try. Although I felt leery and dreaded seeming a fool, I proceeded, worrying all the time that people I loved would find out and do what? I guess not love me anymore. I worried too that I might be delving into dangerous territory but pressed on anyway.

The first evening I sat at my desk with a spiral notebook and pen, relaxed, and waited for the pen to start moving. Miraculously it did but I had no knowledge of what was going to be written. Sometimes I read it as I wrote. The language was very smooth with few errors and definitely not written in my style. I often had no idea what the subject would be. Eventually as I became more accustomed to the experience, I used a typewriter and found no discernible difference between the two writing instruments.

The automatic writing began to reveal personalities distinct from my own. One spirit guide named Emmons announced that he wanted to write a book on reincarnation. Again, I was thrown into a tizzy. Even though I majored in creative writing as an undergrad, wrote some plays and essays, and always wanted to write professionally, I had never until this point in time considered the book as my vehicle. I thought long about whether to allow the book dictation but finally decided it could do no harm to try. I could dump the whole project anytime I wanted.

Emmons and I set an appointment for two evenings a week, and the dictation generally lasted an hour or so. It included messages for me and other people as well as book dictation. The spirit guide named the manuscript *The World Book of Consciousness* and described its primary subject matter as reincarnation with ways to evaluate past life memories to enhance personal growth. Some of the material contained information about lifetimes in England with dates and place names from previous incarnations. This dictation continued throughout the winter and much of 1984.

I received dictation for *The World Book of Consciousness* because I felt compelled to do so. I was torn between a sense of duty to get the information out and a sense of horror that others might ever actually read it. If they did, they would come to conclusions about what I believed or seemed to believe. I did not feel personally anything close to the air of certainty that came across in the automatic writing. I didn't want to mislead people or set myself up as an authority figure. I had no credentials such as a member of the clergy, a priest, or a medium might have.

After I had transcribed all the dictation for the manuscript, I did feel proud of myself for having completed the entire book and fervently wished that I understood the whole experience better.

It worried me a great deal that I might be deranged, copying Jane Roberts without realizing that I did so. Even now, twenty-seven years later I can't definitely swear whether the material came from a being from another reality or from my own subconscious mind. It's equally as overwhelming for me to realize that twenty-seven years actually have gone by since then because the time and emotions of that period are still fresh and a part of my persona. That was an incredibly high-energy time of my life. Ripples spread out from it in ways that still reverberate.

The manuscript that I finally completed contained a memoir, a philosophical treatise, and research results on details of past life information, which I tried to document. I taught full time and worked on the manuscript in the evenings and on weekends. It took a few months to complete. In this phase of the writing process, I found myself relying on familiar skills, the same ones I had developed from directing plays at the high school where I taught: a willingness to work long hours on a project, to redo scenes when they don't work, and to keep on tweaking to make the final product as artistic as possible.

When I felt I had it ready, I sent *The World Book of Consciousness* out to some publishers and failed to get any positive feedback. At the time I thought the reason might be some prejudice against the subject matter or disregard because I wasn't a practicing psychic with a name for myself in the paranormal world.

In any case, I rewrote the manuscript in the evenings over the next few months, changed the title to *Past Lives, Present Hope*, and sent it out again.

Same story all over, so I rewrote it. I believed in the material at such a deep level that I tried again with a third version, *Faces of the Mind*. No luck that time either, despite the fact that the whole experience had given me the confidence and know-how to co-author a supplementary textbook with another teacher. We found a publisher for our textbook without much trouble.

Now in preparing to write this essay, I looked back at that last version entitled *Faces of the Mind*, and I realized it was an awful book. Maybe that's why I couldn't get it published! The long and short of it? I lacked technique, the reason the book turned out lousy.

Paradoxically, even though I've never sold that book in any of its incarnations, it has fueled at least six of the later books I wrote and did sell. The spirit guide Emmons told of a woman who ran an inn in eighteenth-century England. I developed her into a full-blown character with incarnations before and after that century. Her story became a series entitled *Alma Chronicles*. The souls are reborn in different centuries, and it took five books to tell Alma's tale.

Whenever I reread any of these novels, I realize that I could go in many other directions with the material. I could plunge one of my main characters into a lifetime in another century. I could take some of the children from the stories and write children's books or grow the children up and tell their stories for adults. I could take a minor character and develop his story into a new tale. The variations on the characters and themes are seemingly endless.

A major problem I encountered in the early years of my writing career was belief in myself, or lack of it rather, despite the fact that I had written tons of curriculum for the school district, several plays, and some essays. My muse filled me with apprehension. Maybe I set the situation up psychologically so that, if I failed, people could just consider me nuts instead of untalented.

My educational background suited me well to writing books. Besides an undergraduate major in English, I taught composition in high school for several years, requiring me to grade papers, a skill that helps me edit my own work dispassionately. Later, I took writing technique classes and joined a critique group. I have been a member of one critique group or another ever since. With the exception of that first book, no piece of my writing has ever gone out to a publisher or agent without having been through a critique group.

The circumstances of the automatic writing with the messages it delivered still serve as a creative resource for me even though I no longer do automatic writing. I've tried and haven't been successful. I lost the ability to do it through self-doubt. Emmons and the other spirit guides wanted me to become a practicing medium, but I could not bring myself to do so. I couldn't take money or even do for free something I understood so little. Besides, becoming a successful writer remained my original and still pressing goal.

Finding myself the recipient of esoteric knowledge profoundly unsettled me because I've never considered myself a teacher in such matters, rather a learner. But even more, I distrusted the source and doubted my sanity. My inner struggle got in the way of the creative material being given to me and slowed my progress as a developing writer.

On the other hand, without the automatic writing experience, I would never have had the courage to write one book, let alone the ten others I have written since. Even though I couldn't get the first book published but could and did get other books published, I came to believe in my writing ability. Perhaps that need to believe in myself provoked the automatic writing experience, regardless of its origin from this reality or the next.

Mine could be a cautionary tale-use it or lose it, but I prefer to think of my experience in a holistic sense. Automatic writing is a completely right-brain approach. Editing and critiquing are the left brain aspects of writing.

In his book *Write from the Heart*, writing instructor Hal Zina Bennett tells about his own muse, an Indian spirit guide. He quotes his guide as saying: "Your creativity does not belong to you. It is part of the great Creative Spirit that makes us all, that gives us life and that gives the entire universe its form. You have been given your small share of the Creative Spirit, but you are treating it as if you owned it. It is not yours to own. So get the hell out of its way."

Bennett's muse is right, of course, but it's not easy to get out of one's way.

Many authors have had muses or daemons or inner guides. They're called by different names. Carl Jung had a guide named Philemon; William Butler Yeats had a previous version of himself like an earlier incarnation as a spirit guide. I've had some good company, after all.

Over the years without the automatic writing as a continuing resource, I have evolved a writing method that I use for both fiction and nonfiction. It's working so far, but who knows? The next book might require something different.

For now, once I get an idea for a book, I have to incubate it in the back of my mind while I do something else with the front of my mind. I stew about the subject while I clean out closets or go shopping. I try to not think about the book project consciously. Of course, that's a slippery task. Sometimes the idea is all I can think about for big blocks of time.

This phase includes note taking, something I try to organize to accommodate the different ways ideas come to me. I make a folder on my computer using the title of my project. Into that I add a file called Notes. Later I'll add files for each chapter and other items, like research details. Considering that ideas come when I least expect them and sometimes when I'm not at my computer, I keep a paper file folder in my desk, also called Notes. Into this folder I put things I see in magazines, photos, and notes I make while away from home, usually on scraps of paper or restaurant napkins. I try to keep a notebook in my purse, but my purses get too stuffed, so sometimes I fail to write ideas down. However, they often circle back around in my mind when I'm at the computer too. In addition, I keep my dream journal on my computer. Frequently, my dreams contain ideas and details that are useful for the writing project, so I copy and paste them from my dream journal to my project notes file.

After I have a sense of where I want to go, I do research if that is necessary. It's an obvious necessity when I'm writing nonfiction. I spent close to a year in the library and on the Internet doing the research for *Out of the Psychic Closet*. In that research-intensive project I wanted to provide as much scientific support for paranormal subjects as I could find. Because of the book's self-help purpose, I wanted the reader to trust me; consequently, I documented as much as possible to prove that psychic experiences, like precognition, psychokinesis, and ghost sightings, were valid and explainable.

My two eighteenth-century books, *Alison's Legacy* and *Lainn's Destiny*, required quite a lot of research also. I minored in history in college, but I needed to immerse myself in information about the particular time period to adequately convey the culture and mores of England, Scotland, and the American Colonies. For a novel set in the 1980s, years that I lived through, I still needed to do research. For example, I talked to a man at the Navy base in San Diego about the Cessna airplane and what might cause it to explode to make the opening scene in *Angie's Promise* believable.

As a framing device and to anchor me in the project, I do a map of the book, what I think the chapters will look like. This is easier to do with nonfiction where the breakdown into chapters or units is generally dictated by the subject matter. Then I list the subcategories that I think I'll need, but this can change as I go back to research something else or take a new tack. It's important to stay open to the flow of information and insight as much as possible.

In fiction, I always do a synopsis of the whole story, then I continually update that synopsis as the story progresses. That way I have overall direction for the trajectory but can allow characters to have their own way at the same time. If I have my characters well developed in my mind, I generally know how the story will end but not all of the ways to get there. When I wrote *Luke's Covenant* and *The Comet's Return*, I knew Luke had to die. My characters always have to die so they can be reborn. However, I did not know how he would die. One of the biggest surprises in my writing life happened when Melanie murdered Luke. I had thought all along Kegan would do it. But there, only a chapter away from the end of the book, suddenly she did it! Then I thought, *of course, it had to be Melanie.*

Once the incubation phase is finished or I feel like I'm getting close to it, I move on to what I call the creativity dump, which usually involves an alcoholic beverage. That's where I drop ideas randomly into a word processing file without regard for syntax, structure, or cohesion. "Write drunk, edit sober." This saying often attributed to Ernest Hemingway works for me. Some authors say it works the other way around, "write sober, edit drunk," but I can't attest to that.

The above is said primarily for entertainment. I can't get drunk and expect to produce any decent copy although some alcohol allows me to loosen up and prevents me from getting compulsive about editing every single tiny error. Constant editing interrupts the flow of ideas, and I fail to produce original copy. I sometimes get depressed when I start editing in this phase, and I have to just quit and do something else like pull weeds. I have to be pressed to the maximum because I hate yard work above any household chore.

From here I move on to actually writing my ideas into paragraphs and then into chapters. I like to use music to help keep me in the mood required. For example, when I wrote the two historicals set in the eighteenth century, I played CDs of Scottish ballads and Celtic airs. When I wrote a sci-fi romance called *Full Contact*, I played the score from *A Man and a Woman*.

This phase of writing is the most dangerous for me because of my tendency to dislike a mess. I risk deleting something that is useful. I sometimes can't resist the urge, so I have developed the habit of copying and pasting everything I want to delete to the bottom of the file. Or if I want to delete a whole scene, then I drop it into a junk file in the same folder with my chapter. I create a new file for every chapter because that's easier to manage than a long file with all the chapters in it.

Fiction presents a special challenge for me in this stage of the writing process. It's here that the characters are talking, acting, and being talked about by other characters. I may know my characters very well, but I have to make sure that I have them say things, do things, and feel things that reveal their inner natures. If I don't build sympathy in the readers for my character early on, I might as well quit writing because my readers will definitely quit reading. I have to make the character if not lovable at least likable to give the reader someone to root for. They will only have empathy for the character if I reveal the underlying humanity. I do a spot check on this requirement when the chapter goes to critique and ask, "Did you care about the character?" If my critique group doesn't care, I've got a lot of work to do. Often it's here that I use some of those deleted items.

Nonfiction has to pass a different test because there is no character to carry the ideas. The author speaks directly to the reader, at least in self-help and educational materials. It's important to avoid preaching or presuming beliefs that might be far from the reader's mindset. Going on too long, over explaining, or talking down to the reader can also crop up. Here again, the critique group becomes invaluable.

Once I've written the chapter into its first rough form, I print it and edit it on paper. At this point I like to wait a while before I look at the chapter again. The next day generally I input the changes I've made on paper, reread, and make any other changes on the computer. Then I do the whole process again. That's at least two rewrites before I submit the chapter for critique.

I've been in several critique groups over the years. They vary in effectiveness according to the skills of the individual members, naturally. Just about everyone can give input that is helpful. Usually the more sophisticated members can give professional feedback about such things as structure or characterization, but even the novices are intelligent readers, so I listen to all the comments about my work and appreciate them for what they are. I try not to get angry or defensive, but sometimes, what can I say? I'm guilty. For the most part, I profit from what the critique group members say. I always remember that it is I alone sitting at the computer and instituting any changes. I decide what to use and what to lose.

It's probably obvious that I believe in critique groups. I wish I had been in one when I wrote the first version of the manuscript from automatic writing. The outcome might have been very different.

Last, of course, in my writing process comes the editing of the final draft. Once I'm deep into the book and have several chapters, I assemble them into one file. At this stage, I start reading through the whole manuscript, not every day that I work, but every few days.

There's a timing or a sense of movement akin to music that develops in every manuscript. It's the same thing with directing a play. I can hear the theme after a fashion and can sometimes clap my hands to imitate the beat. Maybe the feeling tone of the book, or of a particular scene, is deep and touching or maybe it's catchy and bright. I work for a particular feel, depending on what I want to accomplish, and try to hear the beat. The sounds of words are important because readers read with their eyes and their ears. With dialogue especially, it's important to have this awareness. I often read dialogue aloud so I can hear what the characters are saying to each other.

This last editing step sometimes happens ten times or more, but not always. Some manuscripts go together easier than others. William Faulkner said, "...the writer's obligation is to get the work done the best he can do it." That's always my goal.

Faulkner was my first binge author. At one time I read almost every novel he wrote as well as all of his short stories. I also binged on John Steinbeck, Mark Twain, Richard Bach, and Jane Roberts over the years. I bring this up for two reasons. One, these authors had profound impacts on me as role models. Two, bingeing gets me in trouble with food.

For years my workday required physical activity. Drama teachers especially are always on the move while directing plays, running to the control booth, setting lights, raising the counterbalance system. When I left teaching and started writing, oh my goodness. I gained thirty-five pounds. For me peanuts are thinking food, a real downside to the writing life. I'm now back to my pre-writing career weight, but I'm not fooled. I know if I get really involved in writing something I love, I'm at risk to put the pounds back on.

I used to think the creativity part was the most fun of writing, maybe because I like gin and peanuts, but lately I enjoy editing and revision more. They require just as much creativity and more discipline. Perhaps I've become a perfectionist, but it gives me pride to watch a piece I've written grow in richness and meaning as I hone it to make it the best read I can.

The writing life is not to be chosen lightly. Becoming a writer requires self-analysis, self-criticism, self-adulation, self-doubt. It doesn't matter whether you're writing fiction or nonfiction, the self-inquiry is relentless. I see bits of myself in all of my fictional characters, even the bad guys or girls. I love villainesses.

There's constant potential for hypocrisy in nonfiction even though I'm talking directly to the reader. Memoir is probably the biggest trap, the place where my alter ego shows up most insidiously. My effort to be candid with the reader and reveal myself with transparency sometimes shows up as superficiality. You can bet I will have culled all potential superficialities that I note from this piece before I call it done.

What did I learn from writing my first book? That I could do it, that it was painful, that I had the nerve to try, that there is an endless source of creative potential available to me.

Sometimes I cry when I write a scene, more often I cry when I edit it because I relive the emotions. Every time I read the scene where Alison gives birth to her son, I cry again. I don't suppose I'll ever get over the trauma of Lainn's birth. It's right up there behind the births of my own two living, breathing sons and partly culled from those precious moments in my life.

A writer has to be true to herself. I love magic, magical realism, and paranormal tidbits that hint at a larger reality. The experience of automatic writing is a part of that framework. Some British psychic researchers declare that it contains some of the most compelling evidence for life after death. Here's the web link: http://www.survivalafterdeath.org.uk/articles/barrett/automatic.htm

Did the information in the automatic writing come from me or from a source or sources outside myself? If I was fooling myself, why did I not know it? Twenty-seven years later, the prose in the automatic writing still reads like other-than-Toby composition.

Maturity has not given me the answer. Now I wonder whether I could have accepted any proof as valid. Although I rejected the source and failed to find a publisher for that book, it has permeated many other pieces of my writing. It is a creative wellspring from which I can dip over and over again.

I wish I could time travel to converse with myself in 1983. Would I feel the same about writing my first book? I marvel at how the automatic writing experience has fit into the overall context of my life. It's a powerful memory that helps make me who I am. I suppose it's possible that I might have been suffering from post-traumatic stress disorder. I'd survived a divorce, after all. That's a major life stressor, and it led me to self-evaluation and growth through personal writing in my dream journal as well as public writing in my books.

For me writing is a spiritual path, a vehicle to help me grow in understanding of dimensions of myself. How successful I am is open to question if, after all these years, I still doubt my perceptions. At some level it doesn't matter. Deep in my soul, I have to own whatever comes out of my fingertips onto a page or a computer screen. My attitudes about the automatic writing and about my mental stability during the 1980s continue to evolve. At times, I wonder how I can trust myself, how I can know anything for sure. I'm still looking for causes and solutions.

I am unrepentant about my skepticism. One of the great problems of our time is the propensity of otherwise intelligent people to believe without proof, to depend on someone else's version of reality to frame their own. That includes people considered authorities like priests, imams, teachers, channels, even political leaders. A fundamentalist view in any religion requires acceptance of truth on faith, the blinder the better. That is the exact opposite of my inclination, which is to examine every scrap of an idea.

For me habitual doubt is more honest. I fear for the world I live in because so many claim to know *The Truth*. I long for more doubters in high places.

Nevertheless, I am thankful for the peaceful physical environment that has blessed me while living in Arizona all these years. Without it, I would never have been able to go on my spiritual search. I didn't have to face many outer tornadoes in my path, a security that allowed me the freedom to confront my inner tornadoes.

What I believe? There is one universal consciousness, striving, learning, growing. I am a part of that consciousness, striving, learning, growing the best I can. And so it is.

About the author

Toby Fesler Heathcotte is both mother and grandmother. A former teacher, she now serves as president of Arizona Authors Association. http://www.tobyheathcotte.com

Current release: Out of the Psychic Closet: The Quest to Trust My True Nature. [2011 EPIC award finalist.]

Wings

by Darby Karchut

Blame It on Masterpiece Theater

I never wanted to write a book. But this story slammed into me one day like an avalanche from behind and the only alternative (other than suffocating to death) was to dig myself out and write the thing.

And I blame it all on *Masterpiece Theater*.

In the spring of 2009, I was trying to find information about the next installment of my favorite television program, *Foyle's War* (a gem of a show about the British home front during World War Two) when I stumbled across a website created by enthusiasts devoted to the show.

I hesitated. Okay, I thought, I'll bite, then I clicked on it. And there they were. Stories, written by fans and based on the characters from the show. Fan fiction, they called it. Well, of course, I had to read a few. It was *Foyle's War*, after all. Then I read a few more. Some were incredible, some were ... well ... less so.

Hmmm, I thought. Could I write one? Maybe ... maybe even post it on that website? Yikes! That would mean other people would *read* it.

No, no. Can't have that. Just back away and don't make eye contact. So I quickly turned to other things, trying to ignore the voice in my head. A voice with an English accent, no less.

But for the next week or so, I couldn't get the idea of writing a story out of my mind. I found myself thinking about one vignette after another, and then I would kick myself and go about my business.

After a few weeks of bruised ankles, I finally broke down and wrote a short *Foyle's War* story.

And I liked it. I mean I liked writing (the story was pathetic). Writing was... it was ... fun. And engaging. And stretched parts of my brain I didn't know existed. I re-wrote it a few times, all the while thinking that editing was *cheating* somehow and real writers nailed it the first time.

With much trepidation, I submitted it to the website, then steeled myself. For an entire day, I walked back and forth in front of my laptop, too nervous to check the remarks. What if the other fans hated it? What if they posted it as an example of how *not* to write fan fiction? After many cups of coffee, I logged on and headed to the comments section.

Hey! A few fans read it. And liked it. At least, they didn't hate it. Or were being polite. Two writers even asked for another story. Okay, I thought. I'll try again. I have another idea anyway, so here goes.

And for the next month or so, I wrote and posted about six more stories, all focused on the relationship between the main character, Foyle, and his son. I even exchanged e-mails with other writers. I was perfectly happy to keep my writing at that micro level.

If I had only known what was coming.

One day, the idea of writing my own story, with my own characters, ambushed me while I was running in the foothills near my house. A story about a young hero rising above a brutal past with the help of others along the way, with whiffs of fantasy and history and philosophy and even a love story. Maybe something with ... with ... with angels.

Man, I really should have run faster.

For I already had a career. I taught, and still teach, social studies at a junior high school, and during the summers, my husband and I have been building a modest cabin in the Rocky Mountains of Colorado. A full life. A happy life. A life with some bloody down time!

But the idea of writing my own story would not die. I kept thinking about writing a book. Which is all good and well, except for one problem.

I had never written anything like a book.

I had never written a short story.

I had never written creative fiction (except a few pieces of fan fiction)

I had never written a song or an epitaph or a poem.

Nothing. Nada. Zippo.

I had no idea what I was doing.

Now don't misunderstand me. All my life, I have consumed books. I have read hundreds of books, thousands of books. Mostly fantasy, but also historical fiction, chick lit, biographies, world history, philosophy, science fiction, and young adult books. A metric ton of young adult books.

If my home library was a continent, it would be Asia.

It was similar to having an eating disorder. There's an old saying among writers: you read and you read, and then one day you throw up a book. So to purge myself, I decided to write one, too. About a troubled teen angel named Griffin, and his steadfast father-mentor, Basil.

Because my life was getting just too easy and laid back.

Damn Calvinistic streak.

As I wrote my first book, I did everything wrong. I had two characters, but no plot. No plot as no beginning, no middle and certainly no ending. It was like building a house on an empty lot and starting out by purchasing a coffee table and an ice cream scooper.

But I took advantage of the Internet, my local Borders Bookstore, and other writers, and I learned and practiced the noble craft as I wrote. And rewrote. And rewrote. And rewrote.

Then I broke the rules to make the story better. Everything is about the Story.

Stupid Fate

As well known author, Toni Morrison, once said, "Write the book you want to read."

Best advice ever for any author.

I think I toyed with the idea of writing a book for years, but only on a subconscious level. I was a child of J.R.R. Tolkien, Lloyd Alexander, C.S. Lewis, Madeline L'Engle, and many other classics, so I knew if I ever did write one, it would be a fantasy.

As I said at the beginning, I had never written a story before. Oh, I've written one master thesis, various reports, and a bazillion lesson plans, but I never created a tale, populated with good guys and bad guys having adventures. I did not like or dislike writing. To me, it was simply a means to other ends.

Then, one day in late June 2009, several months after posting my first fan fiction piece, I happened to re-read C.S. Lewis' *Screwtape*

Letters. It is a curious little text in which he explains the basic tenets of Christianity through a series of letters between a senior devil and his apprentice. In the Introduction, Lewis briefly mentions that the opposite of devils are, of course, angels. Warrior angels. Butt-kicking angels. Not the poufy little cherubs that make me believe childhood obesity began during the Victorian era, but real soldiers of Heaven.

I liked the idea. Of celestial warriors. In fact, I found myself wishing Lewis or someone had written such a book. About an angel teaching and training his young apprentice while fulfilling their roles as guardians of humankind, but with an urban twist.

So, off to Poor Richard's, my favorite local used bookstore, for such a book. Searching, searching, searching. Rats. Nothing.

However...

While digging around, careful not to get splinters from the plywood shelves, I came across a battered paperback on angelic lore from various cultures. And there it was. From the High Middle Ages in Europe came a description of a lower caste of angels said to control the four elements: earth, fire, wind, and water. Sounded like Jedi knights with halos.

I was hooked. Fate decided that *I* needed to write the book I was searching for.

Stupid Fate

But I didn't want goody-goody angels. I even wrote, in huge letters across the top of my first page: "No *Touched by An Angel* allowed." I wanted a down-to-earth type of angels who did the mundane, day-to-day guardianship stuff the other angels were too busy to take care of, with a strong emphasis on the delightful friction that occurs when the everyday rubs up against the supernatural.

And I knew the story must incorporate a master and apprentice, knight and squire, father and son type of relationship. The archetypical champion and his wise sage had intrigued me even before Joseph Campbell made me aware of the hero's journey.

So I began writing what was to become my first book, *Griffin Rising*, that weekend; a tale about a young apprentice angel with serious self esteem issues and his coming of age under the tutelage of a larger-then-life mentor, interwoven with a charming love story between Griffin and the mortal girl next door.

And thus angst-ridden Griffin and noble Basil and sweet Katie and everyone else in the book started talking.
To me. In my head.
All the time.
Like children when you are trying to make a phone call.

Earth Angels

Since my angels (or as I sometimes referred to them after a long writing session, *the boys*) had both their feet on the ground (so to speak), I decided they should belong to sub-caste of angels, the very lowest of the lows. *Terra Angeli*: Latin for Earth Angels. Now the belief in angelic beings can be found in many of the world's religions and I borrowed freely from Judaism, Christianity, Islam, and Hinduism. My Prologue gave a nod to the early Christian writing **The Celestial Hierarchy** and with my background in anthropology, any and all world cultures were grist for my mill, to be sure.

For example, the Terra Angeli were inspired by classical Sparta, the Irish myths of Cuchulainne, Finn and the Red Branch, the European feudal system, the Plains Indians of North America, and Great Britain's Royal Air Force during World War Two (and there's a tip of the hat to *Foyle's War*.)

The Four Months

For the next four months, I wrote and re-wrote the first few chapters a dozen times. I knew I wanted it to be a character driven book, but I soon realized my characters needed something to do, by golly! Or it would simply be one lengthy Seinfeld episode.

After wailing to my husband that my book was stagnating like three o'clock coffee at Starbuck's, he dragged me off to the Holy of Holies. Otherwise known as our local Borders Bookstore.

"Look," he said, gesturing to an entire rack of how-to-write magazines. "You could read a few articles about plot. Have a cup of coffee while jotting down pointers, then put the magazine back and pick up another. Voila! Free education for the price of a latte."

I naturally pitched a fit about "the experts" stifling my creativity and that Real Writers learn by struggling on their own (preferably in a quaint cottage overlooking a pastoral scene or deep in SoHo in a hip martini joint) and blah, blah, blah.

When I finished, he nodded like he understood, then said, "Yeah. Whatever," grabbed the nearest magazine and headed for the cafe. Stumping after him, I imagined tripping him from behind and sending him face first into a rack of greeting cards. Too bad he's agile.

After ordering our coffees, we found a table by the window (because a view of a parking lot is always *so* motivational) and I opened the magazine to the table of contents. Okay. There *was* an article about how to outline the plot of your novel. And it didn't seem too long. I even knew and respected this particular author. Fine, I thought. I'll read the damn thing. But don't expect me to follow her advice. I'm not some lemming jostling for a front row position.

You know. That whole creative-stifling thing.

But, by golly, there were some rock solid, down to earth, kind-of-obvious-if-you-bothered-to-pull-your-stubborn-head-out-of-your-butt ideas that made sense. And the author even added a caveat at the end declaring that any advice should always be taken cautiously. Find *your* way of planning or outlining or story boarding or whatever. Any method works as long as it works for you.

I HATE it when my husband is right.

I started going to Borders at least once a week. And I read every writer's magazine, devoured every article. And I started seeing a pattern. Author after author, editor after editor, agent after agent kept repeating the same things: compelling plot, strong characters, crisp dialogue and find your voice.

And I began to develop a writing process. I would write a few chapters, then stop and study the craft of writing. Then I'd go back and re-write them. Then plow ahead a few more chapters and repeat. I wasted a lot of time, but it was perfect just-in-time learning for me. I would study another rule or technique, and apply it immediately. Not just practice it on a short story, but put it to use on the book I was passionate about.

This process quickly morphed into reading every blog, every website, every e-article about the art and craft of writing fiction. Learn, learn, learn. Apply, apply, apply. Fall asleep thinking about the book, the characters whispering in my ears like creepy little stalkers.

All this while teaching junior high school full time. Talk about incredible field research for a young adult author! I would stand around and soak up teenage dialogue, often making notes on my hand if paper wasn't available.

Luckily, I had a friend, another faculty member at my school, who read one of my earliest rough drafts. She was always gracious about my pulling her to one side between classes to ask her opinion, although she looked a bit worried when I asked her, very earnestly, one day: "Do you think Griffin would wear a pink polo shirt?" (Griffin, of course, being my sixteen year old protagonist.)

At least I didn't ask the boxers versus briefs question. That would have been awkward.

Along the Way and Away

The magic of writing is that some days I wrote the story, and a lot of days, I simply took dictation while the characters lived out their lives for me. My subconscious came up with scenes I would never have conceived of, even on my best days. Those were wonderful days.

Known to writers as The Flow. It would be my drink of choice if we could ever bottle it.

Then there were days when every word written was covered in blood and spit. I would struggle with a sentence, a scene, a character, heck, a comma! But those were muscle building days. When I was literally clubbing my book to work; when I fought to use every little trick and skill I had recently picked up. Smashing the craft into my brain and then out onto my work.

Writing is gut-busting, molar-grinding hard work.

And, oh, so sweetly satisfying when it goes well.

Obsessive does not even begin to describe my behavior during those months. Thank goodness, my husband, who is an award winning artist, understood the creative drive. But I had to learn to balance my career and my family while writing. For the sake of my marriage as well as my sanity. (Writing is a marathon, not a sprint. The best advice I can give anyone attempting to write a book: turn off the television. It's all drivel anyway and you might as well be working.)

So I trained myself to write whenever I had a fifteen minute block of time (or longer). Even if it was just a few sentences. Lunch time, after school, during the evening, every weekend. I wrote and I wrote and I wrote.

And I found the more I wrote, the better I got at it.

Well, duh. You think?

One "trick" I learned was to stop just short of saturation for the day. I would stop in the middle of an action scene or during an emotional exchange. That way, I would come back fresh and eager knowing exactly what I was going to work on in the next session. This got me warmed up and gave me a quicker start out of the gate.

Another useful bit of advice I followed was to get a beta reader. A person who would read your work and give your feedback. I did so after a few months and holy cow, was that scary! What if I really did suck? Oops. Sorry. I mean inhale deeply. I had to develop a thick skin and fast.

But I so fortunate to retain my mother as my beta reader. As a retired school teacher, she had the background and time to critically read each chapter as I went along, pointing out weaknesses in the plot as well as discrepancies in the characters. But, being my mother and I, her favorite child, (no matter how much my siblings protest) she was also fantastic at pointing out what was working well. For me, a balanced viewpoint was critical at this stage in my career because I was always looking at what was *wrong* with my story. And I needed to know what I was doing right so I could repeat it.

Day after day, word after word, I plodded along, until I reached the infamous middle of the book. The nemesis of so many good writers. I had been dreading this moment. After reading about writers giving up at this point in their book, I was mentally prepared to slam into the Wall.

Maybe I was geared up. Or lucky. Or maybe all that advice from other authors helped, but whatever it was, I hit the middle of my book, lowered my head and battered my way to the two-thirds section. Came up for air and looked around.

And that's when I knew.

I was going to finish my first book. The plot was slowly tightening up, dialogue was flowing like the Colorado River during the spring melt, and I even knew how *Griffin Rising* was going to end. The adrenaline took over and I sprinted toward the finish line.

After Enlightenment

It was a Saturday morning, in late November, four months after I started, when I typed the words *The End* on the bottom of the last page.

Wow. Cool. I had written a book. A poor one. But a book, nonetheless.

So I hit the save button. Then compulsively hit it again. Then dumped the manuscript on my flashdrive. Then dumped it on a second flashdrive, turned off my computer, and went downstairs for a celebratory cup of coffee.

And I was quite certain that I was now a different person. But I wasn't. I was still just me. I still had to go to work, clean house, shop for food, clean the litter box, and all the other mundane tasks of life. And that was okay. Healthy, even. A famous Zen Buddhist expression kept running through my mind: "Before Enlightenment, chop wood, carry water. After Enlightenment, chop wood, carry water."

Exactly.

(That said, finishing a book remains a rarified thing in this society. There's a popular statistic that although 85% of population wants to write a book, less than 4% of authors get published. And only 0.2% of those get a chance to publish a second book.)

So I refilled my coffee mug, kicked off my fleece lined flip flops and fired up my laptop.

And began re-writing *Griffin Rising* that day.

Because I now had a new goal.

To improve my writing. And make those characters so real, so compelling that they would stop yakking in my head and go pester *other* people. You know. Murmur in *their* heads all night and leave *me* alone.

Winter came and went. And I rewrote Griffin's tale over and over. Some sections just a few times, some sections over twenty times. Added and took away.

I continuously e-mailed new and improved chapters to my beta reader. Than handed the manuscript off to a few friends, including my school's librarian.

And I rewrote it.

I gave it to my sister and brother for their opinion.

And I rewrote it again.

And it was agony. Excruciatingly painful. I found it was more difficult to accept criticism after I had learned a thing or two than before. With my earlier drafts, I would justify negative remarks by reminding myself it was just that: a draft. But as I re-wrote it and found my voice, the criticisms hurt worse because now it was truly *me* they were judging. I would force myself to nod and listen, really listen, and then I would look at the section or chapter through their eyes, and I would have to agree.

But finally, on a snowy day in mid-winter, I found myself jotting down some ideas for the sequel. And I knew I was getting closer to the beginning of the ending of the editing process.

Which, I recently discovered, never really ends.

But I loved editing. I loved polishing each sentence until it gleams, each chapter until it was smooth and sharp. The more I edited, the stronger it became. And the stronger I became. Just like a cross country runner, I found my stride, working my writing into the rhythm of my existence, so that writing was a part of my life, not my life.

Yes, sir, nothing could stop me now.

Until I sent out my first round of query letters.

Okay, those left some bruises. But ice and aspirin helped and I kept working on the manuscript. And the query letter. And sent out another round of query letters.

And finally, eleven months after I began writing my first book, Griffin got his wings with Twilight Times Books.

It Takes What It Takes

So what really, really helped me write my first book? Well, lots of things and lots of people. But the three most important things that enabled me to reach my goal were to read a lot, write a lot, and read about writing a lot.

Read a lot.

The other day, I attended a book talk given by an up and coming young adult author at our city library. As I sat poised with a yellow pad balanced on my knee, ready to mine nuggets of brilliance, my mouth fell open at the following statement from the author: "I really don't like to read that much."

What the ...?!

How can an author not like to read? It's like a cook who doesn't sample his dishes or a teacher who doesn't like children.

Now it used to be the custom, in Europe, that young artists would begin their apprenticeships by studying the works of the masters. For centuries, one would find youths in museums or galleries, feverishly sketching one masterpiece after another, learning the craft by practicing the craft.

Okay, maybe it was different with this guy. I don't know. But like most authors, I read constantly. All the time I was working on *Griffin Rising*, I read three or four books a month, mostly young adult fantasy. I read to relax, but mostly I read to learn from the masters.

But I also read several biographies and even a history of the Battle of Thermopylae.

Read. Read everything.

Write a lot.

As I mentioned earlier, I managed to train myself to write whenever and wherever I could. For me, daily self-discipline was the key to finishing my first draft. Yes, I had to compromise in some arenas, but not as many as I had first thought. Oh, sure. My house was not as clean as I usually kept it, but I soon grew proud of my dust bunnies. The bigger, the better was my motto. And I had to keep introducing myself to my husband so he wouldn't forget who I was.

The two arenas, however, I never neglected were my job and my exercise regime. I still had a life to live outside of my head. And I began to find that when I took a break from my book, my subconscious mind did a lot of work for me, solving plot holes, enriching the characters, and so on. I just needed to give it a chance.

Read about writing a lot.

I continued to study everything I could on how to improve my writing. Everything I needed to learn was available, in books, on-line, in magazine or from the local library. Incredible!

And I am still learning.

Springtime in the Rockies (why, yes, that is an oxymoron)

Finally, in the spring, after months of stalling, I screwed up my courage and attended my first writer's conference. Which I should have done *before* I began my book, but since I seemed to have done everything else backwards, what the heck.

I arrived an hour early and stood around the lobby of the hotel, my knees shaking as I watched other writers milling around, chatting with each other, no doubt discussing their fourth book deal and the outcome of a private lunch with the editor-in-chief at Random House.

You know, they probably all have been writing since they could hold a pencil, I thought to myself. Or they have master's degrees in literature and live in New York City. I gulped and went for my sixth cup of coffee.

But once I was registered and bleeding copiously from stabbing myself with my nifty pin-on nametag (the name tag, which, I was quite sure, said 'Wanna Be' in neon letters under my name), I crept into the first workshop and hunkered down in the back.

When I looked around, I noticed a lot of others had the same deer in the headlights expression as me. The workshop began, the panel of agents and publishers helping the audience lighten up by wisecracking about the foibles of the publishing industry, and as I heard other writers asking the exact same questions I had, I relaxed and just soaked it all in.

Over the next few days, I lunched and talked with other writers just like me, and scurried from one workshop to another, learning a mile a minute, and even met some future friends with whom I formed a critique group. I came away from that weekend with a renewed determination and a wonderful discovery: for the most part, the writing and publishing world is made up of some of the finest, most gracious people in this round world.

Rearview Mirror

My first book was such a backwards journey. I have often wondered if I would have done better to learn more before writing it. I'll never know, because I cannot repeat that first expedition.

Writing is an odd duck of a profession. You do not need have a degree or a license or spend a lot of money. Just determination. And almost every bit of information, from how to write to how to get published to how to market your book is easily and cheaply available.

Since then, I've written the sequel to *Griffin Rising* as well as the first novel in another young adult fantasy series. And I will always strive to improve my craft. That will never change. Writing is infinite; my next book will always be better than the one before and rightly so.

Enough of me.

Now go write *your* book.

About the author

Darby is a member of the Society of Children's Book Writers and Illustrators and the Pikes Peak Writers Guild. She lives in Colorado Springs, Colorado with her husband, where she still teaches at a local junior high school. She enjoys running, biking, and skiing the Rocky Mountains in all types of weather.

http://darbykarchut.com

Upcoming release: Griffin Rising is her first novel. She is currently working on the sequel, *Griffin's Fire*.

The Serendipity Factor

by Linda M. Langwith

Life is full of memorable firsts. Remember the moment your feet finally left the bottom of the pool and you actually swam without any help? Or when your dad decided to let go of the bicycle and you careened across the lawn solo? Graduation, marriage, the birth of one's first child-these are all momentous occasions that happen because we are prepared to live life to the full and embrace whatever comes our way. While you are contemplating all the firsts in your life, what about that first book? Maybe you have a story within you that needs to be told but you keep putting it off because you feel you have too many other commitments.

Family and work are important, but the energy you bring to each can only be enhanced and enriched if you recognize and acknowledge the creative spirit within you. It's never too late to begin. Writing is a process that can lead you on the most amazing journey into yourself, connect you with the people you love in the most profound way and transform your everyday life into a full spectrum kaleidoscope of random impressions, observations and accidental connections. I call it the Serendipity Factor, and if you open yourself up to it, you are taking that first step to becoming an author.

Recently, I attended a little get together put on by the publisher and editor of a magazine to which I am fortunate enough to be a regular contributor. I was buttonholed by an unsmiling woman of a certain age who questioned me earnestly about how I researched my book, what qualifications I had and how I managed to become expert on my topic. It was as if she thought that writing a novel was like a rather dry and academic research paper one did at university.

Well yes, indeed there is often some research required but the creative process is so much more than the marshalling of fact and argument. With both a BA and an MA in English, spanning the study of everything from Beowulf to Shakespeare to the Romantic poets and beyond, with huge dollops of recreational reading on the side in Medieval History and Art History, I am fully aware of the importance of scholarship, critical thinking and research. The study of literature though is really an exploration of the human condition and the creative process is part of that. How could I explain the workings of a writer's imagination, how events, impressions, conversations, chance encounters, emotions experienced over a lifetime can be the trigger for stories that often come unbidden but, once presented in the mind, develop such an urgency to be born that they cannot be resisted?

As my interrogator so obviously lived in the concrete world of here and now, I shared with her a small event that happened recently to me, hoping it would give her some insight into how a story begins. I was taking my usual walk along an oceanfront path that follows the contours of a beautiful bay where I live.

It was early spring and the bluebells, growing wild along the path, were just beginning to show their first green spikes. Having recently moved from a property containing the most glorious bluebell meadow to a townhouse with a small garden, I thought how lovely it would be to dig up a couple of the bulbs and plant them in my courtyard as a tangible link to my former life. When I knelt down to wriggle a bulb from the gravelly soil, I was surprised to see a part of what looked like a blue plastic tarp poking through the loose stones.

Suddenly I was startled by a dog barking and snarling. I whirled around and spotted a woman across the lane standing in her yard with a chunky Rottweiler straining at his leash. She shouted that those were her bluebells. I explained that I only wanted a couple and pointed out that they were growing on a public footpath. She made towards the gate at the front of the garden, as if to let loose the canine intimidator. Not to be deterred, I grabbed the bulbs, popped them in a plastic bag and continued my walk on somewhat wobbly knees, feeling rather unnerved by the aggression displayed.

As I headed down the long jetty that thrusts itself out into the bay, I thought about her reaction, how it was so out of proportion to my 'offense'. Giving free rein to my imagination, I pondered on the fragment of blue tarp and then took it to the next level by toying with the idea that maybe she'd wrapped a body in the tarp and buried it by the footpath. My earnest questioner was left speechless at this insight into how one's mind works as a writer. And yet that is precisely what I find myself doing-looking at seemingly insignificant events, making connections and letting them morph into stories.

When I was a child I was constantly writing little tales -crime, espionage, science fiction, fantasy. At summer camp sitting around the fire, I would read my ghost tales, causing mass goosebumps and nightmares among the more susceptible of my fellow campers. Holding a strong belief that good must triumph over evil, I made sure the criminals always got their just desserts while the spies were inevitably exposed. I also loved to make up stories about the people that I noticed in my daily life. The man who worked in the camera section of our local department store and who took the same bus as me every morning was actually a spy, passing on film to his contact who masqueraded as a customer but who was really a KGB agent from the Russian grain ship that docked monthly in our seaside town. I was sure the fellow in my French class at university was really a war criminal on the run, with a fake autobiography. While he claimed he was in the Resistance, I was convinced otherwise-his accent just didn't ring true, and why would he be studying French if that was his native tongue!

As an observer of people, much like a private detective, there is nothing I enjoy more than sipping an extra foamy latte on the patio of my favorite coffee shop, watching the human drama unfold in front of me. There, in the little corner table in the shade, sit a middle-age woman and a young man. He looks to be an East Indian, and he is sobbing. She tries to comfort him, as a mother would her child. I think of all the reasons he might be baring his soul-unrequited love, a career in ruins, a failed immigration hearing. And I feel such compassion for his distress. As a writer and as a human being I am never without empathy. And what about that older woman who always sits by herself, her back against the wall, watching the entrance as if she is expecting someone who, judging by the unhappiness etched in her face, will never come? Out of her sad solitude evolved my short story *Waiting for Peter.*

The birth of my first novel, *The Golden Crusader,* owes itself to serendipity—a series of accidental discoveries, beginning in the ruins of a Cistercian abbey. My husband and I arrived late in the afternoon at Fountains Abbey in Yorkshire. This was before the creation of the

Visitor Centre, so access was easy. There was just a lone security guard in a small hut. He was about to go home for the day. "The site's all yours," he offered, and with that he headed for the carpark, lunchbox in hand, and left us alone with what has to be one of the most spectacular monastic ruins in Britain. There is something about Fountains that teases at the imagination and plucks at the nerves.

We wandered about the lonely place, paced in awe down the long nave, exploring the nooks and crannies. Coming across the stone effigy of a knight, tucked away in a forgotten corner, I wondered who he was and why he was buried here. His hands and feet were crossed, so I knew he must have been a Crusader. I could still make out his features even though the stone was weathered from the years-if this was a true likeness my knight was once quite a handsome fellow. I was amused to find that I'd taken possession of him somehow. Little was I to know that it would soon be the other way around and he would quite steal my heart!

Within the cloisters, where the monks sat in little alcoves to read their devotions, something began to niggle and I distinctly felt the weight of people circling around us. As the light faded and the shadows grew, so did my unease. When we finally left, a flock of swifts rose up from the ruined tower and the screams they uttered were like the voices of the long departed monks, raging at what had befallen their beloved abbey. I dared not look back for fear we would be pursued into the carpark. It was that moment before the beginning darkness of evening settled into night that I felt the stirrings of a story in my mind, triggered by that most basic of human emotions, sheer terror.

The years passed and when we came again to Fountains, it was with our three children in tow. I searched for my knightly effigy and could not find him. Asking some workmen involved in restoration drew a blank. No one could remember seeing such an artifact. The ruins were full of tourists, as well as school children busy recreating monastic life with the help of 'monk' guides wearing long creamy colored robes. There was even a Benedictine Mass being held in the nave, attended by a sprinkling of the devoted.

It was hard with all this activity to recreate the feelings I'd experienced before, but it was good to see that Fountains had not lost its significance as a place of worship and instruction. Still, I puzzled over the absence of my knightly friend. I might have begun to doubt his existence, but the proof was there in a photograph taken on my previous pilgrimage.

We were living in Reeth at the time, in a grey stone cottage on the banks of the River Swale. The field at the back of the cottage was overrun with dancing rabbits in the early morning and evening, cows munched contently on the rich grass during the day, and the sound of the gurgling river lulled us to sleep at night. The village itself was typical of many hill villages in Yorkshire, with buildings set around a green space, and the usual amenities of pubs, family run restaurants, post office, pharmacy, grocery store, bakery, butcher shop, in short everything one would need to be comfortable without the necessity to seek out the big city. The people were friendly and welcoming for the most part. They loved to gossip—no one could put a step wrong but it would be all over the village by nightfall. Tales about families going back years would still be told with such freshness it was as if the events had just happened. I lapped it all up and stored it away in the recesses of my mind. Reeth would one day become the composite for my village of Srathkeel where my heroine Gemma Ravenscroft experiences a rough homecoming and a rude awakening.

Outings were frequent and fun, encompassing the surrounding countryside, with visits to Richmond, York and other centers. On the way to York, we would pass a set of huge iron gates leading to a site where once a manor house stood until it was burned to the ground, its owner incinerated in the process. Now the space was occupied by caravans belonging to travelers or gypsies. They were eager to tell us the history of the place and about the evil doings of the former lord of the manor. Over the gates was fixed the face of what I was sure was Mephistopheles, the Devil. Some primitive superstition welled up in me and I would not take a photograph of that hideous visage out of a seemingly silly and completely inexplicable fear I never experienced before. I felt that its evil presence would occupy my camera and then escape into my soul. So while I have no photograph to record the encounter I gave it an immortality of sorts since the incident would eventually form part of what I was about to write.

On one of our outings to a nearby market town, we came across a mysterious gated manor house on an isolated country road. A plaque affixed to a set of imposing metal gates announced that this was the Ministry of Social Services, and that trespassers would be prosecuted. A CCTV camera was mounted on the stone pillars at either side of the gate, and an imposing brick wall, with shards of glass embedded along the top, ran parallel to the road and disappeared into thick underbrush. I was struck by the improbability of finding a government office in the middle of nowhere, and of course I couldn't help speculating on just exactly what type of place this really was. Eventually the manor house would find itself in my book for it was here that Gemma ultimately learns the devastating truth about her father.

Characters began to form in my mind. Some were based on composites of people I'd encountered, others were a product of my imagination. I gave them names, identities, physical characteristics, personal histories, added emotional depth and suddenly I was thinking of them as real people. I sketched them out roughly and now I was adding the detail and soon I couldn't wait to bring them all together and watch the sparks fly!

The uncompromising landscape and seascape of Yorkshire seemed the perfect setting, for my heroine would be tested by Nature as much as by mankind. It would allow me to include Fountains Abbey, as it is now, and as it once was—a functioning, vibrant community. My knightly figure would have a major role, allowing me to incorporate my academic interest in monastic life and history, especially that of the Knights Templar-warrior monks-a dichotomy indeed. I wanted Evil to be the antagonist, Evil in the guise of Goodness. I wanted my heroine to know betrayal and the kind of fear that freezes you to the spot, a heroine prepared to take a leap into the unknown and begin to trust and to love. So all of this was building up inside me and the only relief I could get was to start writing it all down.

It was useful to set out my characters as I imagined them in a separate biographical section so that I could refer back when needed and stay consistent with such things as physical characteristics, likes and dislikes, etc., adding any details as they evolved. As well, a firm sense of place mattered a great deal to me. As I wanted a clear picture of Gemma's cottage-the interior and exterior, I made some rough sketches, including the surrounding landscape, the cliffs and the sea below. Oddly enough, the National Trust offers a cottage to rent that is in a similar situation and is featured in my website. My protagonist's cottage was her refuge and I needed to get it just right, to move through the various rooms as if I inhabited them myself, to take the steep path down to her little cove and find the boat just as it was left, to feel the wind in my hair and taste the sea salt on my lips. For as much as this was a work of my imagination, there was a lot of me in it too.

Writing this story was going to be a challenge. The family computer, the only one we possessed, was situated in the living room, in a direct firing line, competing with a noisy television and all the demands that children make. I realized that if I was going to bring this novel to fruition I would have to do it in the bosom of my family, with the many distractions, pleasures and responsibilities that implied. Of course, I did resort to early morning efforts and middle of the night sorties into the creative world, but I also came to terms with my situation rather than using it as an excuse not to write. Once I decided to embrace the fact that there would be no private, cozy little writing room for myself and I would have to give birth to this thing inside me while engaged in all my other roles as wife and mother, it just seemed like a weight was lifted from me. Naturally, there would be those quiet times when my lively trio was at school and I was home from work, and I tried to make those moments as productive as possible, though cooking, cleaning, laundry and the garden were powerful and constant diversions.

Despite all the challenges, I experienced a huge outflowing of creativity when I decided to include my family in the writing process. As I finished each chapter, I would read it to my eager audience who urged me on, asking for more and more. Writing in a white heat, I noticed that the characters took on lives of their own, behaving in ways perfectly appropriate to who they were and the fact that they rang true was of deep satisfaction to myself. There was no time to get bogged down when planning the next twist and turn in the plot, for my fan club was waiting on the edge of their seats for another searing installment. I wondered if this was what it was like for Charles Dickens when he was serializing his stories in magazines, for in a way I was writing to a deadline and a rather fun one at that.

Now of course, people will tell you that your family members are not the best critics, for they will love everything you produce. But if their enthusiasm and support will motivate you to keep writing then that is just what you need at this stage in the creative process. There will be time enough later to mold and sculpt and refine. For me the goal was to write while I was on a roll, and knowing I had an eager audience was great motivation. It kept me focused and committed. At the early stage of any writing project there's no harm done creating a support group of family and friends. In the end you are probably the harshest critic of your work and eventually you will need to turn inward and get tough on yourself, but in the initial burst of creativity have some fun with your project. After all, you didn't start it to win the Nobel Prize surely?

Each of us has our own writing style. I needed to let it all flow out in a great gush. You might prefer to craft each sentence, aiming for immediate perfection. Or perhaps you feel most comfortable roughing out the storyline, knowing the ending before you actually start to write. Many of the pieces of my novelistic puzzle fell into place as I went along. It seemed as if the characters wrote their stories, perhaps because I let them do so. There are a myriad of methods to get that first draft out there. Discovering what works for you can best be achieved by making a start. Just do it!

I now had a finished story, but this was only the beginning of the creative process. Like a quick painting one does en plein air, I needed to take my canvas back to the studio and work on it until I was satisfied it was the best it could be. After all, it was the least I could do for this motley group of imaginary beings living in the dangerous world I'd created. While you could put a rigid timeline on your revisions it may not always be the best approach. Sometimes just stepping back and making some space will suggest refinements that will enhance the story line or move the plot. A prolonged absence from engagement with your creation however can result in that first book lying dormant in your computer's hard drive forever. And that would be a pity indeed.

Certainly in my case it took longer to edit and change than to write the first draft. But I wanted to do it that way. Some things can't be rushed, and this is one of them. Regardless of your motivation in writing your first book, you owe it to yourself to look at every line, every scene, every piece of dialogue, every description to make sure it rings true and helps to move the story along in a meaningful way. We've all read books where there are whole chunks we just want to skip because they are nothing more than fluff and filler, left in by an indulgent editor not wishing to offend his best selling author.

Never believe that one revision is enough, for there is always something that can be made better. I would set my book aside for weeks at a time, letting it mature in my head like fine wine, so that I could come to it feeling refreshed rather than pressured, visiting it anew as if coming to it for the first time. It helped to read each chapter aloud, for then I could get a better feel for the rhythm of the dialogue and the pace of the action. I pretended to be each of the characters so that I could test their reactions to one another. It was then I realized that I'd written the book as if it were a film, because I was always seeing the action and hearing the characters, experiencing the elements of sea and wind and snow.

Rather than just focusing on this one project, I was also writing other things, for this gave me a feeling that I was progressing and moving forward rather than stuck in a revisionist rut. I realized that a book is never finished until the final drafts are done and the editor says 'that's it!' And if there is still a lingering in your mind to tweak it one more time, best to channel your energies into the sequel or embark on a whole new project.

Writing my first book was truly an amazing and exhilarating process. I began with no particular expectations with respect to the final outcome. The journey along the way seemed to be what mattered most. I had a story I wanted to tell. While skeptics and doubters may view writing a book as an act of pure folly and self-indulgence, given the challenges, I say that the creative force running through all of us needs to be acknowledged and nurtured in all its many forms. If you want to write that first book then seize the moment now. However long it takes and whatever highs and lows you experience along the way, may serendipity guide you to a successful and happy outcome. As for my first book, *The Golden Crusader* saw the light of day thanks to publisher Lida Quillen and Twilight Times Books.

About the author

In addition to her mystery thriller *The Golden Crusader*, Linda Langwith is the author of numerous articles, short stories and poetry, featured in various print and on-line publications.
http://www.lindalangwith.com

Current release: The Golden Crusader

The Writing of *Double Forté*: A Gus LeGarde Mystery

by Aaron Paul Lazar

The Motivation

I'd always planned to write a mystery series, but I thought it would happen when the kids were grown and I was retired. I saw myself with my laptop, sitting on the porch of a lakeside cabin, inventing a delightful protagonist and putting him through the wringer to solve bizarre mysteries that only he could figure out.

I was right about the series, but wrong about the timing.

The year 1997 marked the end of a very difficult period in my life, filled with a slew of losses. Eight of my friends and family members died in five years. I'd rarely dealt with death close up, except for the death of my grandfather Sid, when I was eleven. He passed from a heart attack in our home, and although I missed him sorely, I bounced back as eleven-year-olds will do. Strangely enough, the death of my first dog hit me the hardest. My best friend, a little beagle named Sugar, was run over by a truck around the same time I lost my grandfather. It knocked me for a loop, and for years I couldn't pass the site where he was buried near the chicken coop without choking up.

The first to go was my wife's grandfather. I hadn't had the chance to grow close with him, but I'd met him a few times and recognized that being ninety-two, with his Alzheimer's and physical challenges, it was bound to happen. My wife knew he didn't have long to live, but even with the mental preparation of knowing "it could happen soon," when it actually happened, it was a shock. My wife's pain tore a hole through my heart. Little did I realize that it was just the beginning of a barrage of losses to come.

Next to die was our friend and neighbor, Clare, a young woman pregnant with her third child who had watched our two-year-old daughter for us when the twins were born. We'd done the same for her, taking care of little Katie when Megan came into the world. She was hit by a teenage neighbor who'd just received his driving license. Clare was taking a walk on the side of a dirt road with her two daughters after dinner. The boy was blinded by the sun and couldn't see. Why didn't he just STOP? Impossible to know. The two girls were okay, but they grew up motherless.

Shortly after Clare died, my office mate and dear friend of eleven years, Gangaram Patel, succumbed to a heart attack. Ironically, we had walked every day at lunch to stay healthy, to strengthen and protect our hearts. We talked about family and life, and regaled each other with tales of our childhoods. I loved hearing about his youth in India, and the antics he'd pulled as a boy. Alas, I discovered in the end that he'd suffered from decades-old heart damage. I lost my buddy, just like *that*.

Soon, the deaths grew closer to home. My wife, three little daughters, and I had just arrived for a visit in Massachusetts to see our families. We stopped at my wife's parents' house first, where they broke the news to me that my Grandma Hazel had just passed away. With a sense of incredulity mixed with numbness, I drove to my family homestead with tears streaming down my face. The raw pain was so wrenching, I didn't think I'd ever breath normally again.

A year after Grandma Hazel passed, her husband of seventy years followed her. He couldn't stand living without her, and it seemed Papa Ray had forced himself to keep going until he was sure she was safe in God's hands. The doctors said they had no idea how he outlasted Grandma with his congestive heart failure. But he'd always cared for her, since her arthritis had crippled her and put her in a wheel chair. He cleaned, cooked, carried her... whatever she needed, he was there. And he outlasted her out of sheer will to be sure she was okay. When he died, it felt like the bottom of the earth had dropped away and I floundered for a long time, horrified that my family was disappearing so quickly.

When my wife's father passed from Parkinson's, while comforting her, I panicked inside. The reality that one's parents *could* die was too hard to bear. Of course, logically I knew it would happen to us all, but it was easy to ignore when it didn't happen to me. Her father's death brought home the awful truth and while I helped my bereft wife mourn him, my heart twisted inside, worrying about my own folks.

My last living grandmother contracted Alzheimer's in 1992, and by January of 1997, she was gone. I saw her one last time before the illness claimed her. We ate at her favorite local dive. She had a big cold bottle of Narragansett beer and fried scallops, and for one brief moment, we connected. She remembered me, and we sang a favorite song together. It only lasted a few minutes, and then the veil dropped and she didn't recognize me, ever again.

Her funeral was scheduled the same day that my father found out he had esophageal cancer. Nine months later, he died the night before I drove home to see him one last time. I didn't get to say goodbye, and he surprised us by passing the day after they sent him home for hospice.

Just before he died, he looked at my mother and said, "Do you have enough money?" She nodded yes through her tears. He took her hand and said, "Good. I'm going to go now." A look of tranquility crossed his face and he whispered, "Peace. Peaceful." And he was gone.

That was the proverbial straw that broke this camel's back. It crushed me. I couldn't bear it when people were too kind to me, offering condolences. I'd lose it and get all choked up. I tried to bury myself in work, and the numbing effect was somewhat comforting. I took many long walks in the autumn woods. The wind would stir, and it felt like my father was whispering to me, telling me he was okay.

After my walks, I'd go back and write gaudy poetry about the experience. As bad as the poems were, it felt so good to get the words on paper that I craved more of it. I walked more, wrote more. And then it occurred to me. Why not start the mystery series I'd always envisioned, and do it as a tribute to my father?

I modeled my main character, Gus LeGarde, after him. Both men were pianists, music professors, gardeners, cooks, had strong moral compasses, adored French Impressionist Art, and loved kids and dogs. I started writing *Double Forté* with my father in my mind. The process was so soothing, so cathartic, that I craved it every day. Each time I wrote a scene with Gus, I felt like I was sharing a little time with my father. This went on for a few months, until some new family tragedy happened and I simply... stopped.

A few months later, my mother called and said she wanted to know what happened in my book. She'd been reading along as I wrote it, and

I'd left her in the lurch. With that nudging, I picked it up again. This time, however, I was charged with energy, addicted to the process of creation, and I quickly became obsessed with my parallel universe. I lived, breathed, and dreamed about my characters, who came to life in my mind and actually did my bidding. Well, usually. Except when they decided to take the story in directions I hadn't planned.

Another strange thing happened. Since I was writing in first person, Gus started to feel more like me. It wasn't really a surprise, I guess. After all, I was like my father in many ways. I lived in an antique house in the country, had huge gardens, loved my dogs, daughters, and grandkids, and cooked soups on the weekends. I sure couldn't play piano as well as he did, but there were many similarities. After a while, Gus began to take on a personality that was an amalgam of my father and me; and slowly, he grew to have a uniqueness all his own.

The Writing Process

When I look back at the way I wrote *Double Forté*, I was all over the map. I really had no plot in mind, few ideas about the main crime or villain(s), and certainly hadn't imagined the twists or turns that would eventuate. I simply typed "Chapter One" and started writing. I found that when I imagined a scene - like a movie in my head - the words seemed to flow out of my fingers. I didn't worry about style or rules, I just let the words tumble out.

If you want to write, you need to read. It's the best way to subconsciously imprint story line and style on your brain. Years of devouring mystery series had assimilated into my brain and the way a scene flowed, the story line that progressed, the suspense and relaxation that occurred between chapters - it all seemed second nature. My teachers were Rex Stout, John D. MacDonald, Dick Francis, Agatha Christie, Alistair MacLean, Lillian Jackson Braun, Peter Mayle, Helen McInnes, Clive Cussler, Tony Hillerman, Dean Koontz, James Patterson, Stephen King, Laurie R. King, and many more.

Although I'd written lots of stories in high school and college, and had been known as "an engineer who can write," by my peers during my career at Kodak, I was actually a very green writer. I had a great deal to learn as far as fictional technique and skills were concerned. My pages were populated with ungodly adverbs and I allowed myself to go on for too long in poetic narrations. I used the past perfect ("had" structures) ruthlessly, until a mentor pointed out that there was no need to stutter my prose with so many "hads." (see more about this in how-to writing advice articles posted at http://www.aplazar.gather.com) Stephen King's *On Writing*, was one of the most helpful writing books I read, although I also loved *For the Trees* by Betsey Learner.

The first chapter came, then the second, and before long I arrived at the middle and stalled. I remember driving from Western New York to my mother's house in Massachusetts, tossing ideas around with my wife. "What should happen next?" "What would be really scary that would get your heart thumping?" "How can Gus get himself out of THAT situation?"

I bugged her for hours, and she helped me formulate some new threats and twists. Armed with these fun ideas, I took to the story again with enthusiasm. It seemed I needed to simply have the storyline loosely in place, and the rest would follow. Of course, that proved to be the easiest part of the actual "birthing" of a novel.

Developing the LeGarde Series Characters

Gus's family emerged as the pages grew, and secondary characters began to take on important roles as well. In addition, the character of Elsbeth - Gus's first wife and life-long soul mate, who had jumped to her death from the Letchworth Gorge four years before *Double Forté* opened - was a very important character to develop. Using flashbacks, memories, and retelling stories through Gus's dialog, Elsbeth's character began to crystallize as a fiery, independent woman who blazed a dramatic trail through life.

When Gus is introduced to Camille, his secretary's daughter, he fights the feelings of attraction because of loyalties to his dead wife. These conflicting emotions actually follow him through the first three books, until he finally gives into his passion and marries Camille.

Gus's grandson, Johnny, grew from the little grandchild I'd craved for years. My daughters had grown into lovely young women, with whom I had marvelous conversations over lunch, and who filled a different need. But I missed that cute and cuddly stage, and that's when I invented Johnny. A few years later, my real grandson, Julian, was born. Oddly enough, Julian matched Johnny's physical characteristics perfectly. It was as if I'd willed him into being.

Siegfried, Elsbeth's intellectually disabled giant brother and Gus's best friend, came about from a love of movies with big, slow giants who are mistreated or misunderstood. Characters like John Coffey, in *The Green Mile*, and possibly even Forrest Gump, were inspiration for Siegfried's character.

The German element arose from my assignments overseas where I fell in love with all things German. Half Jewish, Elsbeth and Siegfried were children of a woman whose entire family had been held and killed in Buchenwald, a concentration camp. This thread was included because of a deep-seated hatred for Nazis, and to insure that my younger readers never forget the atrocities that were committed against six million Jews.

While writing *Double Forté*, I found that one of the greatest joys of being in charge of creating a cast of characters was the ability to base some of these folks on people I'd loved and lost. Oscar and Millie Stone, Gus's family friends, are closely based on my maternal grandparents; while Maddy Coté, Gus's secretary at the music department in Conaroga, is based on my paternal grandmother. I find that bringing to life characters with the essence of those I still mourned helped me deal with the loss in a creative and therapeutic fashion. These vignettes with Oscar, Millie, Sid, and Maddy ended up feeling like "visits" with my grandparents, as well as becoming a tribute to their lives.

Editing and Rewriting, Rewriting, and Rewriting...

When I finished the first draft of *Double Forté*, I didn't seek representation right away. No, I was so bitten by the writing bug that I wrote four more books, all in several months each. The stories poured out of me, and Gus and his family developed rich histories as their back stories grew more complex and detailed. In hindsight, I realize I probably should have learned "how" to write before dashing off these books that eventually needed serious editing, but I couldn't stem the tide.

After I finished my fifth manuscript, a prequel to *Double Forté*, I realized I'd been totally self-absorbed with the writing process, feeding my need to escape and create, thriving on the sensation of controlling my parallel universe. I'd loved the creating part so much that I couldn't bear to stop and figure out how to get the books published. I'd had enthusiastic friends and family following the series as I wrote, and their encouragement and apparent enjoyment had driven me to continue the saga without glancing outside my blinders at the big, bad, outside world of publishing.

With an inward groan, I began to research what was needed. I discovered with horror that in order to get into a big publisher, I'd need an agent. During that search, I began to network and befriend other authors. I found several superb writers who became my best critique partners. From one, I learned writing tips; another caught my inconsistencies. Another was great at catching typos, and yet another helped me with the concept of head hopping and consistent POV. I helped them as well, and frequently we'd exchange a chapter a day for each to review and comment on. And so, with one hand washing the other, my prose began to tighten, my dialog grew crisper and realistic, and my scenes moved forward with better tension.

With great effort, I tore myself away from the fun of writing and started to seek agents. After a few tries, I landed an agent who fell in love with the manuscript. Alas, it didn't work out, and after that failure, I decided to rewrite the whole book.

I tore into it, realizing there were naive sections that just didn't work. I tossed the plot elements up in the air and shuffled them around. I cut. I slashed. And it hurt, oh did it hurt to eliminate chapters I'd grown to love, but just didn't fit.

I performed a complete analysis of all the books and movies I'd ever loved, documenting which themes I found compelling. I analyzed 'what scared me,' and came up with a list of daunting scenarios that would happen to poor Gus. I realized I wanted to include the themes of unrequited love, the accusation of an innocent man, the horrid fear of losing a child, betrayal by someone close to the family, and additional plot lines that wound themselves into the normally safe and secure, wholesome world of Gus's life. Yet within those chapters, I wanted to keep the consistent flow of a large and loving family, abundant nature, gardens, dogs, horses, and big family feasts. I also wanted to underpin the entire story with classical music themes, since

Gus was passionate about Chopin and played etudes to soothe his soul in times of trouble.

I rewrote *Double Forté* a number of times, but in looking back, I realize it probably was that wild abandon of letting myself simply write for several years without stopping to think about it that helped me craft the skills of storytelling. The writing was freeing, and the practice of creating a chapter a day (my usual output) worked well for me, particularly when I had to write in the early morning hours to find quiet in our house. Once I developed that rhythm, it was a natural progression to adapt and incorporate new writing tips and skills as time progressed. Now I write articles for young writers all the time with writing advice. I list the "forbidden words," give examples of klutzy versus neat prose, discuss what makes up "natural" dialog, and more. The circle is complete, and I love giving out advice that was so generously imparted to me while I was learning.

Of course, I'm still learning. Even as I begin my fifteenth manuscript and look forward to my fifth and sixth books coming out in print this year, I seek new advice and writing mages to help me improve my craft. If I don't get my writing "fix" daily, I feel cheated and get all grumpy. It's become a wonderful source of solace and entertainment, a vehicle to connect with people all over the world, and the best cheap therapy I've ever experienced. Writing is a never-ending process that will continue to challenge and delight me, and I thank God for the opportunity every single day.

About the author

Aaron Paul Lazar writes to soothe his soul. The author of LeGarde Mysteries and Moore Mysteries enjoys the Genesee Valley countryside in upstate New York, where his characters embrace life, play with their dogs and grandkids, grow sumptuous gardens, and chase bad guys.

http://www.legardemysteries.com

Recent release: Healey's Cave, suspense

Writing *Mary's Child*

by Celia Leaman

Looking back over the years, trying to recall how it was, I realize that I never actually became a writer, I always was a writer.

I grew up in a hamlet on the edge of Dartmoor in England, several miles from the nearest town. We had no car, no phone, no television. We were fortunate in that we did have electricity. In such an environment, a child's imagination will be fruitful and multiply. To add to all this, I was an introspective, romantic and sensitive child with an active imagination. And I believe that being an only child contributed to my individualism.

Children realize more than we think. As soon as I was able to piece things together, I perceived that there was something different about my existence. By that I mean a truth that was being withheld from me. It was subtle, but it shadowed my young life. Eventually, after a bully at school revealed that I was adopted, my parents confirmed that it was true.

I had always felt set apart from my peers and this knowledge added to, not detracted from, my feelings of alienation. Consequently, I often chose solitude rather than gregariousness. I shied away from group activities. I wriggled out of my 'Domestic Science' classes at school and spent hours in the art room, mainly painting horses.

I had always adored horses and spent most of my holidays at the local riding school. I never knew why I loved them so much though until many years later when I met my biological mother and discovered that she had ridden while carrying me well into her seventh month of pregnancy.

The first story I remember writing was about a grey mare called Silver Moonlight who led her herd through the American wilderness. She was perfect. She was proud, and she was brave.

At the same time, I was also developing an interest in the North American continent. At school, I had seen a documentary about

Canada. While the other pupils fidgeted around me, I stared silently at the screen, enthralled by the huge trees whose girths took several people holding hands to encircle. I was captivated by the gigantic mountains whose tips disappeared into the clouds. The vastness of it all! The space! It made an indelible imprint on my young mind. Although I could only have been seven- or eight-years old, I vowed one day I would cross the Atlantic Ocean and see it all for myself.

In those days, a child could wander freely and often I would be gone from dawn to dusk, wandering the lanes and the fields or borrowing someone's pony and riding alone on the moors. My parents rarely knew where I was, but I always arrived home safely, and on time, for supper.

I also had a little dog and sometimes I took her for a walk in the grounds of the Manor House Hotel, not far from my village. One day while I was there, I met an American couple who were touring Europe and Great Britain. Seeing how interested I was, they gave me a map of North America. That map, which I treasured for many years, eventually became unreadable because it had accompanied me in so many childhood games.

By that time, the village children had access to a black-and-white television. Enthralled by some of the shows, playing with the local children, mainly boys, I was always Annie Oakley. Or we would gallop through the copse with the images of Boots and Saddles set in our minds. Sometimes, we would pioneer through the Rockies, always consulting the precious map of course and watching out for mountain lions and quicksand. Oh, our imaginations took us on such wonderful adventures.

So, out of all this came my first story. Silver Moonlight, the mare that no man could tame and no man would ever ride. Even in those days I was a bit of a feminist.

My idea was shattered when a horsy lady told me that it was impossible for a mare to lead a herd, although at the time she didn't explain why. I expect she thought I was too young for a lecture on the birds and the bees. I pooh-poohed her comment and insisted that *my* mare would be different! It's funny to look back on it now. What a stubborn and persistent child I could be. I must have appeared so childish and naïve. But of course, I was a child and I expect she realized that and forgave me for my innocence.

In time, I went away to boarding school. I was not a good student. I was a daydreamer, taken up with classical music and reading poets such as Rupert Brooke and John Keats. I believed in romantic love and began to write passionate poetry. Teased by my peers? Yes, I was indeed, but I took little notice of them. While they raved about the Beatles and the Stones, I lingered in the music room to listen to a piece by Wagner, or a Chopin sonata. I thought they were the weird ones, following the trends like sheep.

While my peers might jeer about the prose that was pouring out of me, my teachers encouraged me. I expect they were pleased that at last I had found something to focus on. But their praise wasn't enough for me to pursue and develop that gift. I had a butterfly brain and was rather silly. I regret that now because had I been more sensible and studious, I might have followed my natural leanings and made an earlier career as a writer, or become an editor. Still, I shouldn't really blame myself entirely for my lack of focus. For a girl of my upbringing and class, I did what was expected of me. Further education was never mentioned in our household, and I left school with my diploma, got a secretarial job and later married.

For some of us, and I believe in my case it was because I wasn't truly following my dream, marriages simply don't work out. I divorced after a few years and later immigrated to Canada.

It wasn't until I was in my thirties that I took the plunge and enrolled in a creative writing course at Mohawk College in Ontario. Vigorously encouraged by my tutor, Vin Francis, I received top marks and was encouraged to submit my work for publication. I doubt I would have ever pursued this sometimes arduous vocation had I not met Vin and I will be eternally grateful for his support. Sadly, he has passed on now.

After taking the course, I migrated from Ontario to British Columbia, and it is there I began writing in earnest. I moved to a small island where I no longer had a nine-to-five job. I lived on acreage, grew a garden and kept sheep and chickens. I had time to find out who I was. I had time to think, and time to write.

I also worked outside the home at various jobs, one of which was for a local writer, Jane Rule. I was held in thrall by Jane. For the first time in my life, I knew what I wanted to be when I grew up. I wanted to be like her; to write, and make a living from it.

Knowing I liked to write, after my work sessions, Jane would read my work and we would discuss various aspects. I wish I'd taken better advantage of her experience now, but, not of my choice, my life was changing again and I was facing another divorce.

During this time, I could only keep a journal as I was too upset to focus on longer works. Later, I used those emotional outpourings when writing *The Winnowed Woman*. It wasn't my first book, but it was one of the hardest for me to release into the world.

It is interesting that during the time I worked for Jane, I began the story that would later become my first novel. You must understand that although I loved Canada and had done so ever since I set foot on her soil, immigrating to another country isn't easy. There is always a part of your soul you leave behind and a certain yearning for your old life that never quite goes away. Had I not loved Canada so much, I could have become quite homesick.

There are always the memories, fond and not so fond, that linger for years and it is while the memories of my old home were still fresh in my mind, I began a story about a young girl called Kitty who lived on a farm on Dartmoor called Ford. However, I only got so far with it because of the chaos in my life, and I put the manuscript aside.

I was reminded of it when, after my divorce, I re-visited England in 1993. An old acquaintance and I were chatting about the current events in our lives when I mentioned what I'd been writing before my personal upheaval. When I saw her a few days later, she handed me a newspaper article about Mary Jay and the legend of Jay's Grave.

Jay's Grave is a lonely grave on Dartmoor set at a crossroads between several parishes. Around 1860, men working on the road unearthed what they thought were the remains of a pony, but the bones were later discovered to be those of a young woman. One of the road menders' wives recalled being told by her mother that it was the grave of a young girl called Mary Jay, who hanged herself at a local farm after being crossed in love. In those days, suicides were often buried in unmarked graves outside parish boundaries because of superstition. It was thought that burying them in this way ensured the souls would be lost and unable to come back to haunt the living.

When I read that Mary was sometimes known as Kitty Jay and it was thought that she had been apprenticed out to a farm called Forde, the coincidence between those facts and my most recent manuscript gave me goose bumps. The next day, I went to Jay's grave and sat for a while.

Growing up quite near the grave, I had always been fascinated by it. Passing it late at night when driving home from seeing a movie in the nearest town, I would avert my eyes, dreading that I might see a ghost because some said it was haunted. But that day, in the warm sun, the air scented with heather and bracken, I felt no other presence except that of a wild grey rabbit that hopped around the grave.

Whether it was my own longing or something emanating from an invisible entity that captured my imagination, I will never know, but I left there invigorated, inspired, and determinedly resolved to write Mary Jay's story. When I returned to Canada, I dug out my manuscript and began to write. *Mary's Child* poured out of me like rich cream from a jug.

There are several ways in which I could have portrayed Mary Jay. She could have been a wanton, tempting a young man and suffering the consequences. She might have been a young woman with ambition who sought to trap a man and his means, and her plotting might have backfired on her. Or, perhaps she had given herself in love then been let down and hung herself because of the shame. Yet, after considering each possibility, I discarded it because I could only see her as a gentle victim.

As Mary's life unfolded to me, the story took hold and grew. I fretted a bit because sometimes I wondered if I would ever finish it, and I had no idea how it would end. And then, one morning it came to me. It was also a great ending that fitted in perfectly with the rest of the story. I guess my subconscious knew it all along. This made me realize that you have to give things time to work their way to the surface, and that takes patience.

I have subsequently learned that some endings occur with a trumpet burst; others don't. Sometimes you arrive at a stage in writing a novel that's a bit like one of those dreams where you are running and running and never quite reaching your destination. You keep writing while your characters are doing their thing. You don't always know where they're going. You don't know when they're going to be finished. You have this vague idea in your mind where you would *like* things to go and you see this glimmer in the distance of where the story might end, but it isn't happening; *you're still writing*. This can be disconcerting to say the least, but you must try not to panic.

So I suggest to my students that if they have a problem in finding those satisfactory last few lines, just write what comes to that point and then leave it alone. You see, while your mind is engaged elsewhere, your subconscious will keep working on it and when you return to it later, you will find the ending will occur more easily to you.

My feelings when I finally finished the book were of achievement and of huge relief.

I felt relief, because for a first book it was a big one. And I felt I had achieved something because *Mary's Child* received two readings at Hodder Headline in London. When they turned it down I was terribly disappointed.

That's the thing with writing. You have to have enormous courage and fortitude, and you can't be a quitter. There are times, it is true, when you will tire of the craft and need a rest, but if you are a true writer, there is always an idea or new characters craving to be one day released onto paper.

Although I put *Mary's Child* away, I didn't give up and I didn't give in to despair. Persistence is my middle name so I am told, and I have learned that persistence is a writer's best friend.

I continued to write and submit my work to various publications. When I was rejected, I tried to push past my disappointment and to appreciate the various editorial comments and critique. I learned a lot from my editors, and gradually I began to develop a better sense of what I was doing. I never took another formal course, I just kept writing and submitting. I enjoyed some publication successes and absorbed the feedback.

It was only later when I re-read *Mary's Child* that I realized why Hodder had not accepted it. The story, the plot, was good. But in subsequent years I had learned many things and revisiting the book revealed my first attempt to be amateurish. At this point, I rewrote the book and sent it out again. Epublishing was just coming into being and my manuscript was accepted immediately.

Since then I have had seven books published and I have self-published a book on writing. Also, with these publications under my belt and, after twenty years of writing experience, I tutored for a while for Writer's Digest School, thus partly achieving my ambition to be like Jane. I say partly, because lacking a bestseller, I am still more a struggling artist than a phenomenal success. Having to do other jobs to pay the bills is nothing to be ashamed of though, because most times in this world, it is the artist's way.

As with any artistic endeavour, inspiration and enthusiasm fluctuate. Sometimes, in order to gain fresh wind as it were, you need to rest and do something entirely different. This not only rests your mind, but also allows you to gather strength for the next round—because writing isn't easy. No one knows, unless they are a writer, how draining it can be. Yet, it can also be uplifting and satisfying.

Writing can also be cathartic. For people who have no one to talk to about intimate matters, writing things down can be invaluable. I always say to my students, "When you are happy, or experience a joyous moment, record it. When you are upset or stung by a careless remark, think how it *really feels* and write it down. Record your experiences, observations and gleanings because one day you can bet your life you'll draw on these scribblings for your writing."

Many of my characters derive from my sometimes chaotic and eventful life, yet my own experience is that I'm never writing about a specific person, but a conglomeration of memories that make up a character's personality. You see, a person's perception of someone else might not be as that person really is. We can only deduce and glean from what is shown to us, and what person reveals all to the world? So the rest has to be imagination.

Writing is a solitary craft, so it is important for you to be able to work alone and to enjoy your own company. This means developing self-discipline, which should happen automatically once you realize that procrastination won't write your books.

Writing will sometimes take you by the scruff of the neck and wring you out, leaving you feeling depleted and hopeless. But writing is a passion and altogether a fascinating craft. It can capture your heart and drive you to unimaginable heights.

You will also always never be bored because to the true writer, there is always one more story to tell.

About the author

Local British Columbians can meet Celia personally at the Mayne Island Farmer's Market on Saturday mornings where she has signed copies of her books available, together with her woolen articles. She creates items from fibres she spins herself, using local wools, alpaca and mohair.

http://www.devonshirebabe.com

Current release: Past Present I: web of lies, mainstream

How I Wrote *Shadows on the Desert*

by Beverly Stowe McClure

Beverly, a writer? Who would have thought it? Certainly, not me. Unlike most authors who say they wanted to write from the time they were children, writing never entered my mind. In fact, if anyone had told me I'd be an author someday, I'd have thought they were crazy.

When I was a child I hated to read. School book reports were a nightmare. I was very shy and hated standing in front of the class to tell about the book I was supposed to have read but hadn't. Thank heavens for jacket flap copy. As if the teachers couldn't tell. I struggled through school, reading what was required for my classes and writing the necessary assignments, nothing more. In spite of my avoidance of books whenever possible, I enjoyed school and made good grades.

Even though my eighth-grade English teacher sent my poem "Stars" to a high school anthology and it was published in *Young America Sings*, along with poems from students all over the United States, I hated to write. I only wrote "Stars" because it was an assignment and I didn't want to fail English. At the time, being published in the anthology was no big deal to me. I had no desire to escape to a favorite spot, like a tree house or quiet little stream or secret hideaway, to create stories from my imagination. I was pretty much grounded in the *real* world. What was happening at school, at home. Playing a game of baseball with the neighbor kids. Riding my bicycle with my friends. Going to the swimming pool on hot summer days. Kid things.

However, as I look back on my early years, one thing that might have hinted at a future writing career for me was the radio show *Let's Pretend* that I listened to every Saturday morning. Yes, this was before we had TV or computers. The only cartoons I saw were the ones they showed at the movies, before the main attraction. I always looked forward to Saturdays, where we could sit in the theater and watch the show all afternoon if we wanted to. No one turned the lights on at the end of the show and ran us out.

But back to the radio program. On *Let's Pretend*, actors read the stories of *Cinderella*, *Snow White*, *Sleeping Beauty*, *The Princess and the Pea*, and many other fairy tales. I loved them, the same way many years later, my sons loved the Saturday morning cartoons on TV, and the way kids today watch cartoons on their computers, iPods and all the latest inventions. From radio to the modern means of entertainment, kids in the past and kids today enjoy a good story. I don't think that will ever change. And I did enjoy the fairy tales.

The world of fantasy intrigued me. As I listened to *Cinderella*, I could picture myself wearing the gorgeous gown my fairy godmother provided for me, riding in the pumpkin carriage to the ball, dancing with the handsome prince, fleeing when the clock struck midnight, leaving behind my glass slipper. Then the prince arrived at my house. The shoe fit. And I turned into a princess. Oh yes, for thirty minutes I was Cinderella, living her adventures, dreaming her dreams.

Sometimes I was transported to the world of *Sleeping Beauty* and kissed by the prince who then carried me off to his castle where I lived happily ever after. Or I was Snow White with the seven funny little men called dwarfs. My parents even bought me a collection of what were called "story book" dolls, which were likenesses of different fairy tale characters. Today, I still have Little Bo Peep. The rest have been lost over the years during the many moves from house to house.

As much as I liked the stories, I never read the fairy tale books, but perhaps I tucked those ideas away in a corner of my mind, where they waited for me to discover them when the time was right. Even though my works today are mostly realistic stories, except for a few ghostly beings, I like to think that my modern-day characters have a bit of magic in them. That their lives are filled with adventure, joy, sadness, and love, similar to the lives of the characters that caught my eye so many years ago.

In spite of my rocky relationship with books, I graduated from high school, got married, had four sons, attended Midwestern University where, as an elementary education major, I read more books than I ever imagined possible. For my *kiddie lit* class alone (what we affectionately called our children's literature class), I read one hundred picture books. Then we had to tell one of the stories to the class or to children. At the time I thought the university was training me to be a teacher. Looking back, I now believe my college years were another step in preparing me to be a writer. Of children's books, of course.

After four years of reading too many books and writing too many papers to remember, I graduated cum laude with a teaching certificate. Yup. I became a teacher, another twist in my life that I never expected to happen. My teaching turned out to be the best move I've ever made, because my new profession led to my later interest in writing. Reading to my students and to my sons opened my eyes to what I had been missing: Reading was fun. Who could resist Dr. Seuss and his lyrical books that had me hooked on his prose, right along with the kids? I couldn't. I was caught up in the rhythm, the repetition, the joy of reading. I read Dr. Seuss's books so many times that, like my sons, I could recite the stories from memory.

Then those fairy tales from so many years ago started whispering in my ears, reminding me of other worlds, other times, and other places and what was I planning to do about them. I hadn't a clue. So for a time, I did nothing. I was too busy raising my family and teaching my students to add writing to my life. Or so I thought.

One day as I skimmed through a magazine, I saw an ad for aspiring writers. I wasn't exactly an aspiring writer, but I had been considering writing articles for children's magazines based on activities we did in the classroom, like artwork and science experiments. (I was teaching fifth grade science, as well as reading, spelling, and art at the time.) I just hadn't taken the time to write anything and wasn't sure I was capable of doing so anyway. The timing of the ad seemed like serendipity, however. It sounded exactly like what I needed to give me that final push. My sons were grown and on their own. My teaching duties still absorbed eight hours of each day, except on weekends. But the evenings were mine, so why not write instead of watching TV reruns?

Confidence isn't my best trait. I still doubted whether I was capable of putting coherent words and activities together. I'm more comfortable with a set routine, doing the same things each day. Starting something different took me out of that comfort zone. Still, I kept thinking about the stories I read to my children at home and to my students at school. They flowed so smoothly. It looked easy enough. But looks sometimes are deceiving. Outside of that one poem in my junior high years and papers for my college classes, I hadn't attempted anything else.

I argued back and forth with myself. I wasn't getting any younger. If I was going to do it, I'd better get started while I still had my vision and my brain functioned normally, at least for me. What did I have to lose? If I didn't try, I'd never know. But what if I couldn't put a simple sentence together? What I wrote could end up total gibberish. What would my friends and family think of my literary attempts? Of course, I could always keep my writing a secret, until I either was published or woke up to the realization I needed to stick to my chosen profession. I'd written plenty of papers at the university and made good grades on them. My freshman English teacher even complimented me a couple of times.

But what about writing for children? Was it so different? I worked with children all day and had for years. I could spend the rest of my life debating the issue and still not reach a conclusion, so before I chickened out, I sent for the *Institute of Children's Literature's* brochure and aptitude test. A few days later, I took the test, mailed it, and figured that would be the last of it. Face the truth, I hadn't a clue about writing. Then I wouldn't be disappointed. I was a teacher, not a writer. At least when they rejected me (I hate the word *reject*), my decision would be made. I could stop being wishy-washy. I only hoped they didn't laugh at the pitiful sample I sent and tell me to be sure and keep my day job. Even worse, what if they showed it to everyone they knew as an example of how not to write? That did it. I wouldn't open their reply when it arrived.

A few weeks later, a letter with the Institute's return address glared at me from inside my mailbox. Daring me to open it. Though I was curious, I also was afraid. I tossed the envelope on the table. What I didn't know wouldn't hurt me. Right? Wrong? Every time I walked past that envelope, a magnetic force made me reach for it. But I was strong and overcame temptation. Until the day my hand betrayed me and sliced open that teasing envelope. I read the neatly typed words. I stared and read again. Then I let out a "Whoopee!" and jumped up and down, scaring the cat so that she ran and hid under the bed, thinking, no doubt, that a crazy lady had taken control of my body.

I reread the letter one more time to make sure I wasn't hallucinating. Nope. Right there in black and white. The word *accepted* rattled about in my brain. *The Institute of Children's Literature* accepted me into their program. They hadn't laughed at my story. They said I had potential. My chest puffed up with pride. I had it made. Soon I'd be writing and publishing stories and articles for children's magazines and rolling in dough. Well, it didn't turn out quite that way. Not even close.

The Institute assigned Dorothy Van Woerkom as my instructor. I discovered that the real work was just beginning. I had to actually write the articles first, before they'd be published and I'd become famous. Of course, I knew that. Ms. Van Woerkom, talented, kind and patient, very patient, taught me the basics of writing for magazines. And yes, it was quite different than writing college papers. It was more involved than I thought and not nearly as easy as I had believed. I didn't just sit down and write stories or activities and have the words come out perfectly, the way they sounded in my head when the idea came to me.

For fiction, I needed characters the reader would like and identify with, not some cardboard kid nobody cared what happened to. I needed a plot that kept the kids turning pages. For nonfiction, I needed fun experiments and activities for kids to do, with simple instructions they could understand, and nothing dangerous. So I stayed up late at night, creating short stories and articles according to my instructor's assignments. I then mailed to my instructor my offerings and waited. I soon learned that waiting is part of the game. But my instructor was prompt with her replies. She showed me where my work was weak and how to improve it. When the assignment was spot on, she praised my work, encouraging, mentoring, the way a good teacher does.

To my surprise and delight, many of my articles were later published in leading children's magazines. Not the ones that were my assignments, unfortunately, but articles I wrote after completing the course. My early attempts at writing were lessons learned, preparing me for the future. Seeing my words in children's magazines was fascinating. Picturing students doing the science experiments in my articles or having fun with the art ideas was my reward for the hours spent getting the article just right.

But I got hungry for more. Longer works. Books. Every time I watched my fifth-grade students give their book reports on the Newbery winners or honor books they read, my mind started whirling. Could I write a full-length novel? The students made the stories come alive, sometimes by dressing the part of the main character, other times by talking the way the characters talked or sometimes acting out a scene, complete with sword and boots. How awesome it would be to see children reading my books and liking them enough to give reports on them.

This nagging voice in my head kept asking, "Where is your book, Beverly? Why haven't you written it? Stop making excuses. Don't say 'I don't know how.' Just do it."

I finally listened to my inner voice, but was hesitant about trying something with more words, more pages. I needed more help. So in 1993, I signed up for the Institute's course on novel writing. Again I had a wonderful instructor, Lois Hobart, who taught me about imagery, dialogue, character dimension, viewpoint, and exactly what made a good novel. Under her guidance, I wrote my first book for teens, *Shadows in the Desert*, about the Gulf War in Kuwait.

I chose the war as the subject for my first book because for months earlier the TV had carried pictures of the battles, the soldiers, and a country that I knew little about. I sat glued to the screen, wondering about the people, how they felt, watching their land being destroyed, their lives and families torn apart.

To me, wars, from the Revolutionary War to the American Civil War, World War I, World War II, and all the wars since and between are not about just the armies and fighting, but about families and how they survive conditions over which they have no control. What do they think? How does living each day, not knowing whether you'll have food or water or be safe or even alive, affect them? Slowly my characters formed in my mind: a teenage boy who joins the army and becomes a part of the war, a teenage girl from another culture that my young protagonist meets. What happens to these two young people when they're thrown together in the worst of conditions?

My instructor emphasized the importance of research. Yes, even though my story was fiction, it was based on actual facts and these had to be accurate. The story must ring true. If it doesn't, then the writer loses credibility and the reader probably will mark that writer off their favorite author's list. To keep my story authentic, I read every book I could find about the Gulf War, both fiction and non-fiction. I found very revealing books written from the viewpoint of women who were from Saudi Arabia and other Asian nations that gave a vivid picture of life in those countries. Some of the books were written anonymously, the women fearing they'd be murdered if it was discovered they'd revealed secrets about their society.

I also browsed old newspaper articles and magazines at the library. I studied the customs of the people, the terrain of the land, the culture, the clothing, everything to make the story realistic.

I mailed each assignment to Ms. Hobart. She responded with comments and suggestions of how to make the story stronger. It wasn't easy, but I was determined to succeed. In January 1995, after months and even years of typing, deleting, cutting, pasting, switching scenes, rethinking characters, and all the little details that add up to make a story, *Shadows in the Desert* was complete. Two years of hard work—including pulling out my hair over a scene, waking in the middle of the night with a thought and jotting it down on the paper beside the bed only to discover I couldn't read my scribbles the next morning, moments of self-doubt, moments of joy—and my novel was ready, according to my instructor, to submit to agents and/or editors.

Oh my, that's another story. I count this manuscript as the beginning, the final step in pursuing a writing career. Writing *Shadows in the Desert* taught me discipline, humility, perseverance, patience, and most of all, I think, love of the written word.

Discipline ~ to write every day unless a major disaster occurs in my life, whether I'm in the mood, feel like it, have a blank mind, or can't come up with a plot or characters or even my own name.

Humility ~ respect the intended reader for my work. Without the reader, I am nothing. Give the reader my best stories. Never settle for second best.

Perseverance ~ a bad day doesn't stop me. I type something. Many times I delete it all the next day. Sometimes, a word or sentence, though, sparks an idea, and I'm off and creating a new scene that presented itself.

Patience ~ I write. I send my work out. At that point, it's beyond my control. So I wait. And wait. And wait. Having a temper tantrum does no good. I'm the only one who hears my rants and ravings. And the cat, who ignores me. A sense of humor helps.

Love of the written word ~ This seems odd, I know, considering I was a non-reader as a child. Books were not a priority in my home. I'm not saying this is the reason I wasn't a reader; it's just a fact. I have no favorites from my childhood like most people have. I didn't go to the library and come home with arms full of books. I simply was not interested. My eyesight might have been part of the problem, though I'm not using that as an excuse either. When I was in fifth-grade, my parents discovered I was near sighted and needed glasses. It's amazing how different the world looked to me when they placed that first pair of spectacles on my nose. I could see tiny details in the carpet, the wallpaper, and in people that I'd never noticed before.

To me today, the world is beautiful.

I have other qualifications that help me as a writer, also. I am pretty much a loner. I enjoy being by myself, not having to talk to anyone, just listening to the voices of my characters. I can spend hours in my writing room, at my computer, living in the world of my imagination, ignoring the real world around me. No small children clamor for my attention. My sons are grown and living on their own. My husband sometimes wants to talk and when he enters my sanctuary (the name I call my writing room), I give him half of my attention with a nod here and a grunt there, while my fingers continue typing what my characters are saying and doing. My cat sometimes disrupts my thoughts when she leaps up on the desk and plays kitten on the keyboard. A hummingbird flies in to the feeder on the window, and I pause to watch her eat. These are minor distractions.

I take a break now and then to allow my brain to absorb what my characters are saying and doing and to play it back in my mind. Are they straying off the path I've set them on? Sometimes this is good. Like our *live* children, our story characters have minds of their own. They may be right too. So I listen to what they tell me and see where they lead me. They usually know exactly where they want to go, though sometimes I have to give them a nudge or two.

Music, the TV and the radio distract me, so I seldom listen to them while I work. Unless music is a part of the story, then I'll play the type of music that fits the mood of the story, from Elvis to classical, to country or rock, whatever helps me to envision a scene.

Also, I now respect the work each author puts into his/her novel or nonfiction book. From experience, I know they didn't just sit down, type, and a few hours or days later have written their best seller. More likely they spent months, even years from the concept of the book to those two magic words THE END.

The End is a relief. The End is also sad. When I finished *Shadows in the Desert*, I felt lost. For two years, the characters had been my children. I had guided them, scolded them, and mothered them. Suddenly they were on their own. To face the world. I hoped they'd be treated kindly. Would someone love them the way I loved them? Maybe. Maybe not. The world is cruel. The world is just. They had to take their chances.

This is the story of how I wrote my first novel, *Shadows in the Desert*. You can't find it in book stores or Online. It isn't published. I saved it in a box. Sometimes I take it out and look at it. And smile. Yes, I did it. I wrote a novel. That is quite an accomplishment. Now for two words that show I've accomplished another writing.

About the author

Beverly is a member of the national Society of Children's Book Writers and Illustrators, as well as the North Texas chapter. She lives with her husband, Jack, in the country, where an occasional deer, skunk or armadillo come to visit.

http://beverlystowemcclure.wordpress.com

Recent release: *Caves, Cannons and Crinolines*, YA historical.

How I Wrote *No Place for Gods*

by Gerald Mills

For openers, all the signs and omens were wrong. I was destined to become an engineer, not a novelist.

It's commonly believed that engineers can't write, spell or express themselves beyond grunts and sign language unless they're talking to other engineers, whereupon numbers and formulas join the grunts. Engineers also epitomize the saying "thinking inside the box," the natural opposite of which is "thinking outside the box." They are typically square, structured head-to-toe and fairly uptight. Their typical response to anyone asking a dumb question (dumb from the engineer's viewpoint) is that if that person were to be an engineer, he'd understand.

These traits can often be spotted in high school as any form of disinterest in English, history, the arts and subjects like economics or political science. Business courses are meant for the socially outgoing crowd, not potential engineers. As for languages, most engineers have learned sufficient English by the time they finish kindergarten. What else they ever need when dealing with math, science and mechanics can be learned on the fly.

I must add that budding engineers don't *automatically* hate all those other areas. They suffer through them like all their high school classmates because they have no other options. I didn't know I was a budding engineer at the time, so I suffered less. Math and science appealed to me, yes, but music and math seem to be two sides of the same coin and I was a serious piano student aiming for a career in music without having the slightest idea how I'd achieve it. My immediate family had no money, and there were no rich uncles in the picture.

High school science was simply interesting, and the teacher was excellent. I got decent grades in English and the rest of the mandatory subjects out of sheer stubbornness, but I needed to fill a semester in my senior year and there weren't many choices. I gulped down my false pride and took typing. As I recall it, I was the only guy in the class. *"A, semicolon, S, L, D, K, F, J, G, H..."* Repeat. *"A, semicolon, S, L, D, K, F, J, G, H..."* Arrgh! I never did master the numbers row by touch, but I passed the course otherwise.

Reality came to call at my house that same year, and decided to stay. My family had zero extra money, music schools were expensive and scholarships were small for the lucky few who won them. Any chances of working my way through the least expensive music school seemed improbable at best, even with student loans. That held for colleges in general, so there went any scant interest I held for business or the arts. However, there *were* several engineering schools where I could work my way through, and one was Northeastern University in Boston. A degree would cost me five years instead of four, but I could work in industry half the time after the freshman year. It was the lesser of many evils, better than a trade school, so off I went to learn how to grunt, use sign language, think inside a box and live on roughly $5 a day, including the cost of a shared room.

At that time, a nineteen-cent bottle of warm ginger ale (store brand) and a fifteen-cent box of saltine crackers could fuel six hours of studying and homework, from 7:00 P.M. to 1:00 A.M the next morning. Two English muffins slathered with butter, plus a cup of sweet tea, became a complete, "highly nourishing" breakfast costing just thirty-five cents. It was loaded with carbs and saturated fats - just what the serious student needed to survive. Great for brain function!

Somehow I got through the ordeal. Northeastern grudgingly forked over a small, fancy sheet of paper declaring that I'd earned a Bachelor of Science in Electrical Engineering. It proved that I was finally an engineer even if I didn't feel or act like one. Strangely, I'd learned how to spell many years earlier (which should have disqualified me right at the start,) but my grunting was way below par (girl engineers did it better.) I was an engineer, nevertheless. Hardly anyone cared.

"Fast Forward" three decades. My writing experience during those thirty years consisted mostly of engineering reports, technical proposals and memos. Maybe the occasional personal letter snuck into the lot, but not many. However, some twenty years earlier I'd had a weak moment and sent away for information on the Famous Writer's School. I was just curious and wanted the promised info, but a salesman came knocking at my door and held out something engineers hunger for, called ego booster salve. I think he might have sold used cars in an earlier job. I signed up for the beginner's course, a really bad move! I knew within a few days that it was likely a scam, and it later proved to be just that. All anyone had to do was "follow the bouncing ball", and best-selling novels would come flying off the typewriter. Yeah, right. Never, I vowed, would I be lured in that direction again, and never once thereafter did I think of writing fiction. Not once!

In 1989, wife Lori and I were preparing to take a hiatus away from everything, opting to cruise aboard a forty-five foot ocean-going sailboat until we ran out of money. Then I'd return to my career path, knowing at least that together we'd done something very few other couples do, and done it before we were too old. We sold most of our stuff, including two cars, and put the rest in storage, but for some odd reason I thought it wise to have a laptop computer aboard. Nothing expensive, just something to keep a diary of our experiences afloat. We planned to cruise for at least two years, longer if our investments panned out, and in that time a lot could happen. Secretly, I wanted the thing so I could still feel that connection to the technical world. I could take the laptop out from time to time, blow the dust off and get the same feeling I'd gotten by staring at the degree from Northeastern (which nobody had ever asked to see, and was locked away in a safe deposit box.) It would remind me that I'd finally mastered grunting and sign language.

I located a used laptop, but its mini-screen displayed just fourteen lines, or about seven actual lines when double-spaced. The seller wanted $100, throwing in a really nice cloth carrying case, so I snapped it up. The computer had no hard drive, so any program it ran came from a 3 ½ inch floppy disc, which was inserted first. The program disc was then replaced by another one used to hold the working file. The computer came with a neat little program called Professional Write, or PW. I'd only known WORD up to that point, but WORD in the 1980's was still difficult for all but the most dedicated of secretaries. I hated it. The secretaries I knew hated it, too. PW was a lot easier, in my view. I bought a couple packs of floppy discs on sale, but never once opened the laptop cover until the day after Christmas, 1990, well over a year later.

We were anchored in a little cove near Nassau, The Bahamas, and decided to stay there for several days, keeping company with another boating couple, Brandy and Tom. Brandy had written a novel that Lori was reading, so the subject of novel writing became one of the afternoon's discussion topics. Why didn't I try my own hand at writing fiction, I was asked, now that my life was stress free, with plenty of time and no schedule to keep? All three ganged up on me, even though I immediately fought back with my best grunts and some really cool sign language, even throwing in an impressive mathematical expression - 6.02×10^{23}. That, I announced was Avogadro's number. Heads nodded in awe. Tom was mesmerized further when I also rattled off the number pi (π) to fourteen decimal places, remembering to smile. Engineers do that on rare occasions, and this was one of those.

My ploy failed. Wife Lori declared that I'd be untied from the mast and allowed food and water *only* after I promised to pen the next Great American Novel. I noticed she was softening. Her earlier proclamation had been to maroon me at the top of the mast and not let me down. That was fifty feet up! I pointed out that possible rain would ruin the laptop up there, so she relented.

That night I rehearsed the procedure in my sleep: *"A, semicolon, S, L, D, K, F, J, G, H..."* In order to get fed next morning, I dutifully dug out the laptop and dusted it off, wondering what on earth I would use for my story. I figured on giving myself at least until lunchtime to see what gave out first - my promise to write, my long list of ideas (I had just one at the time) or the computer.

My reason for citing all this background is simply to stress what I now consider a very important and serious point for anyone wanting to write. *You may think you can't write, or that you have no aptitude for writing, or your astrological sign is all wrong, or you're a procrastinator or any number of other negatives such as grunting, but you will never know until you try.* I had so many presumed negatives they were beyond counting, but I'd decided to force myself to make a stab at it so that I could say I tried. I also looked forward to continued breakfasts, which didn't seem a promising prospect if I objected at all.

I made a second cup of coffee and took stock of the few assets I had. One was that I'd been an avid reader since third grade. I'd read hundreds and hundreds of books, many of them way beyond my early years, exhausting school libraries until I reached high school and acquired my own book collection to boot in the years that followed. My tastes included mysteries, westerns, adventure, histories, the classics, even Shakespeare. As a pre-teen, I'd acquired twenty-two of the Tom Swift series, plus perhaps another fifty adventure types, most of which had been given to me by relatives or friends. I'd read many of the classics and classic authors, novels about medieval times, pre-revolutionary and early American times and the Civil War. Comic books were in the picture as well, all the usual heroes - Captain Marvel, Superman, Batman, Plastic Man and, of course, themes popular during the war years. In high school I'd gravitated to science fiction, astronomy, archaeology and ancient history, especially myths and legends. Prior to our sailing adventure, I'd devoured Heinlein, Azimov, Sturgeon and an exhaustive array of other S-F authors. My bookshelves were loaded with Ludlum, Clancy, Forsythe, Crichton and many others too numerous to mention.

Thanks to Lori's reading interests, we had several hundred books on esoteric topics of all kinds, and I'd read many of those. I'd also become interested in things Russian and had built a small file of articles and portions of books that I'd copied. Of particular recent interest was the theory that Russian mind-disruption experiments were behind the tragedy of the U.S. submarine, *Thresher*. It was one of the very few subjects I'd stumbled across in a public library in the years just before we set sail. I couldn't have told anyone why or when, only that the subject intrigued me. I'd probably read a reference to it in one of Lori's books. The same book must have talked of the NRO, or National Reconnaissance Office - a hush, hush U.S. space operation whose very existence was adamantly denied by the Washington, D.C. folks at the time. Maybe I was a closet conspiracy freak in finding those topics interesting, but libraries in general had become foreign territories for me, seldom visited. The Internet as we know it today hadn't yet affected my life.

Other assets included always having been a self-starter, working alone most of the time and using logic to solve most of life's challenges. There were also a few far out assets, such as the fact that I never expected nor sought the support of others. That type of thing might be viewed as a bonus. Also, I'd developed a knack for returning to a project after an absence and being able to dive right back in without a blink. I'd always had that ability even as a teen. Possibly my long association with music would help me in that way.

As a final asset, I'd always finished anything I began. My focus was always on the imagined end product. This had helped me numerous times when setbacks and interruptions threatened to torpedo whatever I was doing. Even when I procrastinated out of discomfort or the feeling of being inadequate, it was usually the image of what I wanted to do (but was trying to avoid) that spurred me into action.

So I *did* have resources of sorts that might help, but I still knew nothing about actually creating a novel unless I could put some of my engineering background to use. Engineers are supposed to know how to define a problem before jumping into any kind of solution. Usually, it involves a list stating all the existing aspects of the problem to be solved as well as those desired of any solution. The mere creation of a list begins a thinking process that often continues night and day in one's subconscious. In my case, bingo! Suddenly a solution would pop into the picture, and away I'd go.

Since a list might help me in this case, I began with things I'd enjoyed reading ever since my boyhood. I'd want those in my world-class novel, of course. Mystery, action, adventure and suspense topped the list. Throw in something from the psychic realm, and maybe have Russia as the big villain? Why not? As long as I was reaching for the stars, why not a whole galaxy? I knew something about the Russian intelligence system from my reading, and I could augment that later on.

Some violence here and there would be good. Shoot 'em up! Sex and romance? Sure. How about astrology? Yes, again. I could use political conflict of some sort, international confrontation or even a doomsday scenario. I'd always liked Edgar Cayce readings, so maybe I could have someone channeling in the story. Telepathy would also work well with the paranormal theme, as would telekinesis and maybe psychometry. I might even throw in Uri Geller, the spoon bender. Lori had actually attended a dinner meeting featuring another well-known spoon bender, Matthew Manning, so naturally she had a few books on the subject. Spoon bender wasn't a demeaning term; it was simply one that people used for the Uri Geller types.

Native Americans? Definitely, especially the medicine man, or shaman. Lori's bookshelf included quite a bit on them.

Espionage? Definitely, again. How about martial arts? Karate? I'd never been a karate student, but karate was a favorite subject in my reading and it had been a companion course to the yoga classes Lori and I had attended years earlier. I added karate. I'd been in the army, so I could draw from that limited experience if needed. At least I knew lots of terminology. I'd always admired how authors brought forces together in a firefight, usually two opponents but sometimes three or more. That would be worth trying for, now that I was simply collecting ideas. Throw in some computer jargon, of course.   The   list was growing along with my excitement. I'd momentarily "forgotten" that the whole exercise was aimed at writing a novel and was treating it as just another engineering problem to be solved. Full speed ahead!

I'd already decided that my male protagonist would have a surprising background, some sort of paranormal power. Somewhere halfway through the list, I got a sudden flash that whispered "Inca." Nothing surprised me by then so I added Inca, along with Peru and more shamanism. Peruvian *indio* supplied shamans, and they spoke Quechua and were even called Quechua, so Quechua went on the list, too. My protagonist might somehow inherit his paranormal powers through that mystical link, even though the Inca were long gone from the scene. Who cared? These were all just possibilities. It also seemed reasonable to play the paranormal theme against standard psychology, so one of the main supporting characters would be a psychologist. I could even place some of the story in Boston, where I'd gone to college. I knew the Boston streets, having been a taxi driver for a time, and had done plenty of solitary walking about the docks and alleys and parks. Those places might fit into the story, perhaps even the street people I'd encountered. I'd always taken particular interest in them.

Maybe I could find a way to get my Inca descendant from Peru to Boston? Nah! Scratch that.

Las Vegas numbered among the many places I'd lived, so I added it. I'd spent gobs of my spare time hanging around in the casinos there, watching people throw away their money and observing them on the city streets at night. There also needed to be a source of money for my hero, something I'd learned from author Robert Ludlum. Money source was added to the list. Maybe casinos? Why not?

Since I was now a sailor, and about to write this masterpiece on my boat, it also seemed proper to include something on sailing, so that went on the list.

Back to Russia. The Cold War was winding down. We'd seen perestroika and glasnost struggling and partially successful. One of Lori's books was titled *Psychic Discoveries Behind the Iron Curtain*. Having read it cover to cover, I knew that the KGB controlled all scientific programs in Russia, and that it had closed the door on psychic research back around 1970, barring any further freedom of information exchange with the West despite glasnost. Anything developed in Russia after 1970 was so secret even *they* didn't know what it was. I could begin the story in 1970, having my protagonist become pivotal to defusing a major international... well, something far reaching years later.

Finally, I needed something so devastating that its destruction or removal would bring society to its knees. My first thought was computers and viruses, but it needed to be more fundamental. Ah, the transistor! What if something developed in Russia could bring an end to U.S. dominance simply by destroying any transistors the something happened to be aimed at? What if huge numbers of transistorized systems suddenly stopped working, our atomic arsenal, for example? If somehow transistors were to vanish, would society return to the Stone Age? I decided that it would indeed, literally overnight, so something central to the story would involve loss of the transistor. I had no idea what it might be, but *something*.

I typed up the actual list on the laptop, in no particular order:
Mystery
Action
Suspense
Adventure
Psychic realm
Paranormal protagonist with esoteric background
Psychologist as a main character
Telekinetics, Psychometry, telepathy
Inca, Quechua, shamanism, Peru
Problem: Peru to Boston?

Russian psychic discoveries
Russia vs. U.S. confrontation
Russian intelligence, especially the GRU (added GRU from my readings)
The *Thresher* cover-up and Russian involvement.
NRO denied by U.S. authorities
Violence
Sex
Romance
U.S. Army
Firefight with several opposing forces.
Boston, Boston streets, street people
Money source for protagonist
Las Vegas, casinos, gamblers
Espionage
Edgar Cayce
Uri Geller
Channeling
Computer jargon
Karate
Sailing
Native Americans and their shamans
Loss of the transistor
Return to the Stone Age

All told, the list was a recipe for a hopeless pile of paranormal drivel, but I'd already convinced myself that it could be pared away once the story was developing in my head. I could only view part of the list at any one time on the laptop screen, so I gave that folly up and wrote it out on paper, tacking the sheet up at my chart table.

At this point, I might have been designing a new gizmo, not writing a novel. Given such a design task as an engineer, I'd first have made a list of all the things making the old gizmo valuable, the things anyone would definitely want in any new version. Then I'd have used that list in a subconscious way to guide my thoughts along certain paths leading to the ultimate prize, the *new* gizmo. Adjustments would be assumed as the project began to take shape. Once the list was done, my next step would be to organize my approach. First I'd need an outline, but here I immediately ran into trouble. With any gizmo design project, I'd know approximately what the outcome should look like. The analogy fell apart when gizmo was spelled n-o-v-e-l.

I started by typing OUTLINE at the top of the laptop page, then sat there and waited for inspiration. Somewhere back in high school, I'd learned how to outline the standard way. (Engineers did it their own way.) It was easy enough to do, arranging thoughts in a logical sequence, but first the outline creator had to have logical thoughts. My list was anything but logical. If I'd been writing something technical, not a problem, but this was fiction. I had no logical thoughts at all, not even illogical ones.

Lori seemed satisfied that I'd started writing; she began making me breakfast after reporting by radio to Brandy and Tom that I was already sitting at the keyboard. I supposed the whoops and giggles were a form of encouragement, but stare as I would at that single word, OUTLINE, nothing came to mind other than what I'd already formed as a basic idea, so I typed *Chapter 1, Scene 1. Boston, 1970.*

Then I stopped. Where did most novels begin, I wondered - at the beginning? As silly as that sounds, it was the question I actually asked myself. In other words, did the story begin in 1970, or should I begin it in the present and supply some sort of history? Maybe it should start even earlier than 1970, since my Inca descendant protagonist needed a background.

Okay, so I'd start the story in Peru. I chose Cuzco as the area. *Chapter 1, Scene 1. Cuzco, Peru, 19???*

New problem. How old was my protagonist circa 1970? And what was the time span of the unwritten masterpiece? How far into the future?

This was nothing like designing gizmos.

I struggled until I had roughly one page of outline, none of which felt right. Still, I absolutely had to have an outline. Didn't I? I could begin with that much and expand the outline as the story progressed. Wrong! My so-called outline lasted ten minutes. No sooner had I typed the first paragraph of Scene One than my mind exploded with new and better ideas. To hell with the outline! I couldn't type fast enough. The only drawback was that I had to learn how to remember what preceded the seven lines I could actually see on the laptop screen. I quickly mastered page-up, page-down to the point where it became automatic. Zip, back ten pages, zip, ahead three. Ahead four. Now back to where I was. The story was writing itself, helped along by the only boy in the typing class and lots of Page Up, Page Down keystrokes.

The masterwork spilling out on my mini-screen included many of the ingredients in my list, plus lots more. It suddenly wanted OUT and I just happened to be the facilitator. Other than the opening scene, which turned out to be Boston after all, everything else came from a place within me I didn't know existed. Names popped into my head without a thought, details and descriptions as well, then a sudden shift to Moscow, where more of the same came spilling out. Where was it all coming from? How did my brain know these things? I hadn't researched anything prior to our sailing, other than that Thresher material, yet much of the information didn't seem to come from books I'd read over the years. It must have, of course, but the whole influx of novel-y-type things had an eerie quality. My subconscious obviously knew a lot more than I could draw forth in the conscious sense. It was creating my eventual story in the way dreams are created, full of details forgotten later upon waking, yet with the knowledge that there had been details, exquisite ones.

All I had to do was step out of the way, remove myself from the process and let that dream-quality knowledge bubble to the surface. Bubble? Ha! A better term might have been gush, as in geyser. I'd stumbled upon an extremely important rule about creative writing: *don't try to drive the story; let it take you where it will!*

At that point I had no title for my story, no plot or subplots and the vaguest of ideas, yet Scene Two was already forming and the list of potential characters grew like Jack's beanstalk. Perhaps this was what was meant by the saying I stumbled across many years later: "In order to start writing, begin." The originator of that gem undoubtedly understood the power of the subconscious mind, once those creative juices began flowing. For someone who'd not yet heard the saying, it was a revelation. *I'd just discovered another truth, this time about the dangers of using outlines as frameworks for writing fiction.* It refuted anything I'd ever believed about outlines, even engineering ones. If

I'd forced myself to stick with my hasty, original one-pager, none of it would have happened, not even if the same outline had been polished over many months. In fact, I'd probably have given up that first morning.

It was only when I obediently and dispassionately followed the whisperings in my mind that my story erupted with a passion. A brand new train of thought would appear - and I'd follow it, even though it wasn't going where I thought things were heading at that moment. Off we went together, frantic touch-typist and mystery-author-hiding-behind-the-curtain, tripping down the new road to see where it would lead. Characters magically sprang forth, fully formed, complete with backgrounds or personalities requiring no thought.

My opening scene at that time involved several street people, all men. They needed names, but before I could even think of any, names appeared on my screen: Turkey, Ivanhoe and Graham Foster. Where had they come from? Other than Ivanhoe, a novel by Sir Walter Scott that I'd studied in high school, the others were a surprise. I remembered no one I knew nicknamed Turkey, or anyone by the name of Graham. (Several years later I realized that I'd read stories by Graham Greene, but I didn't remember the name there on the boat.) Ivanhoe turned out to be John Hough, e.g., "Ivanhoe." Turkey was a nickname for Roy Turcas. Even these formal versions of the names came as a surprise, because they simply appeared in the text.

It was my first taste of what was yet to come. Separate pieces of various puzzles began interlocking in my mind long before they actually converged in the story. In a way, it was reminiscent of my piano-playing days when I could be playing notes on page twenty while mentally thinking ahead two, three and even four pages and actually seeing them in my mind's eye. I found that I was typing one thing on the laptop while thinking something completely different about the story yet to unfold.

Part of the reason for all this may have been the fact that *I hadn't nurtured any really bad writing habits.* No distractions for hours at a time, no procrastination, no TV or entertainment radio, no food cravings. Those things weren't found aboard sailboats, although I did consume lots of Oreos. Days were rated by the number of cookies needed by my psyche. A really bad day, filled with setbacks or physical dangers, rated as many as eight Oreos, called an eight-cookie day. On better days, I could get by with four, which was my norm for the time I spent writing. I had no list of things I'd rather be doing, no children racing around in the next room, no loud neighbors, not even planes flying overhead most of the time. What I did have was lots of free time, quiet time.

I'd heard of writer's block, but it never found me on our boat.

I was in for other discoveries as well. One was output. Even though we did hoist anchor and move our boat a few days after I began writing, eventually meandering our way down along the Bahamas chain of islands, I wrote nearly every day according to Lori's log. "He's writing up a storm" was one of her entries roughly a week after I began. In all, I wrote non-stop for about forty-five days. (Much later, I discovered that I'd turned out 250,000 words in that first draft, more than 5500 words per day!) Some days I didn't have a chance to write, so the actual average was higher. I didn't *know* at the time that real authors rarely spewed out one tenth of that amount, calling it productive by their standards. Nobody whispered in my ear that novelists did their best to set aside at least half an hour each day for writing, or had appointed times when they sat down to create. Probably if I'd known such things, I'd have set aside half an hour each day, sat in the same place in the boat and treated the whole thing like a chore. If I'd missed the scheduled time slot, the story would have languished until the following day, and the day after that.

Some days I typed for several hours, at the weirdest times and places. Days when it rained I might have spent five or six hours going at it. Even the occasional rainy day was welcomed at times. I was admittedly running on a stream of consciousness without regard to quality or any sort of correction as I typed away, and often joked that I typed as fast as I could to see how the story would end. That was indeed how I felt at times. Who cared if the first draft was awful, once done? I certainly didn't, knowing I could fix it later. I'd morphed from reluctant beginner, goaded by others to write anything at all, into a "man possessed."

Further still, the Professional Write program didn't count words for me, so I had no real concept of length. I could see just seven double-spaced lines of copy at a time, period, and I was saving just one chapter per floppy disc, so the pile of discs didn't yield any information on how much they held. Was word count another crutch? If I typed so and so many words, did that mean I could stop for the day? I simply counted floppy discs. And cookies.

Somewhere about the middle of what I imagined the story to be, I began to worry about the final climactic scene and the story's finale. I hadn't a clue to either. At that point, I'd used just about everything in my list of ingredients, including sex and romance. I'd even managed to squeeze in money laundering and gambling casinos. Las Vegas was in there. Native Americans were in there. Shamans... everything! But I'd reached what I imagined to be about the three-quarters mark and still hadn't one *iota* of inspiration about the all-important final scenes.

Notwithstanding mild panic, I was about to reinforce my earlier discovery about writing, one I would later teach to other authors. Stated briefly, it was simply to follow any new road that might present itself; see where it took the story, even if it seemed crazy. Something told me not to worry, that inspiration would arrive when I needed it.

Allow me to describe the situation leading up to the major climactic scene in very few words. My protagonist, Jim, apparently had but one course of action open to him, returning to his solitary existence as a man of the streets, without country, without any traces anyone could follow. In doing so, he'd leave Tricia behind rather than subject her to the dangers and loneliness he'd endure as a fugitive. Now what? Where was I to get the elusive big climax if I allowed that him to take that step?

It was an eight-Oreo question. The story seemed fine right up to that point, but I'd let my logical self get in the way and was mistakenly trying to drive the story in spite of what I'd supposedly learned about staying out of the way. Since I had no inspirations at all, I finally did step out of the way and my subconscious immediately headed Jim right back toward his Oval Office antagonists, this time as the hunter rather than the hunted.

Smoke erupted from my keyboard! Suddenly I "knew" where he'd go, how he'd prepare and what he'd do. I'd known those things all along, of course, but refused to listen to my inner voice. Once again I was several pages ahead of where I was typing. Excitement replaced the panic that had begun to creep into my thoughts, all because I'd allowed my story to choose its own course.

A chapter or so later, my great climactic scene was finally "in the tank," but the story wanted a happy ending and Jim had gone "underground" afterward, as originally advertised, disappearing without a trace and without Tricia. Here again I was at a loss, but *now* I was oh, so clever, so marvelously *smart!* Just recite the requirements, I told myself, sit back and it would all happen. Which of my ingredients hadn't been used yet? There wasn't much about karate, or the Boston streets or "street people", but the story already included a good deal about a fictitious Bermuda. That might be the ideal place to bring Jim and Tricia back together, since they'd met there early in the story. The new problem was that she'd now have to find a man who'd secretly lived his adult life as a non-person in a world of computers and controls. He knew every trick, and she knew none of them.

In my imagined finale, her search would necessarily involve those original Boston streets, would somehow involve street people and karate, and would eventually lead her back to Bermuda and the romantic reunion. It was a tall order, but I resolved to take myself out of the process and jumpstart my subconscious. No more of my getting in the way.

I drew a deep breath, chomped on my first Oreo of the day and typed three words: *Two weeks later.*

Looking back, anything I typed would have triggered the process, because in the very next sentence Tricia was appearing at the door of a karate *dojo*, in Atlanta of all places, gym bag in hand. Where was *this* new road going? Atlanta was the wrong direction. Boston was what I wanted. Once again, I typed whatever came to mind just to see. I'd never have made that jump if I'd been thinking logically. Just one sentence into it and here we were already using the karate ingredient, even though exactly how it was going to figure into the story was still a huge mystery. Everything fell into place thereafter - Boston, street people, more karate, Bermuda and the ultimate happy ending.

How did I feel when I typed *The End.* I was miserable! My most important lesson as a novelist, or so it seemed, had been in learning to stay out of the way. I'd been no more than an engineer in author's clothing, listening to his subconscious. That couldn't be any kind of clue that I could actually write. No one needed to tell me that my methods were all wrong, that real writing wasn't done my way. Others would have used far less effort and reached their goals quicker, I thought, but at least I'd stuck with it, right or wrong. A stack of floppy discs was my confirmation.

Tom and Brandy had long since departed, so there wasn't even a celebration party. I decided to retire the laptop (which was almost limp with exhaustion) and let the story simmer awhile before I tackled the monstrous task of cleaning up the mess, if ever. I'd written enough engineering proposals to know what lay ahead, but it would have to wait indefinitely. Lori and I needed to alter course immediately. Our investments had taken a severe blow, and we needed to head back to the nearest mainland (Florida) where I'd return to the salt mines.

Thanks to this sudden change of plans, it was more than a year later when I finally bought a real computer and popped in the first of the floppy discs. Now I could see *three times as many mistakes* on the screen, the way nature intended. They were everywhere. The first chapter draft was horrendous! Was the rest just as bad? I didn't want to know. I put the floppy away without another glance. Maybe some dim, distant day I'd take another look.

"Dim, distant" turned out to be two days later, when I decided to convert the PW files to WORD, something I could do without actually examining what I'd written. That was when I realized I'd amassed some 250,000 words. In spite of my resolve not to peek at my creation, I inadvertently spotted lots of places where I could trim the length, so I eased into an editing session that eventually got rid of 70,000 words over a several month period. Remarkable! The story not only hadn't suffered, it improved.

Emboldened, I began slashing at everything - dialogue, asides, trivia, stuff that didn't improve the story - and the length dropped another 20,000 words!

I took the new files to a local printer in 1993, plunked down some hard cash and had the whole thing printed out, all 999 pages worth, double-spaced, one side. I still have this printout. It was still *way* too long by my standards, even though I compared it to other long novels I'd read. Ernest Hemmingway had been so right with his declaration that "first drafts were shit," so out came the editing scissors once again.

The first casualty was my whole first chapter. Gone were Turkey, Ivanhoe and Graham Foster. I removed most of the dialogue tags in the remainder, and that saved me another twenty pages. At the same time, I did some research and filled in a few of the sketchy places in the story. Add back a dozen pages. Back and forth, snip here, add there. It was getting better every time I stiffened my resolve, but in fact I wasn't functioning as "the author" any longer. I'd put on my reader's hat. *It was only when I functioned as my own eventual reader that I made serious improvements.* Otherwise, I caught myself changing a word here and there, or rearranging a sentence to make it a teensy bit better or prettier.

Teensy wouldn't cut it. Nor would pretty, or clever, or using 50-cent words.

By this time, I'd discovered a good deal about writing fiction. I made another list of my discoveries. It was short.

- *Discovery one, the one I felt was most important, was the role of the subconscious in creativity.* I don't believe I'm any different than the rest of humanity in that respect, and didn't believe it then. My creativity as an engineer writing reports and proposals seemed to have sprung from the same well.
- *Discovery two was that outlines are detrimental to the creative process when writing fiction.* An outline too easily becomes a stiff-sided box within which the story remains. Human nature resists changing the shape or size of that box, once made, so the author becomes a willing slave to his early creation. The story has already been given a skeleton, and he's now bent on adding a flesh and blood body around the bones, never asking himself if the bones are wrong.
- *Discovery three came in the form of a mantra of just four words: I can do this.* When I discovered that something within my higher self was actually writing the story, I felt empowered. All I had to do was stay in the background and not fear becoming lost.

I can do this! I must have said those words to myself dozens of times in that month and a half. Like the bumblebee that shouldn't be able to fly at all, I shouldn't have been able to write as I did. The bee didn't know he was designed wrong, so he flew. In my case, I didn't know I couldn't write, so I wrote, knowing instinctively that other novel writers weren't doing it the way I was. They weren't blessed with unlimited time and relaxation, zero schedules to keep, and quietude that can rarely be matched mere miles from bustling society. Lori and I didn't have to be anywhere at any particular time. It was wonderful. At the same time, I was mystified as to where all the information had been hiding in my head. Most of what I'd used came tumbling out as though I'd been hypnotized into a regressive state à la Bridey Murphy. I'd described Bermuda, even though I knew nothing much about it, using "place markers" to be filled in later when I knew more. Most of my guesses turned out to be very close to correct. I knew Washington D.C. fairly well and had lived in Las Vegas for a time, but my knowledge of Moscow was limited to old National Geographic magazines. Somehow I'd absorbed enough about all these locations through my earlier reading to supply what I needed for that first draft. We certainly didn't have anything on the boat - ten thousand pounds of essentials, but not a single book or magazine other than my sailing stuff and a few of Lori's treasures.

The manuscript improved some more. Maybe it was time to find someone who could give me a professional overview. Up to this point, no one else had read the story, not even Lori.

A local writers' group held meetings nearby, so I attended one and asked a few kind souls if they could recommend someone as an editor. Several people gave me the same woman's name, so I made an appointment with her and lugged the huge box of manuscript to her house. Our agreement was that she would quickly scan the whole story and give me her valued opinion as to its merits. Was it even worth my further effort to scale it down? Her fee was $35 an hour. I ordered an hour's worth of appraisal, which I could barely afford, but my thinking was that she might indicate portions of the story where I'd gone way overboard, spots where I might simply eliminate whole scenes.

Several weeks later we met again. To my great dismay, she'd completely ignored our agreement and had attacked the first chapter like a proofreader, correcting words here and there, moving a few things about and inserting one-liner examples written *her* way. They were little changes, picky changes. Her way was no better than my way;

her grammar was no improvement over mine. I paid her and took the manuscript back home. No more editors! Much more self-doubt.

This time I hid the damn box beneath a stack of unpacked books we'd trucked down to Florida from storage in Connecticut. A year passed, then two. We were unpacking yet another box of our book collection when the white one resurfaced, immediately haunting me. I took it aside, found some quiet time and re-read my creation. Suddenly I was seeing tens, hundreds, thousands of ways I could do it better. *I can do this!* The only problem now was time and distractions such as my full time job and our growing family of wayward cats.

I hesitantly began once more on page one, only now I was no longer emotional about my "mess-terpiece." I saw the greater value of being completely objective and totally unemotional, becoming my own eventual reader. *This might have been the greatest discovery of all.* I began to see things as my reader would see them - characters, scenes, pace, dialogue. I finally saw myself in the role I'd written for the author in my story, that of being the constant storyteller, and taught myself how to let my characters do the telling instead. If there were a dozen ways to express a thought, I searched for one my reader would like best.

One of my old science fiction books was titled *Occam's Razor*, by David Duncan, building on Sir William of Occam's rule that the simplest explanation is the strongest and best, and that anything beyond that should be "carved away." I put that imagined razor of his to use, carving away huge piles of writing I'd thought was good in favor of much tinier piles my *reader* would appreciate. Character descriptions went from hundreds of words to mere dozens, allowing my reader to supply his own details, perhaps comparing my character to someone he knew. The total word count kept dropping, yet the story kept improving. Everything was still there, the whole list of unlikely ingredients.

Still, something was wrong. After so many years of on-again, off-again editing, length was down to 150,000 words and further reduction seemed impossible. The story flowed as I wanted it to flow, and I'd visited Washington, D.C. and surrounds as planned. I'd completed my research on the Russian side of the conflict, studied Bermuda, filled in all the "place holders" with real facts and descriptions. What was the problem?

The answer surprised me: stage fright. I'd written the story in 1990. It was now ten years later, years filled with agonizing over words and riddled with self-doubt. No matter how I rationalized otherwise, I was still an engineer, not a writer. I'd had no training as a writer. I'd yawned my way through English. The story would undoubtedly be rejected, and how would I react to that? I wasn't good at fielding rejection. Back twenty years or so earlier I'd been out of work during a bad economic period. I sent out more than a hundred resumes, thinking I'd get some polite letters in return, maybe even invitations for an interview. *Not one was answered!* What if the same thing happened again?

I readied myself for the worst, using self hypnosis techniques I'd taught myself several decades earlier during a bout with grinding my teeth while sleeping. Then I learned to write a query letter, whipped up several versions of a synopsis and began mailing. I still have the box of rejection letters, some of which were real whoops. One, with a signature over the publisher's name and title, remarked that the KGB dated a novel. Well, duh! The story began in 1970, as stated on page one. Apparently he didn't bother reading that first page, or maybe he thought the KGB went out with Stalin. Other comments were funnier; some were downright sad. One was filled with misspelled words and missing punctuation, but none deterred me from sending out another batch. I was "rejection-dejection proof." It was one of my final lessons in writing, acquired without trying very hard at all.

- *Work on self-doubts until they're buried.* I was confident in my story, even if my claims to being an author might be suspect. Maybe, just maybe, engineers didn't always have to grunt and use sign language.

Today I'm occasionally asked if I'd change anything in that first novel, given the chance. I've thought a lot about the question, and my answer is always no. Oh, there are little errors that I suppose could be corrected, but taken as a whole I wouldn't change a thing. That impossible list of ingredients reminds me of the Prego spaghetti sauce commercial: it's in there! Every one of the entries in my list can be found in the story, which today has the title *No Place for Gods.*

Is it my favorite of the four in the series? No fair! That's like someone asking which of your children you like the best.

About the author

Shying away from the purely technical, he enjoys writing character-driven stories dealing with human shortcomings, a topic in which he has a great degree of personal expertise. His latest hobbies are gardening and remembering the cats' names. He no longer sails, and the world is a safer place for it.

There are those who believe he should give up writing for the same reason, but so far no one has come forward with an acceptable bribe.

http://www.gerryscorner.com

Recent releases: *The Eden Prophecy*, SF suspense and *Magic for Your Writing: Help for the Aspiring Writer*, non-fiction

How I Wrote *Travels With My Lovers*

by Erica Miner

Reading books has always been my passion. I'm even more passionate about writing them.

I grew up as the daughter of Russian immigrants who loved to read. My mother, a child of the Russian Revolution, was forced to educate herself during that chaotic period when all the schools were closed by devouring every book she could find at the library, from Dickens to Tolstoy. When I was a child, one of the fringe benefits of staying home sick from school was listening to her read stories to me in her exotic Russian accent. My father, too, fostered a love of reading in me from an early age. We trolled the local libraries in my hometown of Detroit, as well as the monumental Art Deco library downtown, and always came home with armloads. I lost myself in historical novels and fantasized about being a little girl during Roman times. I read Dickens, Cervantes, Austen. I remember feeling privileged to "graduate" from the children's section to the world of adult books. Later, in early teenage when I became interested in reading dramas, my father would come home from his library visits with stacks of plays, which I would consume in a matter of hours.

Outside of the home, my teachers built on my parents' influence. When I was seven years old, someone on the faculty of my elementary school must have seen the spark of a writer in me, and I was placed in a special after school Creative Writing program. I can still summon up the image of my writing teacher, an avuncular teddy bear of a man whose warm, kindhearted patience provided me with the inspiration to create with words. After that, a fourth grade teacher who required us to bring in a new poem every day to read in front of the class encouraged me to write a dramatic adaptation of a book we were reading that semester. But instead of acting in the play, I directed it. This was my first taste of the power of words to speak beyond the page.

At age nine, I started violin lessons, which then became the all-consuming focus of my life. Well, almost. My father gave me my first journal at thirteen, just as I was entering high school. I've been journaling ever since. Later in life, when I became a violinist at the Metropolitan Opera in New York, I still continued to study writing, taking courses in my limited but valued free time. The spark that was recognized in my childhood continues to burn many decades later.

My father, who was my first violin teacher, also wrote. He, too, took writing courses in his free time, continued to study writing during his retirement years and kept on writing until his last breath.

The journey to my first book, which was journal-based, was fraught with suffering: not from birthing the book as much as from two painful life-altering experiences that forced me onto an unexpected path.

The first occurred in my previous life as a violinist with the Metropolitan Opera, when my husband of ten years left me for another man. I suddenly found myself struggling to balance a high-pressure career while simultaneously raising two children on my own. Rather than be defeated by a devastating situation, I chose to take life by the reins and do something I had always wanted to do: travel. Each summer I took a respite from my responsibilities at home, my work, raising my two children, to recharge my batteries with a brief sojourn into exciting, uncharted territory. With every voyage, I became wiser and more experienced, and I journaled to keep a record of the fascinating places and people I discovered in my expeditions to these exotic locales. When I returned home, I spent my precious late night hours after opera performances getting my feelings and experiences out of my head and onto the page. I wrote poetry. I wrote about everything that frustrated me: the injustices of being abandoned by husband; the difficulties of dealing with two little kids on my own; the harshness of performing in a high-stakes professional environment; and the joys of self-discovery in my travels. Instead of throwing myself out the window of my ninth floor apartment, I wrote. I survived.

The second experience that rocked my world came several years later, when I was driving home after a long day of opera rehearsals. Fate intervened in the form of a speeding motorist who ran a light, crashed into me, and sent me to the hospital. The injuries I suffered in that car accident ultimately forced me to give up my musical career.

This didn't happen precipitously. I endured almost two years of intense physical and occupational therapy before I finally admitted I couldn't continue with the grueling Met Opera schedule. One doesn't give up such a prestigious position, not easily won and coveted by so many, without a fight. So I fought. I struggled. And ultimately I turned my back on the life I thought was my destiny and sought a new outlet for my creativity. In the process of overcoming my grief at losing my ability to play the instrument that was my passion, I rediscovered an older, more far-reaching passion. I turned back to my lifelong love of writing.

My experience switching back to this former pursuit was a lot like learning to walk and talk all over again. I devoured all the information I could find about writing and screenwriting, took courses in both disciplines, and combed the Internet for wisdom from other writers. I started reading voraciously, everything from novels to writers' manuals to screenplays. As I had done with my violin playing, I was determined to be the best writer possible.

From my travel journals I penned my first novel, *Travels With My Lovers*, which sent me on yet another journey. Ironically, the idea to turn my journals into a novel came to me when I was studying screenwriting in Los Angeles. Having penned several screenplays, I suddenly felt an urge to write a novel. Since my journals were already written, and they recounted experiences that I thought women could relate to on many levels, the time seemed right for this story. My teacher helped me transform the journals from a series of disjointed episodes into a coherent whole. After he helped me build the story, I worked with an editor who was uncompromising in her insistence that I agonize over every phrase, polishing the prose and adding depth to the characters and story line. I was determined to finish the book without setting it aside, rewriting until I could no longer bear to look at the words.

It was like studying a violin concerto: memorizing it, rehearsing it with piano and then with orchestra, until you're sick of it. Then you know you've learned it well enough to get up and perform it for an audience. The same holds true for writing and completing a book. Once you're totally fed up with everything about it, the characters, story line et al, and you can't even go to sleep at night without thinking about it, you know it's ready to be born and pushed out into the world on its own.

In the process of creating my novel, I learned about the differences between novel writing and screenwriting. I discover more about this difference with every novel and screenplay I write. Screenwriting is a far more restrictive discipline than novel writing. The writer is forced to squeeze an entire story, hundreds of pages, into one hundred-and-twenty pages, or, preferably less than that. No long, descriptive phrases, stream-of-consciousness, or getting into the character's head; just streamlined, spare, tight "bites" of dialogue and action. It's the most frustrating genre, and the most difficult to master: very much like trying to learn the violin, in fact. But in spite of my cursing, tearing my hair out, and endlessly pacing the floor, I still love the process.

It also is not an easy transition from novel to screenplay. Most novelists, even the most famous ones, don't write their own screenplays, and vice versa. I do. I drive myself crazy. But I'm passionate about both forms of writing, and since I've studied both and am intimately familiar with my own stories, I choose to write in both styles. Of my three published novels, two screenplays were adapted from the novel versions. My third and most recent novel, however, actually took shape as a screenplay before I turned it into a novel. Either way, each genre of writing informs the other in helpful ways.

The journals on which my first book was based were written over several years, and the book was born after a relatively short gestation of six months or so. But the brief journey to completion didn't mean I felt any less accomplished than if it had taken decades to write the book. All the voracious reading, studying in and out of classes, trial and error, and endless rewriting paid off in the end. Once I started, I couldn't stop. After Mozart premiered his first hugely successful opera, *The Abduction from the Seraglio*, he immediately set upon writing his next one, and the next one after that. A work in progress is the prelude to another work. Before wrapping a film, a director already is planning his or her next *oeuvre*, and a painter is conceiving his next canvas. That's what makes any creative form, and especially writing, so gratifying: the anticipation of crafting yet another story and watching the characters grow and transform on the page.

As writers we're told to write what we know. I certainly accomplished this in my first novel. Inspired by my own experiences traveling through Europe on holiday to some of the most exotic locales in the world, it tells of a woman's journey of self-discovery through five distinct periods in her life, each providing a provocative glimpse into her evolving hopes, dreams and desires. It's also a story about the love of travel. With its multiple enticing worldwide locations, the book fulfills many people's personal fantasies: to go to Europe - and beyond - and maybe even fall in love. It's also the story of the struggle to find someone to love, and everyone can relate to that. The creation of this novel prepared me for the novels to come.

There are a number of reasons why we write. One is for pure self-expression. Having to give up music, my own much-loved form of self-expression, I was then forced to reinvent myself. Writing seemed a natural segue for me, as I'm sure it has been for numerous others, though my own particular journey wasn't at all what I'd anticipated when I started out. I thought I'd be a violinist forever. Life has a way of handing you surprises when you least expect them. It certainly did so in my case.

Many of us write to entertain or put across a message. I am no different. The ultimate purpose of my book was, first, to give people an interesting fictitious journey. But in creating this novel, I soon discovered the message I wanted to present. It was to encourage all generations of women to express their emotional freedom: whether they are single or married; whether they are moms or not; whether they are the first ones on the plane or prefer to travel via the pages of one of the many wonderful books on travel themes.

Since I was forced to give up my professional musical career, writing has been both a creative outlet and a salvation. Creative people do so because they must; life is otherwise unlivable for them. I write because I love the process of creating characters, situations and settings. It comes right down to feeding my soul. We all have stories to tell. I write because these stories vie for my attention constantly, and because I feel other people can benefit from learning about other times, places and people. I give lectures to make my inner performer happy, and also to try to inspire and entertain people and encourage them to write as well. In the end, it all comes down to story. Put simply, where would we be without it? Entire civilizations have handed down stories from generation to generation. I am no different.

There is almost nothing I have written that isn't about my first love, music. I was first a musician, then a writer. I sang before I wrote, but I wrote before I played violin. Every novel, every screenplay, and every poem and essay I've written is infused with the music that has been my driving passion since I can remember. To me, music is a celebration, a basis for joy and edification in one's culture. The fact that I can use my love for it to heighten my stories is an unending source of inspiration for me. The arts are inextricably linked: poetry is music, narrative is music, and even paintings and sculpture are forms of music. These art forms are what I consider to be the foundation of my essence and creative force as a writer.

They say art imitates life and vice versa. I think the two are inseparable. What we create becomes an important part of our civilization, lasting evidence of who we were, what we felt and what we thought. The stories we tell, through art, music, and writing, are the key to the power of our culture. To me, this is what has endured and what will endure. The pen is truly mightier.

About the author

Erica has completed both the novel and screenplay of her suspense thriller, *Murder in the Pit*, which takes place at the Met, and currently is at work on the second novel in her "FourEver Friends" series chronicling four young girls' coming of age in the volatile 1960s and 1970s.

In addition Erica has developed a number of writing lectures and seminars on writing, which she has presented at various venues across the West Coast and on the High Seas. Topics range from "The Art of Self Re-Invention" to "Opera Meets Hollywood" and "Journaling for Writers: Mining the Gold of Your Own Experiences."

Recent release: Murder in the Pit, suspense

How a Rocket Scientist Becomes a Writer

by Stephanie Osborn

My first novel was a science fiction mystery published by Twilight Times Books. *Burnout: The mystery of Space Shuttle STS-281* is a techno-thriller about a Space Shuttle disaster that turns out to be no accident. The blurb:
"As the true scope of the conspiracy is gradually uncovered by the principal investigators, 'Crash' Murphy and Dr. Mike Anders, they find themselves running for their lives, as lovers, friends and coworkers involved in the investigation perish around them. What happened to the Shuttle? Who is responsible for the disaster and why? Why is the government calling it an accident? Why is someone willing to kill to keep it a secret? And how big is the conspiracy?"

There's a loooong story behind the writing of *Burnout*. For one thing, it took me somewhere between 10 and 15 years from the conception of the idea, and the book that's now published with Twilight Times.

Why? Simple.

I was too close to it.

Let's back up a couple decades.

I had just started working in the field when the *Challenger* disaster occurred. The program I worked at the time of the disaster was to have led to a Shuttle mission, and I would have been a Payload Specialist candidate. Shortly thereafter, the next phase of my project was cancelled, however, due to the grounding of the Shuttle Fleet. I found myself moving over into the payload flight control area, and learned a lot.

Over the course of a couple of decades I worked seven Space Shuttle missions, at least four increments on the International Space Station, and a number of space defense programs. That's a lot of experience. You get into some interesting conversations from time to time.

The seeds of *Burnout* began as a conversation between colleagues and myself concerning certain abilities of the Shuttle. It does have an autopilot, and a certain very limited amount of remote control capability. We began discussing under what circumstances a Shuttle could be damaged on orbit and still manage a reasonably safe descent.

Sounds morbid, I suppose. But the first step to preventing a disaster is to figure out what circumstances might cause one, and then work on developing preventive measures and recovery procedures. This means talking about it, working out the details of the malfunction and resulting disaster, then working backwards to "fix" it.

And yes, this did require considerable knowledge of the guts of a Shuttle. Betwixt us all, we did manage to possess the requisite knowledge, though no one person had the whole picture. I don't know that we ever did come to a consensus of whether or not it was possible.

But that was the birth of the idea. What if I wrote a story about a Shuttle accident, and the ensuing investigation? What sort of accident should it be? Should it cause merely a dangerous, or a catastrophic, malfunction?

And then the idea hit: What if it WASN'T an accident?

And that was when *Burnout* was born.

My first Shuttle mission was the first Spacelab flight after the post-*Challenger* Return To Flight. So my research for *Burnout* included all of the investigative reports and such for that disaster. But I didn't want anyone to think I was playing off a tragedy, so I deliberately changed the scenario. Whereas *Challenger* blew during the ascent phase, I'd make my fictional disaster occur during the entry phase - re-entry. And I set to work writing.

Now like I said, I worked in the space industry, civilian and military, for over two decades. I constructed and modified astronaut's experiment operation schedules, sometimes on the fly; I trained them, I trained colleagues, I wrote crew procedures for those experiments. I memorized safety considerations and sometimes helped out in malfunction procedures. One mistake on my part could have meant an injured, maybe even a dead, astronaut.

And here I was, squarely in the middle of said career, writing about a Shuttle disaster. The exact thing that I, as a payload flight controller, did NOT want to see, at least in real life. Certainly not on my watch.

It messes with your head, that.

So I'd write on it for a month or three, then put it aside when it got to me. I wouldn't look at it again for months at a time, sometimes as long as a year or more. Then the "plot bunny" would bite again, and I'd pull it out and go at it for another few months.

Somewhere in there, my husband Darrell introduced me to Dr. Travis "Doc" Taylor, best-selling science fiction author and at that time, my husband's co-worker. Darrell, who is a graphics artist and does all of the artwork for my book covers, had done some cover concepts for one of Travis' books. None of them were used, but they'd gotten to know each other in the process. So when Darrell told Travis that I was trying to get published, Travis suggested he introduce us. Darrell did, Travis and I clicked, and I acquired a writing mentor.

With that encouragement under my belt, I pushed on. Darrell got used to having to stomp up to me when I was writing; I tend to get "lost" in the story and become unaware of my surroundings. A husband suddenly materializing at my shoulder and saying something is apt to end up with him peeling me from the ceiling or detaching me from the ceiling fan.

And technology moved on. When I first started Burnout, I wrote on a low memory desktop computer with dialup and backed up onto 3.5" floppies - one manuscript to a disk. Now I have a laptop with wireless DSL, and back up several dozen books onto a single datastick - and the entire drive backs up onto portable hard drives. And periodically I burn a completed manuscript folder to CD for permanent storage.

Eventually I finished a rough draft and sent it to Travis, who'd promised to read it and give me a helpful critique. When he felt it was polished enough, he'd help me further by submitting it to one of his publisher friends. He said he'd been helped like that, and he intended to pass it forward. I promised him I would, too.

So I sent him the Word file and sat back to wait, glad I'd finally gotten the thing finished.

And then, the unthinkable happened.

Columbia went down. And I had a friend aboard her when it happened.

By that time, I had moved out of civilian work into military work, or my emotional response might have been even worse. As it was, I had to put the manuscript away for a good six months or so—not even look at it. You see, I'd lost TWO friends at one go: KC, and *Columbia*; because that was the Shuttle with which I'd worked the most.

I talked to Travis later; he said it kinda freaked him too, though not as badly as it did me: He didn't know anyone on board or anything. He did go over the whole manuscript in detail, and sent me back an entire list of compliments, critiques, and suggestions. Unfortunately I wasn't in any kind of emotional condition to use them. And wouldn't be for nearly a year.

I seriously considered trashing the entire manuscript. I downloaded the *Columbia* Accident Investigation Board's report and studied it, looking to see if I was way off in left field with my scenario. If I was, then I should probably trash the manuscript anyway. If I wasn't…

I wasn't. In fact, I didn't have to change a word.

In the end, I decided to go forward and dedicate the novel to Kalpana and the *Columbia* crew. I dug up Travis' notes and printed them out. I had to double the size of the manuscript, which meant essentially writing a whole 'nother story. So I wrote several stories, and intertwined them in a series of subplots.

Then I wrote the following:

"Dedication

"This book is respectfully and affectionately dedicated to Kalpana Chawla, and the other members of the crew of Space Shuttle *Columbia* on her final voyage; as well as to the *Challenger* Seven. They were explorers and scientists, first and foremost, and without them, and their gallant sacrifice, our lives would be the poorer. May we always remember that, sometimes, humankind's advances take everything we have to give, of our best and our brightest. May we never take them - our best, or our advances - for granted."

I also wrote an afterward in which I basically swore up and down that the book was written BEFORE the accident. I didn't want anyone prone to conspiracy theories thinking that, as a NASA insider, I'd written the REAL story of *Columbia* under the guise of fiction. And I'd like to reiterate that *Burnout* is entirely a product of my imagination combined with my research and experience.

And THEN… I sent it to Travis.

The first publisher he sent it to rejected it. Not for any particular flaws in the book; it turns out that 1) they weren't taking on newbie authors at that time, 2) it didn't fit the type of book they usually published. That was hard. But that's where I was thankful I had a mentor, because Trav wouldn't let me get down about it. Instead he sent it to Twilight Times Books. I clearly remember his email going out on a Thursday. On Sunday, the editor in chief, Lida Quillen, sent me an email outlining the standard contract for accepting a book. By Monday, I had my very first book contract in my hands, signing it to send back. I was about to become a published author!

Next came a year of reviewing, editing, honing, adding, subtracting, finding a rather large plot hole and plugging it, galley proofs, and being asked to write a book with another author. *The Y Factor*, co-authored with Darrell Bain, the 2nd book of the Cresperia Saga begun by Bain and Travis with the award-winning *Human By Choice*, came out in ebook the same day *Burnout* came out in ebook and print - Tax Day, 2009. Both hit best-seller lists with various sales groups, and both were favorably reviewed by a syndicated columnist in the New York Times.

Burnout has done rather well in the just over a year that it's been in publication. It's been nominated for awards in four different genres—ebook, science fiction, mystery, and thriller—and has garnered some interest from Los Angeles. I already have the contract in hand for the sequel, and a screenplay is in work now for a potential film project.

And in that period of time I was also contacted by a woman working on a Bollywood film biography of Kalpana Chawla, my friend who died aboard *Columbia*. I gave her my own thoughts and impressions on KC, and was pleased that my book helped provide some small memorial for KC and her crewmates.

Burnout's sequel, tentatively titled *Escape Velocity*, is in work. The *Burnout* master script is nearly finished (though the shooting script isn't even begun), and hopefully some producers will be interested in bringing my imagination to cinematic life in the near future. *The Y Factor*'s sequel, *The Cresperian Alliance*, is already out; I'm working on a book with Travis titled *Extraction Point*. And my literary agent (yes, I have one of those now!) has an entire series, the *Displaced Detective* saga, available for placement.

I left the space program shortly before Travis submitted *Burnout* for me. Now I write full time, and tutor part-time (mostly to get out of the house!). From rocket scientist to author in a couple of years' time. Not too shabby, I suppose.

About the author

Stephanie Osborn is a former payload flight controller, a veteran of over twenty years of working in the civilian space program, as well as various military space defense programs.

She is currently retired from space work. Stephanie now happily "passes it forward," tutoring math and science to students in the Huntsville area, elementary through college, while writing science fiction mysteries based on her knowledge, experience, and travels.

http://www.stephanie-osborn.com

Upcoming release: Extraction Point, SF with Travis S. Taylor

How I Came to Write Novels
The Story Behind The Story

by Dr Bob Rich

I became a writer through playing soccer with muddy rubber boots.

This was in 1980, when I had started on the greatest challenge of my life to date: building my own house with my own hot little hands. Just a few years before, someone had called me "the most impractical person on earth," and he was right. I was good at doing research. I could actually capture the interest of a first year university class of several hundreds in whatever the professor told me I had to teach them. This was in the Psychology Department of Monash University, in Melbourne, Australia. I could also run twenty miles without getting puffed. But anything practical, with my hands? Not me. I was competent at changing a light bulb, but when a fuse blew in my house's electrical system, I had to ask the neighbor to show me how to fix it.

And yet, here I was, pouring concrete for footings, laying stone walls, erecting huge posts, cutting joints in timber.

The walls were to be adobe, so the main task was to mix mud and make my bricks. This was good exercise, and although the weather was cold, the activity kept me warm. I worked at making and laying bricks eight days a week, starting before first light (my wife brought me breakfast at the building site), and finishing after dark. I am proud of a few crooked corners that were laid by feel in the dark.

One Sunday morning, I was squishing around the mud in my waterproof rubber boots when a young friend turned up. "Bob," she said, "you know we've got a special 'invite a friend' day, and we want to play a game of soccer, boys against girls, and we've got one more girl than boy, and none of the other adults wants to play and..."

Well, what could I do to resist a command like that?

She didn't even give me time to change footwear. And anyway, I was tough. I was sure I could run around and kick a ball with my heavy boots.

The game went well, and was a lot of fun—until I slipped and fell. My left knee hurt like crazy, and eventually I ended up in hospital to have a torn cartilage repaired.

The worst of it was that my house building had to stop. There I lay in a hospital ward, with nothing to do, bored out of my mind. There was nothing I could do except to think, and all my thinking was taken up by my building activities. I realized that my way of making bricks from mud was different enough from the normal to be of interest to other people. I could make them about four times as fast as the conventional method. Maybe I could write it up. I borrowed a typewriter (a computer in those days filled a huge room), and wrote two articles. I submitted them to two different magazines that specialized in such things.

One replied six weeks later, accepting my article but offering nothing in return. The other, *Earth Garden* magazine, replied by return mail, with a nice check, and a free subscription for a year as a contributor. They even sent me two extra copies of each issue to give away.

Guess which magazine I decided to continue with. I started a regular column on building with *Earth Garden*. Now, thirty years later, I still have an article in each issue. People send me questions on building, and I fool them into thinking that I can offer sensible answers. Occasionally I write an article that's of interest to me rather than a response to someone else.

The funny thing was that I, the most impractical person on earth, had accumulated enough knowledge to be of benefit to thousands of readers. My words struck a spark, and people sought me out to teach them building. I ended up teaching a ten week adult education course on building your own house. It ran successfully from 1984 to 1999.

Money was getting short, because it's difficult to earn the stuff while spending every spare moment on building. Also, in order to go through the many stages of creating a house, I needed to learn many new skills. I solved the two problems in one by getting casual work in the building trades. I worked with a concreting contractor for a while, and wrote a set of articles about how to construct formwork, make footings and slabs. I worked with a friend to lay a timber floor, then did some community work by making a floor for a new school building—then wrote up how to do that. I did some joinery, then made my own window frames, and a set of articles followed.

One day I thought that I must have enough material for a book. Only, I had no idea how to go about publishing one, marketing it, all that stuff. I got brave and wrote a letter to Keith Smith, then the editor of *Earth Garden* magazine, suggesting that he and I should write the book together. By then, Keith had published eight successful books. He also had access to many inspiring articles from the magazine we could reproduce with the authors' permission, and he was very knowledgeable about relevant issues like approaching a publisher. In addition, he had editing and book design skills, which were a complete mystery to me in those days.

I mailed the letter, then checked my post office box. In there was a letter from Keith, proposing that he and I collaborate on a building book. Was it meant to happen, or what?

It took us two years because I kept coming up with things that just had to go in. Keith got us a publisher, and we beat the publication deadline by two weeks. And the *Earth Garden Building Book: Design and build your own house* flew. The first edition came out in 1986. The fourth edition is still in print, and I have lost count of how many hundreds of thousands of copies have been sold.

In 1996, my daughter went traveling around Australia, using an organization called WWOOF: Willing Workers on Organic Farms. This involves living with a family for anything from a couple days to a few months, working with them and sharing their life. It is a wonderful way for young people to travel because they see the real life of a country, rather than just being exploited by the tourist traps. And it reduces the costs of traveling. Look up http://www.wwoof.org on the internet.

About 80% of her hosts owned a copy of the *Earth Garden Building Book*. When they found out that Miss Rich was the daughter of the author, they treated her like a princess. (Mind you, she deserves to be treated like a princess, but in her own right not because she is my daughter. And no, I am not biased.) Many of the houses she stayed in were built by their owners, using my book as the inspiration, following the recipes I had so painstakingly assembled.

Meanwhile, I'd stopped working in the building industry. I found the culture to be distasteful. Commercial building is a business. The aim is to work as fast as possible: get in and get out, and onto the next job. Therefore, everything is standardized, with all the "little boxes on the hilltop" being much the same. Considerable timber is wasted in the name of efficiency and standardization. There is no time to do a fine job, so that a knowledgeable person will see the shoddiness in most commercially built houses. Power tools rule, with their noise and danger. One builder firmly told me: "If you drop a nail, don't pick it up. Your time in doing that costs me more than the lost nail." Since I am a strong conservationist, I hate waste, and this definitely got me upset.

But money was still short. A friend, who was a nurse educator, suggested that I should train as a nurse. Nurses can get part time work anywhere, at any time. Only, to train as a registered nurse, I would have had to do a three year course, during which I would receive no pay. However, there was a more lowly occupation, then called State Enrolled Nurse in Australia. Now it is Registered Nurse Division 2, and is actually higher in training and responsibility than a new occupation that didn't even exist then, called Personal Care Attendant.

The training of a State Enrolled Nurse was one year, and apart from the first six weeks, it was based in a hospital, and the work was paid. So, I went for it.

This meant being far away from home for five days a week. In practical terms, I needed to live in the nurses' home that was attached to the hospital.

Most nursing students are female, and young, and gorgeous. Here I was, surrounded by sexy eighteen year old girls. I had a choice: to make a fool of myself running after them, or to do something constructive with my spare time. As a matter of self defense from activities I would disapprove of, I started writing short stories. I submitted one to a contest, and it won second place. This got me motivated: I like to get FIRST in whatever I do.

During my days off, while at home, one of my hobbies was working with timber. As well as continuing to build my house (an owner-built house is only ever finished just before it is to be sold), I made small wooden objects, toys, little figurines. I renovated furniture, and even repaired my wife's spinning wheel when it needed it.

So, I did an odd thing: I wrote a woodworking book that was actually a chain of short stories. By then, Penguin Books had taken over Nelson, the publisher of the *Earth Garden Building Book*, so I propositioned the relevant person there.

My project was nothing like any other instructional book he had ever seen. How could he publish something that refused to fit into a neat category, or more exactly, it fit into too many? Since most of the stories were autobiographical, this book could be classed as a biography. There were fictional stories, so it could have been a short story anthology. Also, it made people laugh, so it could even have been classified as humor. And yet, every story ended in a woodworking lesson. If you used the book as an instruction manual, you could make a whole range of projects ranging in complexity from a play house for your kids to a rocking chair for your grandmother. It taught you how to use tools ranging from a hammer to a chainsaw.

Penguin Books couldn't imagine how they could possibly market the book, so they declined, but life was too full and too busy to worry too much about a rejection. I worked only as many shifts as a nurse as were necessary to pay the few bills we had, and spent the rest of my time in living a near-sustainable lifestyle. We grew our own food, made for ourselves whatever we needed, entertained ourselves without a television set, and generally felt that we lived like Royalty. Life was good. (If you want to know why I was so stupid as to deliberately live below the poverty line, read my essay on the subject at http://bobswriting.com/essay.html). When I needed some extra money, I worked one more nursing shift a week for a while. For example, a daughter needed braces on her teeth. Orthodontic work costs lots, but I had it all paid off in no time—then returned to working away from home as little as possible.

As a result of the rejection, the woodworking book was put away, more or less forgotten. However, one day, a small publisher contacted *Earth Garden* magazine, and asked for someone they could commission to write a woodcraft book for them. The editor remembered that I had an unpublished woodworking book, and put the two of us in contact. So, my second book, *Woodworking for Idiots Like Me*, was born. The title is apt: if I could learn to be a craftsperson, then so can anyone else. Between 1994 and 1999, the woodworking book sold tens of thousands of copies, which is pretty good for the tiny Australian market. Penguin Books, eat your heart out.

Eventually, the publisher felt the market had been saturated, and ceased reprints. Years later, in 2006, I recast *Woodworking for Idiots*

Like Me into a REAL electronic book. It is like a large web page, with hyperlinks that allow you to skip around inside the book. As a result, *Woodworking for Idiots Like Me* won the EPPIE Award for its category of self-help nonfiction. This is the premier international contest for electronic books.

Part of my relaxation was to continue writing short stories. Over the years, whenever I submitted them to contests, they increasingly won prizes or were at least shortlisted. Before a computer crash a few years ago, I had a list of over forty wins in short story contests. But the list is lost, alas.

Nursing was good for me. The first two lessons were: "It is not your pain. You are not here to share it but to relieve it," and "Before you can care for others, you have to care for the carer first." This training gave me tools for returning to work as a psychologist; not in research, but as a therapist. I apprenticed myself to a friend who is brilliant as a healer of the spirit. Within six months, he told me I was fine to go it alone, and I did. At first, I made sure not to over-reach myself, and stuck to easy problems, but as my experience grew, so did my confidence. Still, the counseling was pocket money at this stage, and I needed to continue as a nurse. It was always too easy to work another shift.

But as my writing focus shifted more from nonfiction to fiction, I developed a terrible problem.

There was Mike, an ex-Vietnam vet who had attempted suicide. Someone had revived him, but too late. He was a veg: incontinent of both urine and feces, unable to move so that he needed two hourly turns for pressure care, arms contracted into chicken wings, no swallowing reflex so he had to be fed through a tube into his stomach... and he was THERE. When I talked to him, I could see understanding and intelligence in his eyes, and he responded to things going on around him. The stuff he was fed on resulted in very evil-smelling feces. When two attractive girls attended to him, they'd make comments about it, and I could see him tense up. When I found a minute to sit by his bed and talk with him, he would relax.

The deadly trap for a writer of fiction was: what would it be like to BE Mike? Anyone interested in a horror story?

Or there was eighty three year old Daisy, who had a rapidly fading body but a mind that was still interested in everything. One day she said, "Bob, there are too many things still to learn. I don't want to die yet! And she died anyway, not long after. As a nurse, I had to be detached. As a writer, I mourned her.

I got to know Jean, who used to be a very proud, private person until she had a stroke. When she became a patient in a nursing home, she was forced to have showers assisted by whichever nurse was on duty, male or female, young and old, and she hated every minute of it. To the other nurses it didn't matter, but I felt her pain.

At the other extreme was Cynthia. She had breast cancer, but had never gone along the medical path for treating it. She was a naturopath, and a Wiccan, and treated herself with herbs and meditation and listening to inspiring music and long nature walks. She managed to keep the cancer at bay for ten years. Then something went wrong. The cancer took off, and she ended up in palliative care, waiting to die in great pain. She refused morphine, because she said she wanted to be fully in tune with the experience of dying. She spent her last week on this planet writing her funeral service. My detachment failed with this lady: hers is the only funeral of a patient I have ever attended. And I wrote a little poem for her devastated husband:

> She will return.
> Having lived the joys and agonies,
> ecstasies and sorrows of this life —
> to do better the next time around.
>
> Will her passing make you a better person,
> as her presence did, by your side?
> Her school is in recess for now,
> for she has passed, though our examination is still to come.
>
> She will return.
> The memory will never fade, but the pain will ease.

These are merely four out of hundreds of such stories I could tell you about. Because of all this second-hand distress, increasingly I wanted out, but needed nursing to live on. And then, Dr Freud stepped into the picture. I had a fall and tore a tendon in my shoulder. Following the advice of my physical therapist I got back all my function, to the point of eventually being able to do 23 chinups and 82 pushups—but no work insurer would pay if I were to injure myself on a nursing shift. And of course, no employer would take me on without worker's compensation insurance.

In the way of the world, as soon as nursing became unavailable to me, my psychological practice started to grow. Soon I was earning far more money than nursing had ever given me, far more than my modest needs. The work was a joy, and still is. People come to me, full of hopelessness, despair, anxiety. A surprisingly few sessions later, they are powerful, confident and able to deal with the problems of their lives. Last year's terrible bushfires traumatized many people in my area. Most of them didn't know they had been affected. For example, one lovely seventeen year old girl was brought along to me months later, because she had changed so much. She used to be a star student, but that year, she was barely passing. She used to be very social, with lots of friends, enjoying sports and parties and dancing. Now, she spent much of her time alone in her room, and couldn't be bothered with doing anything.

I asked her what she had done during the bushfires.

She had no memory of the day at all. Her parents told me that while they were busy protecting their house, she had stayed out in the open, in the thick smoke, in the terrible heat, with burning embers falling out of the sky, with the fire front bearing down on her. She held the leads of four horses on the concrete driveway, saving their lives in this way.

I told them that somewhere within her mind, she had a box with the terrible memories inside it, and she was using tremendous amounts of energy to keep the lid of this box shut. This was why she had no energy left for study or a social life. But, what was in the box was not a monster — only the picture of a monster. She needed to take that picture out, and deal with it. After all, a picture cannot hurt you.

She came alone to her second session. We used hypnosis, and she visited that day in imagination. She relived all of it, in vivid detail. I contacted them again a month later. She had returned to her pre-trauma personality.

Can you see why doing this work is rewarding? Again, I could tell you hundreds of stories like this. Not all of my clients are so spectacularly successful, but I learn from all of them.

If I met you at a party, I wouldn't even remember your name five minutes later. If you came to me as a client and phoned me a couple of years later, I'd instantly remember everything about you, because for a short while, we had shared so much. I have had the privilege of saving people from suicidal depression, supported them through struggles with addiction, helped them to save their marriages, and kept them out of jail with cleverly worded reports. Every session with every client is a new, fresh experience, and it's all fodder for my understanding of the strange animal that dominates this planet.

So, in response to my work as a psychologist, my writing bloomed, and has kept improving ever since.

Another nonfiction book resulted: *Anger and Anxiety: Be in charge of your emotions and control phobias*. It is a self-help book that produces results, and is published by Twilight Times Books. They also have my first short story collection, *Striking Back from Down Under*. This is a fun book with an Australian flavor, in which the powerless gets the better of the bully in every story.

And this was my long and flower-decked passage to my novels.

Way back in the 1970s, I had an idea. I saw a group of teenagers in the forest. They were on a hunt that was to qualify them for adulthood, in the manner of hunter-gatherer societies everywhere. A small group of mounted nomads from the plains intruded on them. They killed the boys and abducted the girls, to be made into slaves. I saw this as a representation of where humanity has gone wrong, and I wanted to write a novel about it "one day."

Well, thanks to nursing and psychotherapy, I at last had the skills to write it. Four volumes of a series is now available, and you can read the first chapter of each at http://bobswriting.com.

Writing has also tumbled me into another profession: editing. I wrote a science fiction book, and was looking for a publisher for it. At that very time, a lady called Ariana Overton joined a writers' email group I was on. She had just been appointed as acquisitions editor of a new electronic publisher so I queried her. She accepted the book, and edited it herself. This book, *Sleeper, Awake*, won the science fiction category of the EPPIE Awards in 2001.

This publisher was run almost like a cooperative. All the editing was done by authors in the group who had some relevant qualification such as an English degree, or experience as a journalist or something like that. Also, each of us authors were asked to read books from the others, and produce reviews. One book was set in the same place I had used in one of my historical series, *The Travels of First Horse*, although at a different time. I reviewed it. In addition to the public review, I sent the author private comments indicating how he could improve the book.

The author was Max Overton, Ariana's husband. She immediately invited me to be an editor for the publisher. That publisher has long ceased to exist. *Sleeper, Awake* is now on the list of another publisher, and I am still getting a steady stream of editing jobs. I have edited many of the best books put out by Twilight Times Books.

So now, I have retired three times (as a research scientist, a builder and a nurse), and have four to go: writer, psychotherapist, editor, and one I took on in October 2009: a Director of my professional association.

And now I'll reveal something even more amazing. I've done all this while suffering from a major handicap: I have no sense of humor whatever.

About the author

Bob Rich is a multiple award-winning Australian writer, mudsmith and psychologist. He has done enough different things to fill a couple of life-times, but is too busy to worry about it.

Bob is cursed with a sense of humor that gets him in trouble all the time, creativity that makes it impossible for anything he does to fit into categories, and an intense empathy for other people, even if they are very different from him. This is his main tool in two very different endeavors: psychological counseling and writing.

He welcomes contact from readers of his books.
http://www.bobswriting.com

Current release: Anger and Anxiety: Be in charge of your emotions and control phobias

Tales of Intrigue, Adventure and Learning

by Dorothy Ann Skarles

In a book club, I once heard an author say, "You have to write a million words before you publish." Well, I must have written my million words, because it took me all of ten years to write my first novel, *Scent of Diamonds*, a mystery/suspense story.

The question of "where did the time go?" is the challenge many writers face. Creative writing takes time, and ideas can send a writer in ten different directions while writing and rewriting. In the interim, a story will often sit in a drawer waiting for inspiration to hit before the writing begins again. Unexpectedly, days, weeks, months, and years fly by without a finished project.

The adventure in learning how to write full-length books did take me a while. My love for writing first started in high school where I worked on the school's weekly, and it was there that I began to nurture a writing career on a newspaper. So when it was time to go to college, I continued the dream, graduating with a journalism degree.

I landed my first newspaper job in my hometown as a stringer. This is where you learn to write what the editor assigns to you. Payment is fifty cents by the column inch for each article you do. When the copy came out in the paper, the story really did get measured with a ruler—write three inches get paid $1.50, ten inches, get paid five bucks.

During my newspaper days, my only claim to fame was an interview with Nancy Reagan when her husband Ronald was the Governor of California. I was so nervous, and she was so gracious, trying to put me at ease by answering all my questions. When the article was finished and in print, I was surprised to receive my very first by-line along with my very first interview.

Trying to write short stories, but never seeming to finish, often grew hot and cold when my work along with family life infringed on dwindling time to write. As my mother used to say, "you have to pick yourself up by your own shoe strings, and keep going to succeed." So, reading short stories to crack this market turned into studying the novel. My discovery was that there were a lot of different ways for a hero to run up the stairs to the bedroom.

However, writing articles for the paper are short, sweet, and to the point, and a glimpse into the fictional novel had all these added scenes with different characters feeding in a story line that was hard for me to write. Now there was plotting. I had to deliver a believable hard-edged hero along with other characters who interacted realistically in a made-up plot that hooked a reader to turn the page. Everyone starts out as a beginner, but where do I begin?

Questions keep coming without any ready answers. What kind of story did I want to write? Where was my hero going? What did the hero look like? How did he feel? What kind of emotions did he show? Was he a good guy or a semi- bad guy? What? What? What? At the time, I called this padding. Not that you didn't need it, but when all the questions were answered, it was a mountain of writing to do. I was in my fiction apprenticeship, and I had to learn.

I began to read a variety of different genres in several different points of view. Mystery books on baffling novels about murder by Agatha Christie to Michael Crichton's suspense, or Elmore Leonard's wonderful way of writing dialogue the way his characters talked to sketching out profiles of major characters. I found that what I liked to read captured my attention and I wanted to become versed in the process.

While reading different genres and how-to books on writing, I started a notebook of subparagraphs. A general framework to jot down the interesting things on how other authors foreshadowed, made up complications and kept the action going in the areas of plot. How scenes moved from a beginning to danger, to climax and to a resolution. Key words that followed into a pattern that provided the reader the transitions needed for continuity to begin a paragraph. Such as: then I heard a man's voice-there was a nasty laugh-the car stopped-his love disappeared like the sunset. Appropriate devices and techniques to link the previous scenes with the new scenes.

Ideas for stories also came from personal experiences of friends who would openly discuss their divorce, troubles with teen age sex, drinking too much or relationships in general. These observations on their searching for ways to solve family problems and change lives would often find a way into another one of my note books. The painful on-again-off-again burdens of others often became a character's 'can of worms' to solve. Giving a reader a person with whom he or she can more easily identify, such as a macho athlete who lost the football game or voluptuous gal with a 44-d problem may be all that is required to hook a reader.

Newspaper headlines are gold mines for finding titles when stumped for a name to give a book. For instance, a title for a story on fish caught my eye. It read "Dangerous When Wet". The sudden thought great title popped into my head for the cover of my book. A story about a championship swimmer fighting the bad guy. The title is even good for a heroine who shoots her lover in the shower. Checking a top news story on a machine-massage parlor murder, or a stripper who gives hints on keeping in shape dancing are nuggets for collecting interesting backgrounds on a character.

Even a single word from a headline in a newspaper can be inspirational when seen how it was tweaked together with another word. Such as in my books: *Scent of Diamonds* for my mystery, *Enchanted Hunt* for my Hawaii fantasy book, and Learning *To Write The Easy Way for Fun, Posterity, Money,* my nonfiction. I also included a list in a notebook of what I thought were sensual words to invoke imaginary images in the mind of a reader. Words such as tongue, jock, hard-on, thrust, tingling. The surprise came when my sons read Enchanted Hunt, the book dedicated to them that included true teen-age adventures that happened to my boys when living on the Big Island of Hawaii, and I had entered them into the book. Those sensual words I thought were so innocent came back to haunt me. "Mother! How could you! You had that gal all over him!"

Eager to keep notes on other ideas of something felt, seen or perceived that I thought were interesting, I kept a "what-to-use book" to have a devil's advocate to brainstorm with, and help create plots for a novel. What I didn't realize at first from trying to write a short story of ten or fifteen pages is a novel would have to continue to grow into three hundred or more pages and have ten to twenty scenes. The uncertainty of adding more development to a story, and going in a door happy, and out the door mad while interacting in a scene with several characters can be mind boggling. Then, when you have to write and rewrite to find out how the process works, it is why your efforts may take ten years to write a novel.

The variations of writing step-by step of riveting creative disorder of storytelling does take time. But, how and when do you begin? Write when in the mood, and organize later? Keep a schedule? Do a page or two a day? Think out what to write while doing dishes or commuting to work? Write an outline? What? Write even on weekends and holidays? Good Lord, my work was cut out for me. I had to launch a game plan to make every free minute in an hour count. A writing goal had to be set.

So, to free this writer from losing anymore writing time, I announced, "I'm taking a needed hour right after dinner to write my novel-no interruptions." Of course, you might know, this didn't always work. The reactions at the dinner table can be summed up in amused smiles and nodding heads. "Yeah, right, mom."

But to keep from getting discouraged and, in lieu of anything better, I started to fill my thoughts with the family trip to Hawaii, and my sons telling stories of their escapades running through the jungle, finding a lava tube and seeing wild boars. Now, I had my vivid setting for what turned out to be my second book titled, *Enchanted Hunt*. When I began to muse on characters and "what and who would be in the story," the three most important characters in any book came to mind-the hero, the heroine, and the villain. I widened the scope to add a true Hawaiian Kahuna that I had met. A whimsical old man with rotten teeth from eating sugar cane and who held the mysteries of bygone days on the Big Island with his love for the fire goddess Pele.

This book took a little over a year to write while getting up in the morning at 4 AM and working three hours for 365 days in the year. I also read a lot of nonfiction books on Hawaii for research. The many brochures I'd saved on places to visit, and stories on Pele gave me a real feel for the Island. The determination to finish what I started really did get me to the end. How else to get three hundred manuscript pages of a story to make a novel with thirty chapters and at the very least thirty scenes?

The way I described the process of writing my two novels is not the only way in the world to write a book. Sometimes the twists and quirks of fate will give you a non-fiction book named, *Learning To Write The Easy Way for Fun, Posterity, and Money*. This third book grew and simmered in a classroom incubator until born with a method of teaching that worked.

I had a journalism degree, but now my teacher's degree would come out of mothballs even though I'd never worked as a teacher... until.....

We moved to a new town, and me without a job, and suddenly luck came to the rescue. I had a writer friend who taught at the Adult School, and said they needed a class in memoir writing, and would I take the job. It only involved three hours and one day a week.

All at once, I needed to get over the hurdle of "how to teach," and penetrate the teaching mystique. Lesson plans had to be made and I was thrown into the creative process. In the meantime my husband advised, "You're a journalist, focus on the journalistic way of using the six basic questions: The who? What? Where? When? Why? How?"

And as the saying goes, I learned by doing right along with my students who, I am proud to say, have sold poetry, articles, short stories on personal experiences, memoirs, and three wrote novels that sold. One student turned his memoir into fiction, another did a children's story, and the third wrote his story of being a black man in the Navy in World War II. He also went on to sell a non-fiction book on blacks in sports. Not only students who wanted to write memoirs signed up for the Memoir Class. Younger students earned three credits to graduate from high school, and learned how to write a query letter to apply for a job. My journalistic teaching did pay off. The nonfiction book, *Learning To Write The Easy Way...* includes all the lessons we did in class.

The company my husband worked for moved him from one end of California to the other and throughout my career, I have worked on three newspapers and five regional magazines. In the interim, I read, studied, and analyzed several kinds of stories and genres while trying to spur myself on to write more than "just the facts, ma'am."

However, my first adventure in learning to write fiction really started when we moved to Long Beach, and I signed up for a course in writing short stories. I soon discovered writing for newspapers or doing article interviews for magazines wasn't the same as writing a book.

I now had to knuckle down to master the finer points in plotting with a germ of an idea, create dialogue, and bring characters to life. In addition, I had to find the right word to use in a sentence, but not fall so in love with it that I used it three or four times in five paragraphs in a row.

"Searching for the right word to use," instructed the teacher, "is a forward step toward selling." She also advised at the time, "write about what you know." A cliché, but it actually worked for me. I sold my first short story called "The Poker Game" with a twist ending on its second time out to a regional magazine. The first time out, I got a rejection, but I did receive a very exciting telephone call from the editor of a gaming magazine who said, "liked the story, but not for us." That was when I learned to study the magazine I wanted to sell to-search out the kind of articles or stories that fill their pages, look at their advertisements and what kind they are, and never ever send a story on smoking if they didn't run at least one ad on cigars or cigarettes. My first short article for a magazine was on cooking, and I received my first fan letter wanting to know if I was related to their family. They had the same last name as mine and came from Greece.

What I really found invaluable from the short-story class was the five-girl- critique group that four had already published, and I had joined. They helped me to hone my skills and become a better writer. Learning to pay attention to a character's name was an eye-opener for me. Their instructions were to never have two names start with the same first letter or have names resembling each other. It only causes confusion to the readers. Get rid of the Robbie and Robert. Finding the right name to fit a hero, heroine or a villain takes a lot of thinking. I changed names several times, and read them out loud before making a decision. I also learned to keep track of characters and what attributes I gave them in a notebook so I wouldn't forget——like what color eyes I gave them or how tall they were so I wouldn't write in chapter ten the hero had blue eyes instead of brown and he only stood six feet instead of six two. Having a critique group helps to write a novel.

In my search to learn the ins-and-outs of writing, I attended my first writing conference where I met the speaker, Walt Morey, who wrote *Kavik The Wolf Dog*. Mr. Morey and I sat on the college steps early one morning talking about how to begin learning to write a mystery. His advice was to read all kinds of mysteries and to study openings, middles, and ends. Then when I found one that I felt I could read several times over, he instructed me to type out the first chapter word for word, smiled at me, and laughed.

When I asked what was funny, he answered. "You probably won't get beyond page four or five before you want to change something. The name of the hero (or heroine), what he said, what he did, or even change characters he meets along the way. Then as you type, you will gain ideas and insights on how to format a mystery story while getting a feel for tone and pacing so you can write your own."

A ream of typed pages proved that his advice worked, and I started to think about the kind of mystery I would like to write. I decided to set my novel in Mexico and write a murder mystery around a few things that happened to my husband and me on our first trip to Guadalajara, the city known as eternal spring. The home of strolling troubadors and mariachi music found on almost every corner. Many of my characters' experiences as Americans in a foreign country happened to us.

It should also be noted that in my story *Scent of Diamonds*, we actually did sit in a Consulate's office for seven days because our travel agent didn't supply us with a tourist card and proof of citizenship to travel from Mazatlan to Guadalajara. Federales did stop us from going into a restaurant and escorted us to the plane going to the United States. The close encounter certainly did enable me to write a feeling of fear for my characters' ordeals.

Some of our other experiences between the covers of my book included a stroll down wide boulevards, seeing museums, beautiful churches, gay fiestas, tasting fiery foods and drinks, and shopping at the Mercado market where you could buy anything from native herbs to hallucinogenic cactus. It also seemed fit to include racing bus drivers on the wrong side of the road polluting the sky with a blue haze. While sight-seeing in Tlaquepaque, known for its famous pottery, my husband bought an unusual, sexually-provocative figurine, and I describe it in the book. And as in the Land of Oz, the city also claims the distinction of being the center of witchcraft known for their good and bad witches and using black magic. Me-I bought picture post cards to write notes on the back of what I wanted to remember using my five senses.

Almost everything from cactus to orchids, and rubbing elbows with delightful people found their way into *Scent of Diamonds*, including my husband who became my model for my Greek hero. As I wrote, and rewrote, my maiden voyage for this would-be writer's first book finally ended with a long sigh. Then the hard-part came. Real courage was needed to send it out and get it published.

The rest, as someone once said, is history, and now begins another start for another book.

Writing what you know from your experiences and travels may be a cliché, but it does build-up credibility, and if you write it convincingly enough, it will open a publisher's door—trust me! Persistence will pay off.

As to my future, I have finished *Temptation for sale*. A comedy of errors with quirky wives trying to get their men in bed and husbands trying to keep the home fires burning. Tarnished reputations for all, with a heroine who finally stands up for herself.

My next goal for a writing project is brainstorming ideas for a murder mystery, *Murder on pudding lake*, to put in a new notebook.

About the author

Dorothy Ann Skarles who writes under daSkarles has appeared in a variety of publications. She has published more than two hundred articles in trade journals, magazines and newspapers. She earned her first byline as a cooking columnist for a local family owned newspaper in California.

Current release: Learning to Write the Easy Way for Fun, Posterity and Money

A Solution and a Seed
Novel Writing as Growing a Crystal

by Daniel C. Starr

Once upon a time, in the summer of 1967: the British invasion of pop music was well underway, the Vietnam War was tearing apart American politics, Richard Nixon was about to become president... and I was oblivious to all this excitement. A suburban sprout of thirteen, I passed the summer between junior and senior high school by drawing fanciful pictures of space ships, making up rather silly stories around them, and dreaming that maybe someday I'd write a science-fiction novel. And in my summer school physical science class, I attempted to grow crystals.

Crystal growing was, and still is, a mainstay of high-school science. It's a process that borders on magic—dissolve some chemicals in a jar of water, drop in a tiny "seed" crystal on a string, and watch as it grows into a small gemstone. Maybe it's the deep blue, prismatic crystal of copper sulfate, or the rich green of a nickel compound, or the back-to-back pyramids of potassium aluminum sulfate dodecahydrate (this stuff is better known simply as "alum," but the long chemical name is so much fun to say). I set my sights on the holy grail of high-school crystal-growing, a deep purple crystal of "chrome alum" at the heart of a larger, transparent crystal of plain alum. If I succeeded, I would create a tiny work of art.

If I succeeded. Alas, while crystal growing is simple in theory, it's remarkably difficult in practice, especially for an impatient thirteen-year-old during a midwestern summer. We'd have a hot day, the solution would warm up a bit, and my seed crystal would dissolve. I'd successfully grow the purple crystal, but when I put it into the second solution, the one that would grow the clear crystal around it, I'd watch helplessly as the clear stuff grew in a disorganized mess. Dust would find its way in, and my single, beautiful crystal became a disorderly hunk of sand. It often seemed that my prettiest crystals were forming among the junk in the bottom of the jar, while the crystal at the end of my string grew into a mess. Worst of all, I'd try to rush things, leading to a crystal that grew haphazardly in all directions. After a frustrating summer, during which I'd grown a few small crystals but failed miserably in all my attempts to grow the crystal-within-a-crystal, I got on with my life. Freshman-year science was biology, and I was delighted to put the chemicals away and begin disassembling small creatures.

Fast-forward to the spring of 1975: disco music ruled the airwaves, the Vietnam war and the Nixon presidency were history, and I was finishing up my bachelor's degree in an obscure area of engineering called "computer science." While I had long since given up attempting to grow crystals, I was still trying to write. In fact, I was trying harder—with my required engineering courses mostly done, I spent most of the year filling out my quota of humanities and social-science electives. After taking a class in science fiction and another in religions of the far east, I signed up for a spring-quarter creative writing workshop.

Because I was (and am) more than a little lazy, my first "story" for this workshop was an account of my run-in with a psychoanalyst-in-training at the college counseling office. The story barely qualified as fiction—I changed some names and exaggerated a few aspects of the would-be shrink's personality, but otherwise simply related what had happened.

The class loved it. The professor went so far as to say I should consider a career in writing instead of engineering (of course, this *could* have been a comment on my engineering skills, but my grades were pretty good). With such support, I decided my next effort would be real fiction, not just thinly-disguised accounts of personal experience.

I started with a more-or-less fantasy story, built around a tall, skinny guy who went by the name "Skornuck." I knew very little about him beyond my one Big Idea: he would be absolutely opaque to any form of mind-to-mind communication. As a result he wouldn't pick up all the little unwritten-and-unspoken rules of behavior that normal people exchange through a kind of low-level telepathy, and as a result of that, he'd be clueless and awkward in social situations. To make a story around this idea, I had to contrive a situation in which his handicap would become an advantage. I came up with a scenario involving feedback systems (about which I'd learned a lot in my engineering classes) and sex (about which I'd learned next to nothing, being an engineering student at an all-guys school), which answered the question of why there aren't more mind-readers walking the streets of our towns.

My other project, started at the same time, was much bigger—a novel intended to riff a bit sarcastically on the popular "planetary romance" stuff that was such a big seller in the SF/Fantasy market at the time. I was going to set up the reader, then make a hard left turn and expose the fundamental flaw in such stories. I was going to be clever and cutting-edge, and while the memories have faded with time, I suspect the word "deconstruction" may have even escaped my lips at some point.

Alas, I had about as much success with these two writing projects as I'd had with my crystal growing eight years earlier. The Skornuck story was just a free-floating idea—as my professor commented, it lacked plot, conflict, resolution, and much in the way of characters. As for the attempted novel, I never got up the nerve to show any of it to him, or to anybody. I couldn't keep the thing under control; the characters wandered, the story grew in directions I didn't want it to go, eventually turning into exactly the kind of tale I was trying to criticize. When I pulled the plug on that project, I had about thirty thousand words that weren't so much a story as a big pile of random, derivative junk. Just what the world needed—another "Barsoom" fanfiction fiasco.

Fortunately, I didn't have much time to mourn the apparent demise of my writing career. Graduation was upon me, followed by a career in the telecom industry. For the next twenty-six years, I worked in the development of big systems that connect phones to each other. Along the way I played a small role in bringing to market an exotic new technology called "cellular" (you might have heard of it), got a patent for an invention that was never built, and invented something that made a lot of money but couldn't be patented. I made a fair income for myself, and a pretty penny for my employers.

And what about writing? I was writing more or less every day. Not novels or stories, though—just piles and piles of memos, proposals, plans, specifications, reports and manuals. Aside from a few papers intended for conference and journal publication (which were heavily revised by the corporate lawyers), most everything I wrote during these twenty-six years was stamped "COMPANY CONFIDENTIAL—NOT FOR RELEASE."

On the other hand, I *thought* a lot about stories and novels. My thoughts and daydreams often came back to the character I'd created in the spring of '75, the skinny young man with the unreadable mind. I continued to try to figure out where Scrornuck (his name had changed a bit sometime in the early 1980s) had come from, who he was, and what his big story might be.

At the same time, I found myself noticing things in the world around me, and storing them away for... well, at the time I didn't really know what for. I've just always had a habit of noticing small oddities in the world around me. For instance, one fine evening in the winter of 1977 (I think), I had dinner in a fast-food franchise joint built into what looked like an abandoned church. The original stained-glass window was gone, and in its place hung a new window, sporting the image of all the company's TV commercial characters, gathered together in a pose that looked like the Hamburger Shepherd And His Flock. Was I dining in the First Church of the Burger? This got me thinking about all the ways in which corporations co-opt religious imagery, and I found myself wondering if a corporation would ever have the nerve to actually declare itself divine (why not? the Roman emperors liked to consider themselves gods). Hmm, I thought, a church built around worshiping a corporate mascot... Might be fun to write about that someday... And then I got back to my burger, and the visit with friends that had brought me to this town in the first place, and let the idea drop out of my conscious mind.

But these ideas didn't disappear completely—the idea of a corporate church went into what a friend dubbed the "cesspool of knowledge," along with all the other strange, funny, cool or otherwise interesting things that passed before my eyes. From time to time, things would return to the surface in unexpected combinations—an observation I just dropped into the "cesspool" would hook up with something that had been in there for a while, and I'd find a new floater. I recall seeing a fairly bad movie based on the Arthurian legend of Sir Gawain and the Green Knight. For some reason, the beheading game that brackets the legend caused the title song from the John Waters film "Hairspray" to float to the surface, and I found myself wondering: *how might somebody use a can of hairspray to win the Knight's game?*

As I dumped ideas into the "cesspool of knowledge," I daydreamed about my imaginary friend Scrornuck (note to aspiring novelists: only as a writer can an adult spend time with imaginary friends and not be considered crazy). In time, I found I had come to know the guy pretty well—who he was, where he came from, what was his favorite beer, and so forth. I had a fair collection of his adventures percolating away in the back of my head—Scrornuck slays a dragon, Scrornuck plays the beheading game, Scrornuck gets abducted by aliens—but, to my frustration, I found I still didn't have a story. I was no closer to becoming a novelist than I had been in the spring of '75.

Fast-forward a little further, to the fall of 1999: Disco was pretty much dead, the tech-stock bubble was fully inflated, I was discovering the joys of elite frequent-flyer status, and the idea of writing a novel was about the farthest thing from my mind. Until, one Thursday night...

I had just returned from the Team Building Meeting From Hell—four days holed up in a room fifteen hundred miles from home, with a half-dozen coworkers and a consultant who was supposed to assist us in becoming a better Team. Instead, we'd ended up squabbling and bickering, and by the end of the week, most of us weren't talking to each other and all of us wanted nothing more than to get home. Naturally, my flight was delayed, and when finally I arrived home in the late evening, I wanted nothing more than to wind down with some mindless entertainment and hit the sack.

My daughter was (and still is) big into Japanese animation, so I sat with her in the basement, watching the last few episodes of a series she happened to have on videotape. It was relaxing, it was pleasant to be back home, and the story was entertaining enough. And, as the cartoon finished, a thought crept unbidden into the back of my mind: *I could have written that final scene better.*

Thoughts like that are dangerous, especially at bedtime. I found myself running the scene—or more precisely, my rewrites of it—through my head all night long, with different variations. Shut up, I told myself, go to sleep, you've got to go to work tomorrow. But nothing, it seemed, would shut off the compulsion to go over and over and over with that scene. So, around four in the morning, I gave up, got out of bed, went downstairs and opened up the laptop computer. By six, I had a scene of a couple thousand words written. At eight, I called work, told them I was having a jet-lag problem and wouldn't be in today, and went back to bed.

When I awoke and read what I'd written after my night of temporary insanity, I found it wasn't a rewrite of the *anime's* climactic scene—it seemed to be the climax of some other story, a story that had yet to be written. And, I realized after I read it a few more times, the main character of this scene was none other than my old friend Scrornuck. Perhaps, after twenty-four years of knocking around in the back of my head, he had grown impatient. Maybe my restless night had been him yelling, "Enough waiting! You are going to make me live, you're going to tell my story, and you're going to do it *now!*"

The only problem was, I had no idea what Scrornuck's story might be. I had nothing but this one scene—no idea how things got to this position, no idea who the other characters were, nothing. This scene was like all the other little "Adventures of Scrornuck" I'd daydreamed about over the years—not a story, just some things that happened to the character. At least on the surface, it seemed no more destined to become a real live novel than any of my other daydreams.

There was one difference, though: the other adventures existed only as daydreams, while this one scene existed as two or three thousand actual words. That seemed significant: for the first time since the spring of '75, I had something *real*.

So I considered my options: I could do the sensible thing, and simply file this scene away, to be revisited when I was retired and finally had time to write. Or I could follow the scene and see where it went. I chose the latter, though in all fairness, I'm not sure how much real choice I had in the matter—if I'd chosen to file it away for later, I might have found myself up all night the next night, and the night after that, until I finally gave in.

So, for the next six years, I worked on the book that finally became *The Last Protector* (and I mean "finally" in the most literal sense—the book didn't receive an actual title until I was ready to start submitting it to publishers. Up to that point, I simply thought of it as "the Scrornuck book"). Most of the time I had no idea what the story was. But as I struggled, argued and played with my steadily growing collection of imaginary friends, the story slowly revealed itself to me.

It was a messy and often frustrating process. Things wouldn't stay where I put them. Scenes that started up near the beginning insisted on moving to near the end. Secondary characters came into existence, only to disappear when I found alternate ways to move the plot along. Whole scenes—whole series of scenes, tens of thousands of words—just disappeared entirely. That climactic scene, the one that had triggered the whole process, got rewritten so many times it was barely recognizable after its last revision.

As I struggled with the story, I found things floating up from the "cesspool of knowledge" just when I needed them. At one point, I discovered I was writing a time travel/alternate universe story, which left me with a problem: I had yet to read a story that accommodated time travel, free will and causality in a satisfying way. While I was stewing over this, the concept of activation energy—something I'd learned in high school chemistry—floated up and demanded my attention. Aha! Just what I needed!

To my surprise and delight, many of the "Adventures of Scrornuck" that I'd been daydreaming all those years also floated up and found their place in the book—even the combination of a beheading game and hairspray turned out to have a home in the story!

Of course, there were also very practical obstacles to getting the book written—work, of course, often got in the way. I seemed to get my best ideas at the most inconvenient times, like in the middle of a serious corporate meeting. I suppose I was fortunate to be regarded as something of a brilliant eccentric—otherwise, I might have seen more than just a few raised eyebrows when I started scribbling furiously because I'd just figured out how the peculiar arrangement of fire escapes in our building could be used to resolve a chase scene. Things didn't get any more convenient when I took early retirement in '01 (after the tech-stock bubble popped)—on many occasions, my Harley was pulled over on the side of the road while I scribbled down yet another note to myself.

Because the muse was so unpredictable, I found myself looking for ways to bring a proper writing device with me at all times. Some of these experiments worked better than others—the blueberry-colored iBook survived a two-thousand-mile motorcycle trip (though I lost a lot of saddlebag space to the padding I put around it), but the attempt to put the whole manuscript into a PDA for a week-long conference was a disaster (I lost a week's worth of work when the security people at the Eugene airport set their X-ray machine for "Microwave Burrito, Well Done").

After six years of writing, revising, rewriting, to the point where I had files on my computer with names like "Chapter 7 Version 34F," I had a complete novel, a hundred eighty thousand words that I thought were good enough to be submitted to a publisher. So, in 2005, I started collecting rejections, and after a year or so of that, I got a contract with Twilight Times Books. After another two years of edits and revisions, *The Last Protector* hit the shelves in the spring of 2008.

Looking back, I tried to figure out just what had happened. How had this process that seemed to begin with a sleepless night and a scene scribbled in the wee hours ended up producing a book with several characters, a pretty complex plot, and all those little details that the reviewers so enjoyed?

I pondered on this question, and eventually realized I'd come full circle: in writing *The Last Protector*, I hadn't just written the novel I couldn't write in the spring of '75; I'd also grown the crystal I couldn't grow way back in the summer of '67. And it wasn't just an ordinary crystal—with Scrornuck's origin story folded into his here-and-now adventure, I'd grown the crystal-within-another-crystal that had been my ultimate goal.

Well, in a metaphoric sense, anyway: crystal growing is about preparing a *solution* with the right amount of chemical dissolved in it, and dropping in a *seed* around which the crystal forms. In the case of my book, what I'd called the "cesspool of knowledge" served as the solution, and the scene I'd written in that sleepless night was the seed. And in both cases, the stuff that's in the solution attaches itself to the seed, one little bit at a time, until the seed's grown into something big and (we hope) beautiful.

If that's the case, then I ought to be able to look back at my experiences and find in the crystal growing failures some lessons for the aspiring novelist (and vice-versa, but this is ultimately an article about writing, not growing crystals). Let's see what we can find.

The first insight could be that *the solution has to be prepared first*. Drop a seed crystal into a jar of plain water, and it just disappears. You've got to dissolve the proper chemicals in the jar first.

I think this is why my early attempts at writing fizzled. I had ideas, but I didn't yet have the experience to turn the ideas into a story. The Skornuck story went nowhere, perhaps, because the idea (about mind reading, feedback loops and sex) needed to play out in the context of a romantic relationship—an area in which my experience at the time was approximately nil. My novel also involves a romantic relationship, but by the time I started writing it, I was forty-five, married, and considerably more experienced in how men and women get along. The abortive novel was supposed to be about responsibility and the misuse of technology, but to a senior in college, these are just theoretical issues, bones with no meat on them. By the time I tackled unintended consequences in *The Last Protector*, I had seen firsthand how the best of intentions can still lead to the worst of results, and so could develop these themes more realistically (well, realistically within the context of a society that worships a cartoon character, anyway).

Setting up the solution takes time. Some things dissolve faster than others. In the case of my "cesspool of knowledge," it took at least a quarter-century to get the solution ready. Of course, I wasn't aware that I was preparing a solution—if I'd known I was loading up the solution that would one day condense into a book, I'd have done some intentional research instead of just letting stuff accumulate as I went through life. On the other hand, in some ways I was consciously doing a sort of research—when I noticed things that seemed a bit odd and worth remembering, I tended to play around with them, ask myself how they'd work in a story. I wasn't just having experiences. I was stirring them into the "Cesspool," to make sure they'd properly dissolve.

Of course, no matter how much stuff is in the solution, nothing will grow until you drop in a seed. It's actually possible to create a "super-saturated" solution—one containing more of the chemical than can in theory dissolve in that volume of water. The stuff remains in an uneasy solution until you drop in a tiny crystal, around which the bigger one will grow.

It's the same with writing—you can wander around with a head full of interesting ideas, observations, details, jokes, whatever—but until you drop in some kind of a nucleus for the story to condense around, you won't have a novel. In the case of *The Last Protector*, the "seed" was a short scene from a Japanese cartoon, a scene I thought I could have written better. Even as I was writing it for the very first time, at five in the morning after a sleepless night, it was changing, growing, picking up bits and pieces from the solution around it.

I wonder now whether those various little "Adventures of Scrornuck" that I daydreamed during the '80s and '90s might have served as seeds had I written them down. I might have ended up with a much different book, much sooner. Then again, they might not have been good seeds, which might be why I left them unwritten. Ah, if only the alternate universe stuff were real—I could visit another universe in which I had written one of those adventures down, and see what story crystallized around it!

Crystals don't grow from the top down, or the bottom up, of course. Neither do novels, at least not in my experience. I'm told there are authors who can sit down, type "Once upon a time..." and then proceed straight ahead till they reach "...they lived happily ever after." No doubt there are such people, but I'm not one of them! I seem to write everywhere at once. The "seed" for *The Last Protector* was a sort of climax to the adventure, appearing near the end, but I didn't simply write backwards from that climax to reach the beginning. I wrote beginnings, I wrote endings, I wrote middles, I wrote scenes without the slightest idea of where they'd eventually wind up.

If you could watch a crystal growing at the molecular level, you'd see it's not a simple process of molecules coming out of the solution and attaching themselves to the crystal. All the time, everywhere on its surface, some molecules are coming out of solution, while other molecules that were part of the crystal are deciding to dissolve again, perhaps to reattach themselves later on the other side of the crystal.

This was also the normal state for *The Last Protector*. Scenes, lines, and events rarely stayed where I initially put them. I'd be absolutely convinced that a particular event fit *here*, in the conclusion, and a day later I'd find it actually belonged at the beginning. I'd delete a scene, quite certain it had no place in the story, only to put it back in a few days later in a place I'd never thought it might fit. It is more than a little unnerving to have pieces of the story—sometimes quite large pieces—seemingly move by themselves to new locations, or take themselves out of the story only to put themselves back in again, but that seems to be the way the universe works. It's a logistical nightmare to keep track of where things are at the moment—which chapter is that scene in? Or is it in the "deleted scenes" file? It's gotta be somewhere...

One of the most painful lessons I learned in my crystal-growing days was that the process goes at its own rate. The rate was always slower than I wanted it to be, and there were days when, because of changing temperatures or humidity, nothing seemed to happen at all. These days were dangerous, for they tempted me to try to make something happen. On more than one occasion, I had a pretty nice, small, slow-growing crystal, and tried to speed up its growth by oversaturating the solution. The result was a disaster—a mess of jagged angles and veils, something so unsalvageable that I ultimately broke it up, re-dissolved it and started over. I've found the same thing about writing. At least for me, the book gets written at its own pace, and if I try to force things to go faster I'll just make a mess that I'll eventually throw out. I've come to accept that there are days when I'm not going to write anything, at least not anything worth keeping, and on those days I give myself permission to *not write today*. Yes, I know, this goes against the advice of many who say you must put in two hours each day, writing your favorite dirty word a thousand times if you can't think of anything else. If the underlying problem is a lack of desire or self-discipline, I suppose this is good advice. But in my case it seems that most of the time, an inability to write is a sign that things are stirring and mixing in the "solution," and the best thing for me to do is wait till the next batch of molecules are ready to stick themselves into place.

There were days when the crystals didn't seem to grow at all, and there were even a few days when they seemed to shrink—more molecules were leaving the crystal than were sticking to it. On those days, it was easy to believe the whole enterprise was doomed and the most sensible thing for me to do would be to flush the whole mess down the sink and give up. But, if I resisted this temptation and kept at the task, in time I'd find things growing again. When working on *The Last Protector*, I had many such days. I'd wake up in the morning realizing there was a huge, unfixable plot hole, and quickly convince myself the entire project was an unsalvageable mess and my best move would be to walk away and forget the whole business of writing a novel. Oddly enough, this often turned out to be the best thing to do—walk away for a little while, maybe get the Harley out of the garage and go for a ride. Most of the time I'd return a few hours later with an idea of how to fix the hole, and over the next few days it would usually turn out that the problem wasn't anywhere near as bad as I'd thought. Of course, I didn't know for sure that I'd fixed the plot holes until the book was actually finished—and in truth, I still don't know for sure!

There's always scrap material at the bottom of the crystal-growing jar, and some of that scrap seems to grow into prettier crystals than the one growing at the end of the string. It's frustrating to see such nice crystals in the scrap, and it's certainly wasteful to have it down there, but the process just doesn't seem to work without some discarded material at the bottom of the jar. I found the same thing happening in my book—I'd create what I thought was a beautiful scene, only to discover a bit later that it just didn't fit into the story. But, just as in crystal growing, the creation of these scrapped scenes is an essential part of the process. Writing scenes that didn't make it into the book taught me a lot about the characters, their motivations, and their history. These were things I needed to know so that the scenes that did make it into the book were consistent and believable. At one point I found I had written something over thirty thousand words of scenes in which the bad guys plot their next step—and then, I decided to keep a tight focus on the hero, which meant these scenes all went away. But the work of writing them wasn't wasted—even though the hero (and therefore the reader) weren't shown what the bad guys were doing, *I* needed to know what they were up to. And some of these scenes went on to a sort of second life—I took a selection of them (scenes that weren't spoilers) and stuck them on my website. Just about every DVD that comes out includes a set of deleted scenes. Why shouldn't a book do the same thing?

So, if I did everything right (which I rarely managed to do), I'd finally pull a finished crystal out of my jar. And after all the writing, submitting, and re-submitting, I finally got a publishing contract for my book. Hooray! Pop the champagne, we're done... right?

Not yet. Just as that crystal has to be cut, polished and mounted before it becomes a piece of beautiful jewelry, the "finished" book needed to go through editing and revision. *The Last Protector* spent two years in editing after we signed the contract—and that's in addition to having been carefully scrutinized by four other trusted readers before I even thought about submitting it to a publisher. It's absolutely essential to get a fresh look from somebody who's not familiar with the story (that is, not the author—unless you've run into the Mister Smith and his "neuralyzer"). Editors and reviewers ask hard questions, uncover holes in the story, and deliver the bad news that the flaw you were hoping nobody would notice... uh, it just got noticed.

For me, editing and revision were the most difficult part of writing *The Last Protector*. For one thing, it was the final barrier between me and publication. For another, my editors found holes that were damned hard to fix—for instance, in a scene where the bad guys had just taken Scrornuck captive, my editor had noted, "Of course they will tie him up." Oops. Hadn't thought of that. I hit this comment while on a cross-country motorcycle vacation. Each night for the next week, I'd check into my motel, fire up the computer, and try to figure out how to get Scrornuck untied. I eventually did, but it involved rewriting half a chapter.

Sometimes, like a jeweler, an editor will suggest simply cutting off a chunk. I had labored mightily on an expository story near the end of the book, one that neatly explained and tied up all the loose ends. I wasn't happy with it—I still thought it was too long—but couldn't figure out what to do with it. Then my editor suggested simply cutting it out and letting some of the loose ends remain untied (after all, that's what sequels are for). It was the right decision, but cutting several thousand words was difficult—even though they weren't all that good, I'd put so much effort into them!

So far, I've discussed how my experience in writing *The Last Protector* reminds me of my adventures in crystal growing. But the metaphor only goes so far, and I want to note one very important difference: crystals pretty much assemble themselves. You set up the solution and the seed, and the laws of physics and chemistry do the rest. The molecules move themselves into position, drawn by their electric charges and the random movement of the water. So, if temperature, humidity and the general contrary nature of things dictate that the crystal will only grow at three in the morning, it's no big deal. The crystal will grow while you're asleep.

But while stories come together like crystals, the words don't write themselves. Every word in my novel got there because I put it there, and those words had a habit of wanting to be set in place at the most inconvenient times. The little scene that served as a "seed" for the book insisted on being written down at five in the morning, after a sleepless night. Many an evening, I looked at the clock (a little before midnight, again?), saved the file, put the computer to sleep, turned out the lights and headed up to bed... only to find myself waking up the computer and re-opening the file because some idea had just informed me that it needed to be written down *right now*. People who took motorcycle trips with me got used to my occasionally pulling over, yanking out a slip of paper and writing down some idea or phrase that had just come into my head and would soon disappear if not recorded. It's said that the story will write itself, but remember, it's going to use your fingers.

With *The Last Protector* finished and in print, I'm working on my next book. I wondered whether my second book would come together in a more orderly and controlled way than the first. After all, I learned something about how to write a book, didn't I? Well, so far the second book seems to be coming together the same way—I've got pieces all over the place, everything seems to be in constant motion, and I just sent several thousand words that I really liked over to the "deleted scenes" file.

Looks like I'm still growing crystals.

About the author.

Daniel retired from the telecom industry in 2001 and now lives on the banks of the Fox River outside St. Charles, IL. In addition to writing he spends his time paddling his kayak, touring the country by motorcycle, practicing the bagpipes, and substitute-teaching at his local high schools, where he is viewed as the "coolest sub ever."

http://danielcstarr.blogspot.com

Current release: The Last Protector, fantasy

About the editors

Anne K. Edwards loves a good mystery with interesting people and complicated plots. She is also an author, enjoys meeting people and lives with a herd (not clowder) of cats.
http://annekedwards.com

Lida E. Quillen is an author, editor, publicist and publisher. She is the founder and owner of Twilight Times Books, Paladin Timeless Books, and Twilight Trade Books as well as Twilight Times ezine.
http://twilighttimesbooks.com

Contributing Authors

Christine Amsden (My Million Words of Crap)
Christine Amsden has been writing science fiction and fantasy for as long as she can remember. She loves to write and it is her dream that others will be inspired by this love and by her stories. Speculative fiction is fun, magical, and imaginative but great speculative fiction is about real people defining themselves through extraordinary situations. Christine writes primarily about people and it is in this way that she strives to make science fiction and fantasy meaningful for everyone.

At the age of 16, Christine was diagnosed with Stargardt's Disease, a condition that affects the retina and causes a loss of central vision. She is now legally blind, but has not let this slow her down or get in the way of her dreams.

Christine currently lives in the Kansas City area with her husband, Austin, who has been her biggest fan and the key to her success. They have two beautiful children, Drake and Celeste.

http://www.christineamsden.com

Darrell Bain (The Story Behind *The Pet Plague*)
Darrell Bain has always been a voracious reader and always wanted to be a writer but didn't get serious about it until he bought his first computer, a Tandy 1000 at age fifty, seventeen years ago. Being a very naïve and trusting soul, he struggled for years with crooked agents and publishers which very nearly ended his writing career. Finally he turned to e-books and became almost an overnight success. Subsequently, he has won every major award offered in the e-book publishing industry.

Darrell Bain is the author of more than forty-seven novels and non-fiction works, ranging in genres from humor to adventure and thrillers to science fiction. He is also the author of more than two dozen short stories. He has collaborated with several authors, most notably and recently, Travis S. "Doc Travis" Taylor. These days Darrell concentrates mostly on science fiction and suspense/thrillers with SF elements.

He left school in the ninth grade and served thirteen years in the military, including two years in Vietnam. After leaving the army he attended college and has a B.S. in Medical Technology. He worked as a laboratory manager in Louisiana, Texas and Saudi Arabia then settled down with his wife Betty. They ran a Choose and Cut Christmas tree farm on their acreage in east Texas for many years. The farm became the backdrop for much of his humorous fiction and non-fiction. When back problems intervened, they closed the farm and Darrell became a full time writer. Within a few years his name became an icon for e-books, synonymous with success in E-book publishing and with most of his books now out in trade paperback he is rapidly gaining recognition in print.

http://www.darrellbain.com

Bob Boan (How I Came to Write *Bobby becomes Bob*)

Bob Boan has been an active member of the space community for over a quarter of a century. He has worked on a variety of manned and unmanned space programs at different levels of responsibility over that time. Prior to his space experience he was a member of academia. He taught courses from the high school level through graduate school, primarily chemistry.

Dr. Boan has authored a number of technical publications including peer reviewed articles. He coauthored An Introduction to Planetary Defense: A Study of Modern Warfare Applied to Extra-Terrestrial Invasion, BrownWalker Press, 2006. He has written three novels, Bobby Becomes Bob, Williams Lake Was Once the Center of the Universe and Don't Tell Brenda.

http://bobboan.com

Mayra Calvani (Tips on Writing Your First Novel)

Mayra Calvani is the author of several books. Her stories, articles and reviews have appeared in many online and print publications in the States, England and Puerto Rico. In addition, she is assistant editor of Voice in the Dark newsletter, where she writes a monthly column. She has lived in America, Asia, the Middle East, and is now settled in Brussels, Belgium, where she lives with her husband, two children and a variety of pets. Her hobbies include playing the violin and astronomy/sky observing.

http://mayracalvani.com

D Jason Cooper (Understanding Numerology)

D Jason Cooper was born south of Toronto, Canada, grew up in Buffalo, New York, and now lives in Perth, Australia. He has a wife and two children, a girl, Shadra (aged twelve) a boy, Darius (aged eight), and two cats.

He holds a BA from the University of Western Australia and is the author of six other books, including *Understanding Numerology*, *Using the Runes*, *Esoteric Rune Magic*, *The Power of Dreaming*, *Mithras: Mysteries and Initiation Rediscovered* and *The Astral Grail*. He is a regular on Perth radio and has occasionally appeared on TV.

Lee Denning (Two Beginnings)

Lee Denning is the pen name of a father-daughter writing team. Denning Powell (dad) has been a soldier, scientist, engineer and entrepreneur. Leanne Powell (daughter) is a psychologist and corporate researcher by day, and a poet and mystic by night. He lives on the East coast, she on the West. They correspond, with love and hilarity, exchanging ideas and outlines and drafts by email. Somehow it works. The first two books of their *Nova sapiens* trilogy (*Monkey Trap*, in 2004; *Hiding Hand*, in 2008) will be followed by the third (*Splintered Light*) sometime in 2011. At this writing a first draft is out for review.
http://www.monkeytrap.us

Susan Goldsmith (How I Wrote *Abithica*)

Susan earned her Bachelors Degree in Journalism from the University of Arizona. She was selected to serve as Rep. Morris K. Udall's Assistant Press Secretary and was honored by handing his resignation to the Senate Press. Later she became an Undercover Private Investigator at Pinkerton, worked as an outside Sales Rep at Dun and Bradstreet and spent five years in pharmaceutical sales.

She met husband, Bryan, in Mr. Ledezma's biology class, at age 13, setting off fireworks that still light the sky over Madera Canyon, AZ, to this day! Those presently enjoying the show include her daughters Riley and Reagan, 3 1/2 dogs, 3 cats and a parrot who she's trying to teach Shakespeare and failing. Note: Her 210 pound English Mastiff, Teddy Bear, counts as 1 1/2 dogs.

Presently a stay-at-home mom, she stumbled across a pondering personal question after reading Thomas Moore's *Care of the Soul*, that being her own worst fear. Losing her husband and children was the answer, arriving while she vacuumed the living room. What if she were to be taken from them without their knowledge? What if another soul was inserted in her place? She'd look the same, but oh, what would happen then?

The question soon became an obsession, the idea of 'soul switching' was born, and the result was her first novel, *Abithica*.

http://susangoldsmithbooks.com

Ginger Hanson (Ten Lessons I Learned from Writing *Quest for Vengeance*)

Ginger Hanson is a former college history instructor who found writing historical romance a natural outlet for her love of history. While *Lady Runaway* (2009, Twilight Times Books) is her first foray into the Regency period, her two award-winning Civil War era romantic adventures were published in 2004. The release of *Feather's Last Dance*, (2010, The Wild Rose Press) marked Ginger's entry into the contemporary romance field. *Ellie's Song*, (January 2011. TWRP) is the second in what she hopes will become a series set in the fictional small town of Tassanoxie, Alabama.

In addition to writing fiction, her feature articles have appeared in magazines, newspapers, blogs and ezines. She also spent several years as a clean up writer/copy editor of FAA handbooks. An experienced presenter, she has taught workshops at local and regional writers' conferences as well as Romance Writers of America's national conference.

After a vagabond life as an Navy brat and Army wife, Ginger convinced her husband to retire in southeast Alabama where they now live with various rescued pets. When not writing, Ms. Hanson volunteers with the Friends of the Library, often staggering home beneath a pile of books she has "adopted." She also practices the art of Tai Chi, masquerading each week as a set leader

http://www.gingerhanson.com

Toby Fesler Heathcotte (The Manuscript from a Mystifying Source)
At the age of seven, Toby lost her best friend, Marcia, in a car accident. Three months later, Marcia peeked over a cloud and said she liked her new world. Toby's family dismissed the episode as mere imagination, and she grew up distrusting her own perceptions.

Unable to reconcile this and other psychic experiences, such as precognitive dreams and seeing astral forms of people, she became a lifelong student of the paranormal. Her personal library contains over four decades of volumes from Bridey Murphy and J. B. Rhine in the Sixties to current studies by the Institute of Noetic Sciences and the American Society for Psychical Research. Her dream journals span the same time period and serve as resources for her life and work.

Repeated psychic experiences forced Toby to learn some coping strategies. She sat in development groups and experimented with techniques like psychometry, automatic writing, and dream analysis. As she came to terms with her nature, she wanted to share what she'd learned to help others with any self-doubt or concerns about their sanity.

Toby taught high school speech and drama and college English. Now her primary interests rest in understanding her psychic abilities and writing projects that incorporate that learning. A mother of two and grandmother of three, Toby lives in Arizona where she serves as president of Arizona Authors Association.

Fiction titles - *Alma Chronicles: Alison's Legacy, Lainn's Destiny* (an Eppie Finalist), *Angie's Promise, Luke's Covenant*, and *The Comet's Return*[2011 EPIC award finalist.]

Nonfiction titles - *Program Building: A Practical Handbook for High School Speech and Drama Teachers* (a San Diego Book Award Winner) and *Seeds for Fertile Minds: Eight Curriculum Integration Tools* with Betty Joy, *Out of the Psychic Closet: The Quest to Trust My True Nature* [2011 EPIC award finalist.]

http://www.tobyheathcotte.com
http://www.outofthepsychiccloset.com

Darby Karchut (Wings)

All her life, the archetypal hero and his journey have enthralled **Darby Karchut**. A native of New Mexico, Darby grew up in a family that venerated books and she spent her childhood devouring one fantasy novel after another. Fascinated by mythologies from around the world, she attended the University of New Mexico, graduating with a degree in anthropology. After moving to Colorado, she then earned a Master's in education and became a social studies teacher.

Drawing from her extensive knowledge of world cultures, she blends ancient myths with modern urban life to write stories that relate to young teens today.

Darby is a member of the Society of Children's Book Writers and Illustrators and the Pikes Peak Writers Guild. She lives in Colorado Springs, Colorado with her husband, where she still teaches at a local junior high school. She enjoys running, biking, and skiing the Rocky Mountains in all types of weather.

Griffin Rising is her first novel. She is currently working on the sequel, *Griffin's Fire*.

http://darbykarchut.com

Linda Langwith (The Serendipity Factor)

In addition to her mystery thriller *The Golden Crusader*, Linda Langwith is the author of numerous articles, short stories and poetry, featured in various print and on-line publications. For Linda, family life is everything, and she is blessed by the love and support of her husband, two daughters and a son. The recipient of a B.A. (Honours) and an M.A. in English, her passion for history, art and architecture sees her heading to Britain, Ireland and Europe whenever the opportunity arises, to discover and explore places that nourish her imagination and nurture her soul. In addition to her writing, she has enjoyed careers as an arts grant officer, academic advisor, community resource coordinator and university researcher. Blissful distractions include gardening, hiking, painting, playing the piano and listening to English choral music.

http://www.lindalangwith.com

Aaron Lazar (The Writing of *Double Forté*)
Aaron Paul Lazar wasn't always a mystery writer. It wasn't until eight members of his family and friends died within five years that the urge to write became overwhelming. "When my father died, I lost it. I needed an outlet, and writing provided the kind of solace I couldn't find elsewhere."

Lazar created the Gus LeGarde mystery series, with the founding novel, *Double Forté* (2004), a chilling winter mystery set in the Genesee Valley of upstate New York. Like Lazar's father, protagonist Gus LeGarde is a classical music professor. Gus, a grandfather, gardener, chef, and nature lover, plays Chopin etudes to feed his soul and thinks of himself as a "Renaissance man caught in the 21st century."

The creation of the series lent Lazar the comfort he sought, yet in the process, a new passion was unleashed. Obsessed with his parallel universe, he now lives, breathes, and dreams about his characters, and has written ten LeGarde mysteries in eight years. (*Upstaged* – 2005; *Tremolo: Cry of The Loon* – 2007 Twilight Times Books; *Mazurka* – 2009 Twilight Times Books, with more to come.) The author is currently working on his fifteenth novel.

One day while rototilling his gardens, Lazar unearthed a green cat's eye marble, which prompted the new paranormal mystery series featuring Sam Moore, retired country doctor and passionate gardener. The green marble, a powerful talisman, connects all three of the books in the series, whisking Sam back in time to uncover his brother's dreadful fate fifty years earlier. (*Healey's Cave*, 2010; *One Potato, Blue Potato*, 2011; *For Keeps*, 2012) Lazar intends to continue both series.

Lazar's books feature breathless chase scenes, nasty villains, and taut suspense, but are also intensely human stories, replete with kids, dogs, horses, food, romance, and humor. The author calls them, "country mysteries," although reviewers have dubbed them "literary mysteries."

"It seems as though every image ever impressed upon my brain finds its way into my work. Whether it's the light dancing through stained-glass windows in a Parisian chapel, curly slate-green lichen covering a boulder at the edge of a pond in Maine, or hoarfrost dangling from a cherry tree branch in mid-winter, these images burrow into my memory cells. In time they bubble back, persistently itching, until they are poured out on the page."

The author lives on a ridge overlooking the Genesee Valley in upstate New York with his wife, daughter, son-in-law, four grandchildren, mother-in-law, two dogs, and three cats. He finds grandfathering one of the most precious and important times of life.

Lazar maintains several websites and blogs, was the Gather Saturday Writing Essential host for three years, writes his monthly "Seedlings" columns for the *Voice in the Dark* literary journal and the *Future Mystery Anthology Magazine*. He has been published in *Absolute Write* as well as *The Great Mystery and Suspense Magazine*.

See excerpts and reviews here:
http://www.legardemysteries.com
http://www.mooremysteries.com

Celia A. Leaman (Writing *Mary's Child*)

Celia's novel, *Mary's Child*, was a Reviewers Choice Award and Frankfurt eBook awared nominee. *PastPresent I: Web of Lies* is Celia's latest release. Her other novels include *Unraveled*, a lighthearted mainstream novel with a touch of fantasy and humor written around a fictional Gulf Island, and *The Winnowed Woman*, a collection of essays, poems and journal entries, which received the WordWeaving Award for Excellence.

Local British Columbians can meet Celia personally at the Mayne Island Farmer's Market on Saturday mornings where she has signed copies of her books available, together with her woolen articles. She creates items from fibres she spins herself, using local wools, alpaca and mohair.

http://www.devonshirebabe.com

Beverly Stowe McClure (How I Wrote *Shadows on the Desert*)

If anyone had told Beverly she'd be a writer one day, she'd have thought they were crazy. When she was a child, she hated to read. Even though her eighth-grade teacher sent her poem "Stars" to a high school anthology, and it was published in Young America Sings, she hated to write. No favorite stories come to mind from her childhood.

In spite of her rocky relationship with books, she attended Midwestern State University and became a teacher. Reading to her students and to her sons introduced her to Dr. Seuss, and she made an amazing discovery: books were fun. She also started to write. To her surprise her stories and articles were published in leading children's magazines. One of her articles was reprinted in a Scott Foresman PreK anthology. Her breakthrough article about her writing journey appeared in the June 2007 issue of the *Writer* magazine. *Caves, Cannons and Crinolines* is Beverly's fourth young adult novel. Her other novels for teens are *Listen to the Ghost, Secrets I Have Kept,* and *Rebel in Blue Jeans.*

Beverly is a member of the national Society of Children's Book Writers and Illustrators, as well as the North Texas chapter. She lives with her husband, Jack, in the country, where an occasional deer, skunk or armadillo come to visit.

http://beverlystowemcclure.wordpress.com

Gerald Mills (How I Wrote *No Place for Gods*)

Gerry spent most of his first sixteen years studying the piano, reading everything in print and ruining as many staged events as possible just by appearing in them. His promising career as a concert pianist came to an end when he found it involved hard work. Instead he entered Northeastern University. In return for his promise never to return there, he was handed a degree in electrical engineering. Misreading that as encouragement, he began a career in avionics engineering. When the engineering industry learned his true value, he wisely switched to sales, but divorce unhappily followed. He later met and married Lori, continued in sales, then launched his own business, selling it ten years later.

The high-speed automation and robotics industry kept him occupied until 1990, when he took a brief sabbatical with Lori, his bride of twenty-eight years by then. They set out on a 45 foot ocean-sailing yacht, managing to terrorize most of the Canadian Maritimes and eastern seaboard for over a year before ending up in the Bahamas, where fortunes ran out. Not one to fret, he immediately wrote his first novel, Then Is The Power, typing furiously to see how the story ended, while Lori plotted a course for Florida.

While in Florida, he worked in automation and learned to herd nine cats.

Shying away from the purely technical, he enjoys writing character-driven stories dealing with human shortcomings, a topic in which he has a great degree of personal expertise. His latest hobbies are gardening and remembering the cats' names. He no longer sails, and the world is a safer place for it.

There are those who believe he should give up writing for the same reason, but so far no one has come forward with an acceptable bribe.

http://www.gerryscorner.com

Erica Miner (How I Wrote *Travels With My Lovers*)

Violinist turned author Erica Miner has had a multi-faceted career as an award-winning screenwriter, author, lecturer and poet. A native of Detroit, she studied music at Boston University, the New England Conservatory of Music, and the Tanglewood Music Center. After experiencing a variety of highs and lows in her quest to forge a career in New York City, Erica won the coveted position of violinist with the Metropolitan Opera Company, a high-pressured milieu but the pinnacle of her field.

Her life became even more challenging, however, when injuries from a car accident spelled the end of her musical career. Searching for a new creative outlet, she drew upon her lifelong love of writing for inspiration and studied poetry and screenwriting, winning a number of awards in both categories. After moving to the west coast, Erica honed her screenwriting skills with author and script guru Linda Seger of *Making a Good Script Great* fame and with Ken Rotcop, the author of *Perfect Pitch*. Erica's ten screenplays, one of which is based on her award-winning debut novel, *Travels with My Lovers*, have won awards and/or placed in such competitions as WinFemme, Santa Fe and the Writer's Digest. Her essays and articles have appeared in *Vision Magazine*, *WORD San Diego* and numerous newsletters and E-zines.

Erica has completed both the novel and screenplay of her suspense thriller, *Murder In The Pit*, which takes place at the Met, and currently is at work on the second novel in her "FourEver Friends" series chronicling four young girls' coming of age in the volatile 60s and 70s.

In addition Erica has developed a number of writing lectures and seminars on writing, which she has presented at various venues across the West Coast and on the High Seas. Topics range from "The Art of Self Re-Invention" to "Opera Meets Hollywood" and "Journaling for Writers: Mining the Gold of Your Own Experiences."

Stephanie Osborn (How a Rocket Scientist Becomes a Writer)

Stephanie Osborn is a former payload flight controller, a veteran of over twenty years of working in the civilian space program, as well as various military space defense programs. She has worked on numerous Space Shuttle flights and the International Space Station, and counts the training of astronauts on her resumé. Of those astronauts she trained, one was Kalpana Chawla, a member of the crew lost in the Columbia disaster.

She holds graduate and undergraduate degrees in four sciences: Astronomy, Physics, Chemistry, and Mathematics, and she is "fluent" in several more, including Geology and Anatomy. She obtained her various degrees from Austin Peay State University in Clarksville, TN and Vanderbilt University in Nashville, TN.

Stephanie is currently retired from space work. She now happily "passes it forward," tutoring math and science to students in the Huntsville area, elementary through college, while writing science fiction mysteries based on her knowledge, experience, and travels.

http://www.stephanie-osborn.com

Bob Rich (How I Came to Write Novels)

Bob Rich is a multiple award-winning Australian writer, mudsmith and psychologist. He has done enough different things to fill a couple of life-times, but is too busy to worry about it.

Since 1972, his main preoccupation has been to try and preserve a future for coming generations. The trouble is, he doesn't believe in salesmanship, the missionary spirit. This approach is part of the problem, so mustn't be part of the solution. So, he has lived a low-impact lifestyle for twenty years. When things go bad, he can at least say, 'It wasn't my fault!'

Because of their commitment to a sustainable lifestyle, Bob and his wife Jolanda decided to live on as little money as possible. They have successfully raised three wonderful children, while way below the official 'poverty line,' and they consider themselves to live better than Royalty. If this seems crazy to you, read Bob's essay on the subject.

Bob is cursed with a sense of humor that gets him in trouble all the time, creativity that makes it impossible for anything he does to fit into categories, and an intense empathy for other people, even if they are very different from him. This is his main tool in two very different endeavors: psychological counseling and writing.

He welcomes contact from readers of his books.
http://www.bobswriting.com

Dorothy Skarles (Tales of Intrigue, Adventure and Learning)

Dorothy Ann Skarles who writes under daSkarles has appeared in a variety of publications. She has published more than two hundred articles in trade journals, magazines and newspapers. She earned her first byline as a cooking columnist for a local family owned newspaper in California.

Along with her love for writing daSkarles also loves animals. She once owned a 99 percent wolf from Alaska who lived to be thirteen years old. She hopes one day to write a book about her experiences with this wonderful wild animal.

Dan Starr (A Solution and a Seed: Novel Writing as Growing a Crystal)

Daniel Starr began writing his first novel in 1975, but stopped when he graduated college and and got a "real job." He began his second novel in 1999, and Twilight Times Books published *The Last Protector* in 2008...

Stop. Wait. You already know these things. They're in his article. There's no point in repeating them. Instead, here are some Fun Facts that didn't appear in the story of how he wrote *The Last Protector:*

If you make phone calls in North America, you're probably using a gadget he invented. In 1985, he came up with a performance enhancement for AT&T's 5ESS® switching system. A few years later, a small army of engineers turned the "Communications Module Processor" into a reality. Several thousand of these went into service, and remain to this day, helping you reach Uncle Jake.

If Daniel's name sounds vaguely familiar, you might have caught his Fifteen Minutes of Fame. In the spring of 2002, a Chicago-area newspaper featured him in an article about men who wear kilts, a wire service picked up the story, and soon Paul Harvey mentioned Daniel Starr, a ong-haired, bearded, tattooed biker who rides a Harley and wears a kilt. "Are you going to tell him he can't?" Mr. Harvey asked. Over the summer, Daniel was interviewed by several radio stations in the US and Canada. Alas, he had no book to promote at the time—let this be a lesson to other first-time authors!

While *The Last Protector* is his first published novel, Daniel has published a number of articles on software technology and project management in such places as *STQE* and *Software Development* magazine and the *Projects at Work* online journal. These range from "war stories" based on his experiences in the telecom industry to an article comparing the project management skills of Aragorn and Frodo... thereby demonstrating that SF/Fantasy and Project Management are often the same thing.

Since retiring from Bell Labs in 2001, Daniel's been working at the high schools in his home town of Saint Charles, Ilinois, where the students say he's the "coolest substitute teacher ever."

More about Daniel, including links to his other published works, stories of kilts, bagpipes and motorcycle adventures, plus deleted scenes and songs from *The Last Protector*, are on his website.

http://danielcstarr.blogspot.com

Order Form

If not available from your local bookstore or favorite online bookstore, send this coupon and a check or money order for the retail price plus $3.50 s&h to Twilight Times Books, Dept. GB311 POB 3340 Kingsport TN 37664. Delivery may take up to two weeks.

Name: _____

Address: _____

_____

Email: _____

I have enclosed a check or money order in the amount of

$_____

for _____ .

> ➤ Learning to Write the Easy Way
> for Fun, Posterity and Money
> by Dorothy Ann Skarles
> (1-931201-98-6, $16.95 US)

>> ➤ Magic for Your Writing
>> by Gerald W. Mills
>> (1-60619-147-0, $15.95 US)

If you enjoyed this book, please post a review
at your favorite online bookstore.

Twilight Times Books
P O Box 3340
Kingsport, TN 37664
Phone/Fax: 423-323-0183
www.twilighttimesbooks.com/